Mary Howitt

Jacob Bendixen, the Jew

Mary Howitt

Jacob Bendixen, the Jew

ISBN/EAN: 9783337136680

Printed in Europe, USA, Canada, Australia, Japan

Cover: Foto ©ninafisch / pixelio.de

More available books at **www.hansebooks.com**

THE JEW.

FROM THE DANISH OF GOLDSCHMIDT

BY MARY HOWITT.

LONDON:
CHAPMAN & HALL, 193, PICCADILLY.
1864.

TO

ESTHER LEVY BENSUSAN,

WHOSE COMPREHENSIVE MIND EMBRACES ALIKE

CHRISTIANS AND JEWS,

This Translation

OF

A WORK WHICH PRESENTS A FAITHFUL PICTURE
OF THE INNER LIFE OF HER PEOPLE,

IS

AFFECTIONATELY INSCRIBED.

TRANSLATOR'S PREFACE.

At the moment when we are searching into the social and moral condition of all classes, a faithful transcript of the life and feelings of the Jews, presented by one of themselves, cannot fail of being welcome. The heart of the Jew has hitherto been to us as a sealed book; for even D'Israeli, with all his wit and talent, and Grace Aguilar, with her fine womanly sensibilities, describe to us the life of the Christian in preference to that of the Jew. The following pages, however, written by a man of unquestionable genius and originality of mind, unlock, as it were, to us this mysterious and sealed book, and enable us to peruse the history of a human soul, which is as interesting as it is new, at the same time that it makes us familiarly acquainted with the domestic life, manners, and feelings, of a portion of the community which is, in general, as little known as if it belonged to another hemisphere.

LONDON,
Dec. 10, 1851.

JACOB BENDIXEN.

CHAPTER I.

"What noise is that?" said Philip Bendixen, in an under tone, as he carefully unbarred the shutters and opened the casement in the early summer morning.

He saw many people hurrying down the street, and beckoned to the nearest of them, but they passed on without regarding him, and he did not dare to shout, lest he should disturb his sleeping wife.

"I fancy I hear a drum," said he, and closed the window; "what can be the meaning of it?"

He stole softly down-stairs, and went into his shop, where his servant Benjamin, still half asleep, although dressed, was about to unfasten the heavy iron bar from the door.

"Don't stand sleeping there, you simpleton," said Philip Bendixen, in a suppressed and angry voice. "Run over to my brother-in-law's, and find out what is amiss in the city."

Benjamin hurried himself, and in his hurry let fall the iron bar, which he was about to set down.

"Bad luck of the world!" exclamed Philip, "what a din is

that for my poor wife! God of Israel, stand by her!—Hark! now she calls, you have woke her, you wretch!"

"What's amiss with your wife?" asked Benjamin.

"I don't know at what hour I may have to send for the mid-wife!" said Philip, angry at his servant's phlegm—"don't you know that, fool?"

In a moment the shutters were taken down, the door was opened, and Benjamin hastened across the street to the house of the brother-in-law, just opposite.

Shortly after the brother-in-law, Isaac Bamberger, came over with his wife. They went cheerfully into the room, where Mrs. Bendixen was seated at the breakfast-table.

"Now, how are you, madam?" said he, addressing Jette. "Be so good as to keep up to-day. We have no time just now for fool's play; the Spaniards are running away. You might be frightened at the firing, although there would be no danger to you."

"Schema, Yisroel! (Hear, oh Israel!) She is ill!" exclaimed the sister-in-law, and running to the door she called the maid-servant.

Philip drew Isaac Bamberger from the room. "How thoughtless it was of you," said he, "to talk so and frighten her."

"Thoughtless?" repeated Isaac, "does not she know me well enought to be sure I would to be sure I would not frighten her? —Hark now! How they are drumming and firing! Was it not the best to prepare her for it?"

The drums beat so loud in the street that the casements shook; after the drummers marched the armed citizen corps, whose teeth chattered with terror in concert with the casements. Cannons were heard to thunder at intervals, no one knew where, and bewildering shouts sounded from the neighbouring houses.

In the midst of all this noise a cry was heard from the sleeping-room. Isaac Bamberger's countenance became very grave, and without saying a word he crossed over to his own house. Philip Bendixen ran first, in his anxiety, to the chamber door, but turned round and hastened into the yard. His soul, however, was in the house, let its body be where it might. He then went into the cow-shed, to the cows, and filled their racks with fodder; next to the pump, and pumped a bucket of water; but every time the bucket was full he emptied it out and filled it again.

At length the upper half of the kitchen door opened, and an old woman presented herself. She beckoned, and said, "A son, Mr. Bendixen! a son! I congratulate you!"

Philip sprang away from the pump. "A son!" exclaimed he, and laid his hand upon his head. "Adaunoi Elauheinu! Lord, my God, blessed be thy name! A son! a son!"

With tearful eyes he hastened into the house, following the midwife. "Let me come in, and kiss my son and his mother," said he.

"Yes, indeed!—No, go out, and get to your pumping again!" said the woman, and locked the door.

"I must be patient," said he, "I must give them time. God has sent me a son! I am the father of a man child."

He hastened into his shop.

"My wife has got a son," said he, and embraced and kissed Benjamin.

"God be blessed!" said Benjamin.

"Yeschkanach, Rabbi, Benjomin! Thanks!" exclaimed Philip, in his unspeakable joy.

"Hear, Benjamin," said he, a moment afterwards, "it is best that you go instantly over to Rabbi Jokuf; he must be maul (godfather). Also, inform Simon Nasche, and the other Jews in the town, that my wife has got a son. Where is my brother-in-law? True, he went home. Run across to him, and tell him that he may now come back. Stop a moment, Benjamin," cried he, when the man was just out of the door, "take a pound of coffee and a couple of pounds of sugar, and a little rice and groats, and this money, to old Martha. Tell her that I send it for her to rejoice with on the occasion of my son's birth.—My son! oh, I have a son!"

Almost as quickly as this was taking place within the house, were the citizen corps relieved from their terror. They had been out, and had seen the Spaniards safely on board the English vessels, and it now might be a question which were the happier, the Spaniards or the citizen corps of that little Funen town.

It was now the Jews' turn; for as they had not joined the warlike body they were now called cowardly wretches, who had neither patriotism nor yet were good citizens. Many a little group, on their way to the public-house, stopped for a moment before the houses of particular Jews, and made known their dislike by loud exclamations.

"Komech (the Christians) are in reality an extraordinary people," said Isaac Bamberger, when such a little group had sent in its greeting to Philip; and as he said this he cast an ironical glance after them. "They cannot bear that the Jews should be enrolled with them in time of peace, and as soon as there is war they abuse the Jews because they do not serve. I think I must go and scold my house-dog, because he never goes out."

"Who troubles himself about them! Let them shout!" replied Philip Bendixen, as he listened to the noise outside from his wife's chamber.

CHAPTER II.

EIGHT days afterwards, and the little family was assembled round the bed of the mother, and congratulations passed from lip to lip, on occasion of the child's being received into the Jewish community. Every one naturally expressed admiration of the boy's healthy and lively appearance. The old Rabbi Jokuf laid upon the cradle a horro—a gold coin, on which was inscribed a Hebrew benediction, and which would defend the child against the evil eye; and in so doing he said solemnly, "He shall be strong as Judah, and blessed with riches like Ashur."

Isaac Bamberger drank a glass of wine, and exclaimed, "Yes, it is very good; but still I continue to assert that it was not a very rational time to be born in. If the lad had been a Christian, then the disturbance which prevailed at his birth might have foretold that he was to be a great hero; but as a Jew it may give him a twofold aversion to war and commotion—he may become so determined a coward, that even the Jews may call him one."

All laughed, except the mother; for all women have by nature a chivalric feeling, and would rather give birth to heroes.

"No, no, Isaac," she said; "if the lad grows up under thy eye, and looks every day at thy great sword, he will, perhaps, not be so very timid after all."

"So be it," exclaimed the uncle; "I will bring him up. Do thou rear him, for that I cannot do; and then he shall come to school to me."

It is best that we now make the reader more nearly acquainted with this uncle, who took upon himself the part of Aristotle towards the Funen Philip's son. He was, which is not often the case among Jews, a tall and very strong man. It was related of him in the town, that once, when two peasants began to fight in his shop, he took them up, one under each arm, knocked them several times together, and then threw them out of the door. Although he was hated as a Jew, and envied as a rich man, still he always inspired his fellow-townsfolk with respect when they saw his powerful figure among them, and his lively gray eyes observing them with their half-merry, half-sarcastic gaze. His hair was already gray; he was somewhat above fifty. In his youth he served in the German army against the French, for he was a native of Germany; and after various adventures and changes of fortune, removed to Denmark, where he intended to end his days peacefully, and where he married. His wife brought him no fortune; ill-luck set in against him, and he was reduced to the extreme of poverty.

He was accustomed, in his later years, to tell with a certain pride, that for one whole winter he maintained himself and his wife on a capital of two rix-dollars, which he laid out in goods, and with which he set off into the country. When, however, on the first Friday evening he came home, he found his house burned down, his wife ill, and their only child dead. Notwithstanding all these misfortunes, he held his sabbath with due solemnity, buried his child on Sunday, and again set out with his capital, in a bundle of old clothes, under his arm.

Now, however, he lived in a large house, and was a rich man; but he seldom failed to remark when he saw a small piece of gold, that his large house was built from such pieces of money; and hence it was, probably, that he came to have an almost superstitious respect for gold.

Philip Bendixen, the father of the young child, was a quiet and peaceable man. The domestics, who very often give the most accurate description of their employers' characters, only thought ill of him when he was angry, because, if once offended, he did not easily forgive. There was a report, that in his youth he had lived too freely, and had outstepped the bounds of the Jewish ceremonial; but it was a dark and indistinct rumour. This, however, was certain, in any case, that after his betrothal and marriage, he returned with twofold zeal to the ordinances of his religion, and severely blamed all such as disregarded them.

Late in the evening of the above-mentioned gratulation-day, Philip Bendixen entered the little bedroom. His wife slept calmly behind the white curtains. The Jewish matron who had undertaken to watch had fallen into a gentle slumber in her chair; the rosy-lipped child slept in its cradle, and the night-lamp threw its quivering light on the snowy pillow.

Philip enfolded with one long glance his precious happiness; his heart swelled with emotion, and covering his head, he prayed:

"Almighty Father! ruler of the world! I thank thee that thou hast given me a son to read kadisch (prayers for the soul) over my grave. Whenever it is thy will, let this be:—take, if it please thee, all happiness from me, and give it to my son! I will bow me in the dust, and bless thy name, if only he be happy!"

Such was the prayer which was spoken by the cradle of the child who is the hero of this story.

CHAPTER III.

As the child grew, the father still uttered benedictions over him.

"He must not go to school; he must not have to endure the Jew-persecution from the other boys, neither must he learn their rude ways. When he is old enough, I will myself teach him what a Jew ought to know; then afterwards I will send him to Copenhagen."

Nobody was more pleased with this determination than uncle Isaac Bamberger, for he was thus able to occupy himself either according to his humour or pleasure with the boy. Often he came over, took the boy from his mother, and carried him home with him. Arrived there, he took him into an adjoining chamber, and locked the door upon them both, so that any one might have believed he was about to practise some kind of witchcraft; and if they had watched and listened to what went forward within, they would have been strengthened in this belief. First, he would leap about with the little lad in his arms, and howl in his ears, and make noises as of trumpetting and drumming; he would imitate the neighing of horses, the lowing of cows, and the barking of dogs. If the child laughed loud at all this, and scratched him in the face for joy, he set him down, and let him ride on his knee with such vehemence, that the little Jacob, after some vain attempts to find it entertaining, began to cry.

His uncle would then seize him by his ears, and stare gloomily at him till he was still, saying, "I will teach thee to be afraid, boy!" and so would continue staring at him and making faces, until both burst forth into roars of laughter. On this he would spring up again, dance the child round, and clasp him so lovingly and yet so firmly to his breast, that he again wept, and insisted on going home.

"Only be quiet, Jacob," said Isaac Bamberger—by that time somewhat tired himself—"and I will tell thee stories. Don't tell them at home that I teased thee, wilt thou?"

"No!" sobbed the little lad.

"Brave comrade, though thou art so little!" cried the uncle; "now listen."

And he told him about warriors and knights, and foreign lands, or else Biblical stories about Jewish heroes; so that the child, in later years, did not remember to have learned these histories. They seemed almost to have been born with him.

The father soon said, when he saw Isaac with the child:

"The lad is too much with thee, Isaac; at length he will not know who is his father."

"I can always be as good a father to him as thou," replied Isaac. "He gets sense when he is with me; only look what a knowing countenance he has already."

"Dost thou really think that he has got that from thee?" asked Jette archly.

"If he has not been out of the town to steal it," exclaimed the uncle, "how else could he have got it? He can already say his Krieshmo (the Jewish creed), by heart. I will now teach him to say the grace after meat."

"Yes, yes, Isaac," said the father, "thou mayest have him till he is six years old; and then it will be my duty, as a father, to teach him what a Jew should learn."

"You have already taught him too much; you talk too

rationally with him," said the mother, anxiously. "The lad would like rather to talk rationally in his own way, with other children, and tumble about in the fresh air."

The child looked at his mother as if he understood her—as if she had prescribed the right medicine for that longing desire which made his cheeks pale.

"To-morrow morning," said his uncle, "I will take him a long way into the country."

CHAPTER IV.

Happy human beings who can say, "That was one of my playfellows!"

Reader, do you indeed know the full meaning of those words? They recal to you green meadows, where you gambolled in the excess of childish delight, and the little yard where you had a rendezvous with the neighbour's lad, and where you fought and wept. How willingly would you thus weep again! Or of the dark room, where you were told to be good, and play quietly, because of the old grandfather who slept just by, and where you did play quietly, until all at once, having forgotten the old grandfather, your merriment rose to its height; and then, behold! the old man stood at the door, and besought you to let him sleep only a quarter of an hour longer! They recal the thousand tricks which you played later as schoolboys—the greengrocer's oranges, which, piled pyramidally in his window, suddenly came rolling down, to his great amazement, because you tapped on the panes—the couple of bladders which you tied to the cat of the old woman who lived in the cellar, that she might have to chase after it, as after her canary-bird. They recal to you the little girl for whom you both of you would gather flowers, and for whose sake you became enemies, although you yourselves knew it not.

That was the time when you received your first drilling to fit you for the active scene, called the world; that was the time when the heart was prepared to nourish and bring forth the flowers of life, friendship, and love; and that was the time also, when you were all pressed into the same mould, until your characters presented the same uniformity as your dress.

Jacob grew up a solitary child. He had no playfellows, because the other Jewish families in the town had no children of his own age, and Christian children derided him when they saw him. Although he was called Jacob, they nicknamed him Moses; and when he approached them, they made signs with their hands under their chins, as if laughing at his beard. If ever he did chance to play with them, it mostly happened that by degrees they turned him into ridicule, called him Jew-smaus,* and struck at him. When their derision became more than he could bear, he left them, stood at a distance, and with longing looks watched their sports. All this began so early, that it never occurred to him to inquire the reason of it; it was just as little a cause of wonder to him as that he was born and lived. He was, indeed, born with it; he believed that it must be so.

On one occasion, his maternal uncle came from another town on a visit, and brought with him his little son. The boy advanced kindly towards Jacob, who drew back in a reserved manner. As, however, the stranger still maintained his friendly demeanour, and came nearer, Jacob riveted his large brown eyes upon him, and asked:

"Why do you not call me Jew-smaus?"

All present were shocked by this unexpected question.

"They have been abusing the poor lad," said his uncle Bamberger, at length.

His father went up to him, placed a hand on each side his

---

* The term *smaus*, applied derisively to the Jews also in Germany, is probably a corruption of some Hebrew word or words of salutation, which, being caught up by the populace, was applied to the Jews as a term of derision and scorn.

head, raised his face upwards, and kissed him with trembling lips. His uncle, however, exclaimed,—
"Who called thee Jew-smaus, Jacob?"
"The boys down by the shore always do so," replied he.

The next day his uncle took him to the shore; but when the boys saw the tall man that was with him, they were naturally silent. Isaac Bamberger could not, however, control himself; he rushed among them, seized one, and hurled him into the midst of the crowd. When Jacob saw this, it became all at once clear to him why his father, on the preceding day, had kissed him, and why his uncle had now accompanied him to the shore. The recollection of the unkindness he had received at their hands rushed hurriedly through the mind of the child. He sprang like an unfettered tiger on another boy, rolled over with him, and clung to him as if frenzied. The uncle, who regarded it as a regular fight, applauded him; but when he saw that blood was flowing from the Christian boy, he separated them, and hastily carried off his nephew. When he saw Jacob's deathly pale cheeks and pallid lips, his teeth set rigidly together, his eyes as if starting from his head, and his hands grasping hair which he had torn from the head of his antagonist, he believed that he was ill, had him put to bed, and sent for a physician. The child slept many hours, and then woke as if out of a swoon, evidently without any recollection of what had happened.

Isaac Bamberger was, however, summoned before the magistrate, by the parents of the boy whom he had attacked, and who had received an injury by his fall, and only got off by the payment of some of his precious gold pieces. Furthermore it was decreed, that to prevent any similar occurrences for the future, the little field belonging to Philip Bendixen, which ran down to the shore, should be enclosed by a tall wooden fence.

Within this wooden fence Jacob now sat for many an hour,

separated from all the rest of the world, and with nothing but the broad Belt, with its scattered shipping, outspread before his eyes. Solitary and in silence walked he among the flowers and trees, and watched the proud sea, as it joyously spread its calm bosom to the sun, or dark and threateningly hurled itself against the coast; or he sat for hours within the large pleasant summerhouse, where, during the celebration of the Feast of the Tabernacles, the family arranged the leafy tent, and here, in its deep and magical solitude, he created for himself a world, in which were no other persons than those he knew, among whom that one individual played the principal part about whom he occupied himself most—namely, himself. Whenever he suffered any disappointment or mortification he fled hither, and found consolation by describing to himself some other state in which things would go on better.

These little episodes developed themselves by degrees into connected stories, in which every new occurrence of his life furnished material for a new chapter. But the most important of these still remained to be the remembrance of the boys on the shore; his longing after them, and his indignation against them. If by chance one of them met him in the street, and saluted him in a friendly spirit, he went down into the garden and imagined all the good things that he would give to this boy. He related to himself histories of how this boy was in danger, how he himself rushed in and saved him, and finally how this boy showed his gratitude by climbing every day, at the risk of his life, over the tall wooden fence, and playing with him.

But if—as was most frequently the case—one of the boys from the shore, made bold by the absence of his uncle, repeated the opprobrious epithet, as he hastily rushed past him, then he went down into the garden, and spoke to himself in thise wise:

"I will set fire to their corn-fields, by catching foxes and fastening firebrands to them. They pursued me, but every time they came I put them to flight. But once, when I slept, they came upon me, and bound me; and then they set me in their temple, between the two pillars on which it rested, and in that way they thought they had me safe, so they leapt round me, and shouted 'Jew-smaus! Jew, canst thou eat bacon and cream?' But with that I grasped the pillars with my strong arms, so that the whole house fell—fell upon them and upon me with——."

A cold thrill passed through him; he closed his eyes, he felt a faintness and a weakness come over him every time he arrived at this point, however various the occasions might be. He was unnerved, and wept for grief, at being obliged to kill them, even though they were his enemies.

CHAPTER V.

These ideal phantoms grew and became too strong for the lad; they were like spirits which he had evoked, and now knew not how to control. They lay like mist in his brain, until he himself approached the spot which was their home and birth-place; then they assumed a living shape, flapped their wings, and overpowered him. He was guided by them; his head began to be dizzy, and his nerves to quiver, and yet they had so mysteriously seductive a power over him, that whenever he was alone he hastened to that lonely spot in the garden which was peopled by them.

One day as he sat there, with his eyes convulsively open, and terror trickling through his veins, his father, who had no business to occupy him either in his shop or at home, came walking towards him.

"What art thou doing there, Jacob?" asked he, addressing his son.

"Nothing," replied Jacob; and rose up.

"It is high time that thou learned something useful," said Philip; "thy uncle crams thy head full of stories. Come with me, and we will begin with the Hebrew alphabet."

An instinct told Jacob that in his father he should find the best defence against these frightful images, and joyfully he grasped his hand.

"I have not yet given thee thy arbakampfoth,* although thou art in thy seventh year," said his father, and shook his head at his own negligence; "we must make haste, Jacob. From this time thou must know that thou art a Jew, and become acquainted with thy true religion."

"Yes, father," said Jacob, secretly proud of the maturity which all this implied in him.

From this time the father continued daily to instruct his son with great zeal, and Jacob employed himself in impressing his learning still more deeply on his mind; for so long as his thoughts were thus occupied the phantoms had no power. He revived like a plant which has had water, and his cheeks again became blooming. His mother, however, often scolded, and said that the boy had too much to do for his strength."

"Nothing of the kind," said the father to her, on one occasion; "he has himself a desire for it. Besides, he knows what I have promised him, if he is industrious."

With these words he looked at Jacob, as if there were some great secret between them.

"Now, what have I promised thee, Jacob?" asked the father. "Canst thou not remember what I promised thee when thou couldst say the eight prayers? Canst thou not remember? What have we on Monday?"

"Purim!" exclaimed Jacob; "shall we be disguised, father?"

"No;" but thou shalt go with me to the synagogue, and hear about Esther and Haman, and shalt have leave to strike Haman."

"Who is he, father? and why should I strike him?"

"Dost thou not know him? He it was who wished to

---

* A square piece of cloth, with a hole in the middle to draw down over the shoulders. In each corner are twisted threads—zizis. It is the token to the Jew of his pure religion, and of his covenant with God.

murder all the Jews in one night; but our Lord was with the Jews, and Haman himself was hanged. See, this is the way the thing is done; if thou pull the string, the hammer falls and strikes upon the name of Haman. Every time, therefore, his name is read to-morrow in the story of Esther do thou pull the string and strike him."

I would rather strike the real Haman, father," said the boy.

"He is dead, my lad," said the father, and laughed, amused at his son's earnestness; thou "must strike upon his name when we elders read it aloud.

"No, I cannot," said Jacob.

"Why canst thou not, Jacob? Whouldst not thou smite Haman, who wished to kill the Jews?"

"No, I cannot," repeated the boy, and began to weep.

"No! then thou mayst let it alone, if though hadst rather; but thou must not cry about it," said the father, and clapped him kindly on the back. "But be industrious all the same, and then thou shalt sit by my side at Pesach (Easter) to read the Exodus, and I will then tell thee all about it."

"Oh, tell it to me directly?" besought Jacob, and dried his eyes.

"No; they only talk about that at Pesach," said the father.

"How long is it to Pesach, father?" asked Jacob.

"Four weeks; but thou must be very industrious and well-behaved till then," said he.

The anxiously expected Easter was at length come, as might be seen many days beforehand by the preparations which had been made. There had come thither by ship, from Copenhagen, a well-closed cask, containing the unleavened bread, which had been carefully conveyed to a secure place in the garret that it might not come in contact with anything unclean. All the articles of Glass in use in the family had been laid in water for three days; copper and iron vessels had been purified with fire;

and upon the day which immediately preceded the feast, the whole house had been cleansed, and all utensils, which were made of porcelain or wood, and could not therefore be thoroughly purified, set aside, and those which were duly cleansed taken from the closet, where they had been kept for a whole year.

Towards evening, when the first stars made their appearance in heaven, the father went through the house with a quill in one hand and a wooden bowl in the other, that he might clear away all scraps and refuse that he should find, and thus assure himself of the cleanliness of the house. Crumbs of leavened bread were purposely scattered about by the mother; under the sofa, however, she hid a large pot of butter, in order that she might have it for family use after the feast had begun.

When the father, quietly repeating prayers to himself the while, had cleared away all the crumbs, and was about to leave the room, Jacob, who had followed him attentively said:

"Father, mother has hidden a pot of butter under the sofa."

"Be still, child!" exclaimed the father, and went towards the door; "I must not know anything about that, else I must take it away and burn it."

"But, father," persisted Jacob, "thou wilt then do as the exciseman did, when thou gave him a gold piece."

"For God's sake, child! thy tongue may bring me into trouble," said the father, greatly annoyed, and left the room.

The following day, Eref Pesach, passed in solemn preparation for the festival. The father fasted in the name of his son, because on this day the angel of the Lord had slain the first-born of the Egyptians, and preserved the Jews unharmed.

"To-day, and yet for some years, must I fast for thee," said the father affectionately to Jacob; "when thou art thirteen, thou wilt bear thy own sins before the Lord."

The rest of the family might not taste of leavened bread, nor even of unleavened bread, before they were consecrated, which would not be until night, when the stars shone forth from heaven.

When it was dark, Isaac Bamberger and his wife came over, as they had no children to prepare the feast for; and all then went into the saloon, where the table of the passover was spread, and was blazing with light.

An elevated seat, well supplied with cushions, was prepared for the master of the house. On the table stood the basket of unleavened bread, covered with a brilliantly white napkin; a large dish of Matzaus; a knuckle of lamb, cooked with sweet and bitter herbs; and for each person was placed a bottle of the sweet raison-wine.

The father took his place of honour, wearing a white robe— that garment of fine linen, which the bride presents to the bridegroom on their wedding-day, and which, besides the feast of the Passover, he only wears at Yohmkipur, or the great feast of reconciliation, and when he is laid in his coffin.

After a fervent thanksgiving to the Lord, who established the feast of the Passover, the bread, wine, and herbs are blessed. Two large pieces of passover-bread are laid upon the seat of honour, to be afterwards divided among the persons present, as amulets against danger by sea and land.

After this, the Hagoden, the book of the captivity in Egypt, and of the Exodus, was read aloud by the father to the little devout community. At the enumeration of the plagues in Egypt, the hearers all dipped their little fingers in the wine, and let fall a drop on the floor for each of the plagues.

When he came to that portion which described the deliverance, he paused, and made a sign to Benjamin, who, amid deep silence, arose, and opened all the doors in the house. This done, the father poured out a glass of wine, and broke a piece of unleavened bread, both of which he placed beside him, as if expecting another guest.

Benjamin having returned, and taken his seat, they all suddenly and with one voice uttered a fervent prayer, that God would send deliverance and happiness to all people who at this moment opened their doors to receive his mercy.

All sat bowed over their books, and without lifting their eyes, that they might not behold that which at this moment was supposed to enter through the doors.

When the prayer was ended, the doors were again locked, and the wine and bread placed upon an adjoining table, where it remained all night, in order that the house, through the whole of this night of the festival might be prepared to receive with hospitality Eilio Novi—the prophet Elias, the Messiah of the Jews.

The house being now filled with mercy, and sanctified to receive the messenger of God, the father cast a glance of joy over the assembled family, and stretching forth his hand, gave the time of the great hymn of the Jews, which all present joined in singing, and the chorus of which is as follows:—

    Adir hu! jivne beishro bekorauv!
    Bimbeiro!
    Bimbeiro!
    Bejomeinu, bekorauv!
    Eil benei!
    Eil benei!
    Benei beishro bekorauv!
    Boruch hu, godaul hu, dogul hu, hodur hu!

    Great is God! he will quickly build his temple!
    Let it be quickly!
    Let it be quickly!
    In our days let it be builded!
    Erect thy house!
    Erect thy house!
    Build the temple in our days!
    He is chosen! he is great! he is a host! he is mighty!

and so on; this enumeration of attributes being continued through the whole alphabet.

The joy inspired by this hymn increased, and became almost wild. They sang in Danish, German, and Hebrew, all at once. Every one gave the loftiest and most endearing names to God:

> Sweet God! Great God! Blessed God! God of prayer! Mighty God!
> Build thou thy temple Schiro!
> Und also ban!
> Und also schier!
> Og byg Dit tempel Schiro!
> Eil benei, &c.

Louder and louder rose the song; the elders sang with tears in their eyes,—the child kept time upon the table, with a glass in one hand and a bottle in the other, and wept for joy till the tears trickled down his cheeks.

The frugal meal was over; for on this particular evening, in opposition to every other feast, nothing is taken but the simplest food, because their ancestors on this night, arrayed in travelling garments, ate in anxiety their last hastily-prepared meal in Egypt; and they now delighted themselves by calling to mind all the wonderful acts which God performed for the Jews. The father described in strong colours the captivity and sufferings of the Jews; how the king sent out his messengers, who took away their male children and slew them, that the Jews might not become too numerous, and rise up against their oppressors. "But," said he, "out of this very cruelty came the deliverance of the Jews; for Moses was by this means brought into the court of Pharaoh, and trained to be their leader and lawgiver.

"The wicked king Pharaoh soon foresaw what he had to fear in Moses. He was warned against him by an evil dream; and, without the support of God, the child would have been murdered. The king called together his interpreters of dreams, and took counsel with them, and they advised him to try the child in this manner: 'Let two dishes be brought in,' said they, 'the one filled with gold, and the other with live coals. If the child snatches at the gold, it is a bad sign, and he must die; but if he snatches at the fire, then is he harmless, and the dream betokens nothing.' It was done as they said. When the two dishes were brought in, Moses was about to stretch forth his hand to the gold, but God's angel held it back, and directed it towards the fire. The boy took up a glowing coal, and when it burned his tender finger, he put it, as children do, into his mouth; and thence it was that Moses never was a good speaker,"

"And," said the uncle, smiling, "thence comes it, also, that Moses's people are wise, and always seize upon gold, rather than upon fire."

"That may very well be," replied Philip, and laughed.

It was now late; and when the customary table-prayer was repeated, all retired to rest.

When Jacob went to his bed this night, he had no fear of phantoms, which still, at times, were accustomed to present themselves in the dark. He had now another object than his youthful persecutors to occupy his mind with and to long after, and that was the beloved Being that they called God.

He said to himself, as he laid himself under the coverlet, "I will now no longer desire to punish the boys; if they deserve punishment, God himself will do it."

CHAPTER VI.

The Jews' festivals are always doubled. Their calendar is reckoned from the creation of the world; and they assert that nobody can come so very near as to say, within one or two days, when the world was positively made. In order, therefore, not to neglect the right day, they hold two holy. On the next evening, therefore, the father told the history of Joseph and his brethren; namely, of the journey to Egypt, and of the endeavours which the brethren made to have Benjamin released. "As they could not manage it by good words," said the father, "the brethren grew angry, and determined to show Joseph what sort of people he had to deal with. Napthali, therefore, ran in an hour into all the cornfields of Egypt, and reckoned up how many sacks of corn there were; but Joseph sent out his son Ephraim, and he quickly did the same. Judah then shouted so loud that all Egypt trembled, and the king fell down from his throne, and broke his leg; but Joseph's son, Manasseh, shouted quite as loud as Judah had done.

"On this, Judah turned round to Joseph in amazement, and said, 'Thou art not an Egyptian; thou art one of us. Thou art Joseph, whom we believed dead.' And thus Joseph was made known to his brethren.

"There are now no more such heroes among the Jews," said Philip, sorrowfully; "therefore is it that we too are oppressed."

"But there's uncle Isaac," exclaimed Jacob.

"Dost thou think so, thou little thing?" said the uncle, well-pleased. "No, no! Besides, it was only in those days when such roaring could be borne; one should now get into trouble with kings, if one shouted so loud."

"But it was very wonderful that Judah could shout loud enough to make the king fall from his throne," remarked Jacob.

"In my time," said Isaac, turning himself with a mysterious air to Philip, "whilst I was in Germany, the Frenchmen shouted so loud, that their king fell down from his throne and broke his neck."

"Yes, the plagues of Egypt at that time passed over the mighty ones!" said Philip.

"Yes, and then they were kind towards us Jews, and called us patriotic," said the uncle.

"What didst thou say, uncle?" asked Jacob.

"It was nothing, my lad; it was only something that we Germans fought for with the French."

"Oh! uncle," exclaimed Jacob, "do tell us something about the French, as they used to do. Tell us the story how they took thee prisoner, and thought thou wast a girl? Thou promised to tell me long ago."

"Not to-night, my lad; on Yohmtauvim" (the great feast-days), "people do not talk about such things. But now I will tell thee why the Jews at Gnesen do not wear the linen garment at Yohmkipur," (the Feast of Reconciliation).

"What linen garment, uncle?"

"Such a linen shirt as thy father has on this evening," replied the uncle. "You see the Jews at Gnesen had, for a long time, no peace in their houses. Every night something came walking in at the door; now it was at one house, and now at another, and always the next day somebody was ill in the house where it had happened. The priest then ordered that everybody should set up a new Mezuossoth,* because the old folks were become unclean, and that might be one cause. A short time afterwards came Yohmkipur, and at the moment when they were saying Maskir-neschommos," (the prayers for the deceased of the community) "there was a great throng in the synagogue. A crowd came rushing in at the door, and filling the whole place, until the congregation at last were almost trampled to death. Neither could one person know another, for they all wore the white linen garment, and the thallis over their heads, because the dead had all been buried in theirs. The priest, on this, made his way to the tabernacle, took out thence the sacred parchment roll, and stretched it forth towards the congregation, saying, in a loud voice, 'In the name of Almighty God! let all those who belong to this place take off their linen garments!'

"This was done, and immediately the space was cleared; but since that day the Jews of Gnesen have not worn the linen garment at Yohmkipur."

"But really, did such a supernatural thing happen?" asked Jette.

"Did it!" exclaimed Isaac Bamberger, warmly; "was not I myself very near buying a horse from the devil?"

"Oh! tell us about it, uncle," prayed little Jacob.

Uncle Isaac needed no pressing, for the incredulous expression of Jette's face was sufficient; and he began:

"What I saw with my own eyes nobody shall persuade me out of; and as sure as I hope to see once more my little Rebecca (may she rest in peace!), so certain is it also that I saw that which I am about to relate. Before the war broke out, when I was a young chap of twenty, as tall and strong as I am now, and not afraid of anything, I bought a horse from a French horse-dealer, who was at Frankfort. One Thursday afternoon,

* A sort of charm which is nailed over the door.

—I remember that afternoon as well as if it were to-day,—I came riding to a public-house, which stood three miles on this side of Sachsenhausen. I was to have been at home that same night; but as there were some people at the public-house who offered me a horse, it was almost dark before I had concluded the bargain. When I was about to leave, they advised me rather to remain there over night than to go in the dark through the little wood which lay on my road.

" 'Do you think I am afraid?' asked I, with vexation.

" 'Even if you are not afraid, Mr. Isaac,' said the landlord, 'it is as well to be prudent.'

" 'Oh! I am content,' cried I; 'even if the devil himself should come to me in the wood!' and, ordering my horse to be brought to the door, rode away.

"Now I cannot deny that I secretly repented of my last word,—really repented, the very moment I had said it. Human beings ought to be humble and not defy God.

"When I came into the wood, I would very gladly have turned back; but I was ashamed, and said to myself, 'Fie! Isaac, hast thou not a good horse and a clever fist? Don't be afraid.'

"If I had put my trust in God, instead of in my horse and my hand, and prayed a Schema Yisroel, that would not have happened which did happen afterwards.

"Well, I rode on; and very strange my feelings were, that I don't deny; and very glad I was when I heard the rapid sounds of horses' hoofs behind me,—I might thus expect to have a companion on the road. I pulled up my horse, that the stranger might join me. He saluted me with a friendly 'Good even;' I did the same, and we soon got into chat. By chance I happened to say that I was a horse-dealer, when the stranger asked me whether I had any inclination to buy his horse.

"'In the high-road?' asked I, smiling; 'one must see a horse's mouth before one buys him.'

"'That you may do directly,' replied he; 'a clever horse-dealer never refuses to trade. Look at my horse's teeth, Isaac Bamberger.'

"I was amazed that the stranger knew my name; but, without making more ado, I leaned down over my saddle-bow, and, taking hold of his horse's head, opened its mouth.. Adaunoi Elauheinu!—flaming fire flashed out of the horse's throat!

"Without speaking a word, I clapped spurs to my horse, and galloped without stopping to Sachsenhausen."

"But that might be naturally explained," said Jette.

"How so?" asked Isaac Bamberger.

"For instance, by supposing that you did not see very clearly," said Jette, with a roguish smile.

Isaac, however, wrinkled his brow, and said:

"Thou knowest, Jette, that thou canst say to me whatever thou wilt; but remember that I asseverated the truth of what I say by the name of my little Rebecca, who was burned!"

"There are incomprehensible things in nature," said Philip, with quiet gravity; "is not every leaf which is put forth from the tree an incomprehensible thing, although we see it so regularly that it appears to us quite simple? But even Thora (The law of Moses), teaches us that there are dark mysteries which it is not well to pry into. Did not Moses change his staff into a snake, and dust into living insects? But if he did it by the immediate aid of God, how came it that his enemies did the same thing by the wisdom of the Egyptians? And the truth of this is not to be doubted because it is written in the laws of Moses. There are still people who can practice such arts. Do not the Jews of Lemberg still say, every Friday evening, an especial prayer because of such black arts?"

"What was that?" asked Jette.

Jacob scarcely dared to breathe.

"There lived in Lemberg," began Philip, "a rabbi, who, as the Christians say, knew more than his father did. He had not the means of keeping a servant, and therefore he made himself a man of clay, and by putting a piece of parchment, on which were written certain holy words, under his tongue, he gave life to him, and he worked for him six days in the week. Every Friday evening he took away the parchment with the holy inscripton, and the clay lay as if dead, until he had repeated his avdolo (the prayer which closes the Sabbath), when he again laid the parchment under his tongue, and he again lived. One Friday evening, however, when the rabbi had remained out in the town later than usual, and the Schabbas lights were lit the in synagogue, the clay man became unmanageable. He rushed into the synagogue, and killed the people with a single blow of his heavy arm,—and he would certainly have killed everybody, if the rabbi had not come in at the right time and taken the holy words out of his mouth. Thus he was again dead; and at the earnest prayers of a congregation the rabbi never more restored life to him. But still the Lemberg Jews repeat an especial form of thanksgiving, because they were delivered from this misfortune."

"Certainly there are dark and mysterious things," continued Philip, after a pause; "are we not a mystery to ourselves? But the believing Jew has no cause to fear. If my repose is mysteriously disturbed at night, of this I may be sure, that it is a warning sign, which the Lord permits the dead to give me, because the tokens on my door-posts are become unclean. If I bear my *Tephilim** with me, I may go safely over land and sea, and sleep with Goijim. The Lord, the God of Israel, is with

---

* Strips of parchment, on which are written the deliverance of the children of Israel from Egypt, and which are fastened every morning, with a certain form of prayer, by means of leather straps, round the head and the left arm.

his children. See, my son, we are but a weak and subjected people; and yet, for all that, how has it gone with our enemies, and those who have lorded it over us? The Emperor Titus, who burned the temple, was slain by his own brother. Antiochus Epiphanes, who would compel the Jews to sacrifice to his gods—the plagues of Egypt be on them—how went it with him? Did he not see in his lifetime his own flesh eaten of worms? And the late King of Prussia, Frederick William the Third? Although he knew that the Jews dared not dig up their burial-ground, yet some years ago, in 1806, he commanded that all the Jewish burial-grounds should be desecrated at the end of the month of October; and before the end of October Napoleon had taken the whole of Prussia, and he had scarcely a burial-ground left for himself. And lastly, the mighty Napoleon himself? As long as he was a Turk among the Turks, a Jew among the Jews, a Christian among the Christians, so long went it well with him, and the Lord was with him in the battle. But when, a few years since, he called together rabbies from every corner of the earth, that they might reform the Jewish religion, and change it—change that of which every particle is immoveable, and shall remain so while the world stands—what happened? In Russia his whole army was frozen to death. And let us see how long he will still hold out, now that Zion's God has turned from him."

"But yet Napoleon is a great hero, greater than either Joab or Abijah," remarked Jacob, warmly.

"Oh! what great art is there in keeping quiet and striking down armies with great cannon?" said Philip; "nor was even that done, excepting by the very qualities which the good God gave him. No! the Jew Eleazar was a greater man than he. He also was a warrior, but he sacrificed himself; he stabbed the elephant in order to kill the wicked king who had desecrated the temple, although he himself must die when the huge beast fell. My son, when the hour of need comes to Israel's children, the Lord sends a champion; and every one, therefore, ought to hold himself in readiness, lest God should choose him. Say thy prayers every morning, over thy tsitsis, so that thou may'st be well-pleasing to God."

"The Christians talk of one who resembled Eleazar," remarked the uncle. "He was called Whitfield, I believe. He leapt into the air for the good of his people."

"Then he was a great hero," said Philip—and bowed his head in reverence. "Self-sacrifice and humility are greater heroism than victory in a thousand battles," added he, according to the Jewish manner of adding a moral to every conversation.

"My friends, let us give thanks to God for our meat!" exclaimed the house-father, after a pause, and according to the formula with which the precentor leads the thanksgiving after meat, when two or three Jews eat together.

The uncle and Benjamin, as well as little Jacob, covered their heads, and repeated the thanksgiving; after which all retired to rest.

The little family group, in whose midst Jacob lived, slept peacefully and soundly after the stories of the evening. With him, however, it was not wholly so. The mysterious power which the stories contained, or which he perceived in them, left a strong impression on his soul. For many nights afterwards he saw terrific shapes; the fearful Judge who sat in the dizzy height, and held a threatening thunderbolt ready to hurl down among poor fearful human beings; the horse of fire which pursued his uncle; white-garmented figures which thronged onward in an awful mysterious crowd; but still, amid the very terrors which made his hair stand on end, he seemed to hear the gentle voice of his mother saying, as if to pacify him, "Perhaps it may be explained by natural causes."

CHAPTER VII.

What is there to relate about the years of childhood? The life of the child is a constant taking in of knowledge; for it exists only events; and its history is the relation of all that which happens round it. But it is from these events and this condition of things around it, that the soul of a child derives its nourishment, even as with the tender plant of the earth, water and air prepare the future blossom. Will these blossoms be beautiful and refreshing, or will they be unsightly and noxious? Will they be gathered by joyful human hands, or wither neglected on their stalk? Yes; for the plant it is inevitably fore-ordained by nature, and the poisonous weed is cradled as joyously and as blamelessly upon its stem as the pleasure-bringing violet.

The human being, on the contrary—he creates for himself his own flavours—philosophers call it human free-will. Merciful God! did I create for myself my own blood, with its mysterious sympathies and antipathies, with its seasons of calm, and its wild tempestings of passion; did I choose for myself the earth, the air, and the light from which the roots of my life should derive their nourishment?

Jacob grew up, tended by loving hands and always alone. He wandered about like a hart in a fenced-in garden, gazing with his brown eyes abroad into the great landscape—yes, that may truly be said; like one of the creatures of the wild; because, however much he might be surrounded by affectionate beings, still there were in many respects, in all that regarded his childish feelings, no intelligible language between him and them; they were like the palings that fenced in his little demesne, and denoted its boundaries.

This solitude gave rise to a circumstance which produced an untold effect upon the whole of his future life.

It was mild spring weather; the sun shone upon the twittering sparrows of the roof; the cat lay on the cellar shutter, and turned herself, snapping at the lively flies with eyes half closed. Around a great heap of rubbish and brick-bats, which had been accumulating from time out of mind in the street, a great number of boys had collected themselves, and with paper caps on their heads, and wooden swords in their hands, made a desperate attack upon the fortress, which was equally desperately defended. Loud cries of onset, shrieks of pain and laughter were mingled together. Jacob sat and gazed at all this glorious sport through the bars of a Venetian shutter; he watched the number of hearty blows that were given and taken, as a thirsty wanderer on a hot summer day gazes on the distant sea.

Many a time he hastened from the window down into the garden to begin a similar game by himself; but every time he turned back dejected, for he found himself as much alone in the garden as in the chamber.

Suddenly a happy idea came into his head, which he as suddenly acted upon. Outside lay the beautiful cat; Jacob seized her and set her upon a board in the garden, which was to represent the fortress, and he himself the attacking army. In order that the cat might not run away, he tied her to the board—a praiseworthy forethought in the commander of a fortress. The cat, however, made such forcible resistance that Jacob's hands and face were covered with wounds, from which the blood flowed, though not exactly in torrents. After some time, how-

4

ever, the cat became so accustomed to the sport, that as soon as she saw the board she sprang mewing up to it, and seemed impatiently to await her adversary.

At length Jacob found that it was not satisfactory in all respects; the cat was far better armed than himself, and the whole war appeared to him unnatural, inasmuch as that no one fell, either upon the side of the attack or defence. Perhaps, also, there mingled with this dissatisfaction a secret pity for the cat, with whom he always concluded a peace; and although his hands and face were bloody, purchased reconciliation with, at the expense of a good meal.

However that might be, Jacob did not rest until his uncle had furnished him with a little dagger, a memorial of war, and armed with this he commenced the combat afresh. The cat soon saw, as Hector did of old, that his adversary, by one means or another, had come into possession of an irresistible weapon, but dared nevertheless to fight to the last drop of blood.

Philip Bendixen came in at that moment when his son, for the last time, struck his dagger into the breast of his enemy, and, he exclaimed, "But what dost thou take thyself for, my son?"

Jacob, who was terrified at what he had done, answered with confusion, "I want to see what more is inside the cat."

The astonished father stood silent for some time, and then said gravely:

"My son, I see in this an indication from Heaven. I early intended thee for study; but latterly I had partly given up the idea, in order that thou mightest assist me in my trade. But now I know that thou art called to be a physician, as Rambem was, who was also impelled by nature to dissect animals and plants, that he might hence acquire knowledge."

"Who was Rambem?" asked Jacob,—ready to hear a story,

and glad that the murdered cat should be put out of his own and every one else's remembrance.

"Rambem* was a great physician among the Jews in the East. So unwearied was his search after wisdom, that when tidings reached him of a still greater physician living in another country, he straightway sent messengers to him, and begged him to receive him as his disciple. But the other physician, fearing that any one should learn his secret arts, replied, 'No.' On this, Rambem disguised himself as a servant, and engaged himself as such to the physician, by whom he was employed to wait upon him, carry his instruments, and other such service. On one occasion, he was called to a sick man, who had a worm in his brain, and he took Rambem with him, that he might hold the patient during the painful operation. When the brain was laid bare, the physician extended his forceps to take out the worm; but Rambem suddenly held back his arm, saying, 'Great master, wilt thou not rather lay a green leaf over the brain? The worm will of its own accord, and following the impulses of his nature, betake himself to the leaf; in the other way, he will make resistance, and perhaps cause the death of the patient.'

" The physician turned in amazement to Rambem, and cried, 'Of a truth, if thou art not the devil, thou must be Rambem!'

"'I am not the devil, but Rambem,' said the wise man, and bowed himself humbly before him.

"'No, no;' cried the old physician; 'it better beseems me to kneel to thee, who art the superior.'

"My son," concluded Philip Bendixen, "become as great in learning as Rambem, and, at the same time, remain as humble."

After many consultations and discussions with his mother and his uncle, it was decided that, immediately after his barmitzvo,† Jacob should be sent to Copenhagen to study. As regarded his

---

* So called from the first letters in his name, Rabbi Mausche Ben Meyer.
† A sort of Jewish confirmation.

further education, and the sedulous observance of his religious duties, all this was to be entrusted to his paternal uncle Marcus, who lived in the capital.

"And now," said the father, "we will seriously set to work on *Gemoro*, that when thou comest to Copenhagen, they may not think that we, out in the country, are fools."

"My Jacob," continued he, as he took down a large volume from the shelf, "prepare to approach with reverence the treasures of wisdom which the great and learned men of old have laid up. There is no branch of human knowledge which they have not examined and studied; and everywhere wilt thou find traces of these researches. They may be often expressed in dark language, and, for the laity, may be hidden, as it were, in riddles."

Now began, for Jacob, the study of the old, subtle, hair-splitting, rabbinical expounding of the law, interwoven with interesting histories, legends, and anecdotes, which lightened and gave a fascination to the otherwise laborious study.

But if, during this period of extreme mental exertion, study was coupled with amusement, so was every amusement coupled with study.

Jacob walked with his father outside the town; they came into meadows where sheep were feeding with their lambs. It was a great delight to the boy; he ran among them, that for once he might play with creatures of his own size.

"Jacob! come here; I want to tell thee something," said his father, with a pleasant smile, as if he had found an agreeable surprise for his son.

Jacob gave up his own pleasure resignedly, and took his father's hand.

"Canst thou answer me this question?" asked Philip. "All men eat lamb's flesh, but few eat the flesh of swine. The Jews do not, the Mahommedans do not, neither do the Hindus; and even among the Christians, this flesh is eaten principally by the poor. Further, a sheep produces only one, at most, two lambs; on the contrary, a sow has six, seven, nay, even nine little pigs. There are thus brought into the world many more pigs than lambs, and there are eaten much fewer; and yet there are more sheep in the world than swine. Canst thou expound that riddle?"

Jacob beat his brains to find some reason for this striking fact, but he could not succeed.

At length his father expounded: "See my son, this is a new proof of the righteousness of the Jewish religion. The dear God gives not his blessing to that which, in consequence of his law to the Jews, is unclean; spite of all its prolificness, the swine does not thrive."

And with this the father launched out into the regions of the expounding and comparing of the law, and his son listened devoutly until they reached home.

Thus was Jacob given up to the mysterious learning of his people.

The world in which his spirit now moved seemed to him like a row of quiet cells in Solomon's temple, where holy men, with long white beards, sat and prayed. It often seemed to him as if he stood in the long, low temple, with its small windows, and all its internal rich, golden decorations, which transformed themselves into strange representations, and wild, dark figures; while from the porch of the temple he heard the crowd of the faithful murmuring prayers around the High Priest, and the God of Zion speaking softly with them.

Through all this, however, there sounded at times a foreign, but living melody—the songs which his mother sang, when, as often happened, she walked up and down the room with him in the twilight. When the moon cast her soft beams in through the window upon him and her, as they often sat together alone on the sofa, she would rise, take his hand, and sing with her sweet voice the songs which she had learned in her youth at the theatre, and among her friends. She would sing with a quiet, rapt enthusiasm, as if she were entertaining herself with recollections of those times, through their melodies. They were, for Jacob, voices as if from another country and another race; yellow locks and blue eyes seemed to rise up on those billows of sound; they gazed on him with such a foreign aspect, and yet there seemed to be a mysterious acquaintance between himself and them. A melancholy longing seized him, but a resistless figure stood in the way. Or when his mother sang, with a clear and rejoicing voice, one of those gay songs in which the rhyme dances and rings like the golden spurs upon the dainty heel of the female dancer, and heaved and sank like the bosom of a young girl,—one of those songs where the lively images intertwined themselves with each other like the tones themselves, —then was it, as if by some unnatural manner, the enormous loss of all childhood's delights made itself perceptible to his soul. He was unconscious of the workings of his own mind,—but still it was to him, not as if he looked out into life, and longed, and longed in vain, but as if he looked behind him upon a barren and joyless life; and then that sense of loss and pain overwhelmed his heart, and he burst into a violent fit of weeping.

"Why dost thou cry, Jacob?" inquired his mother, amazed.

"Because the song thou sangst was so sad," sobbed the boy.

It was unintelligible to the mother; but a mother's tenderness cherishes more than her experience, and a painful foreboding stole into her heart, when she thought that her only child was to be sent out into the world.

CHAPTER VIII.

These melodies took the place of the wild phantoms which had formerly haunted him, only that these had no existence excepting when his mother sang. These wonderful creations were called forth, but the figures were always the same; they danced in the air around him and his mother, played in the corners of the room, and under the ceiling, and gladdened and amused him; anon they sprang merrily out of the window; anon they advanced mournfully nearer, and then died upon his mother's lips.

It was a long time before Jacob could hear these airs with sufficient calmness to distinguish the words from the melody; and it was not until he had learned the accompanying intelligible words that the aërial figures assumed shapes of flesh and blood, and lost their magic power. He then learned music himself, and he, too, might be able to call up these living pictures. His mother gratified him cheerfully in all that lay in her power; and when Jacob, having learned these, yet demanded more and more, she sought up old books, the remains of her youthful days, and gave them to her son, and taught him to read in them.

Thus she also became his teacher, without knowing it; and she taught him that which he never forgot. She gave him the most beautiful gift which he took with him from his paternal home into the world,—a knowledge of his mother-tongue, as pure and clear as that which rung through the rhyme of the poet.

His father was displeased when Jacob began to translate "Gemoro" into Danish instead of German; but his mother came to his assistance, and said:

"Dost thou, then, wish to make the lad a rabbi? Ought he not to know the language which the Christians speak, if he is to go among them?—Consent to it."

The books which Jacob thus became acquainted with were comedies, collections of songs, descriptions of travel, and so on, and which had lain in the house disregarded. Out of several the rats had gnawed great pieces; others had been more or less plundered for the shop; some wanted a beginning; others an end; and a great number of them both; but, as far as Jacob was concerned, this only excited attention, and woke a mysterious presentiment of the life beyond his limits, and where he thought that the continuation was to be found.

Amid these various studies time passed onward with as much uniformity as the circuit of the heavenly bodies, which brings night and day. The new moon brought with it the great day of rest,—which formed, as it were, the mile-posts of the year; and now and then, though very seldom, a comet arose on the horizon of the family life, to make for it an epoch. This was one of the travelling Poles,—one of those extraordinary visitors who suddenly would present himself in the town, without any one knowing whence he came, and who vanished again, after a short stay, without any one knowing whither he went. But what a holiday it made in the house when Philip Bendixen brought home with him from the synagogue a Pole whom he had met there!

There were many reasons to rejoice over the arrival of such a guest. In the first place, they had Minyan,* or the full ceremonial, at the synagogue.

* The full service is not permitted to be performed in the synagogue in the presence of less than ten Jews.

The number of Jews in the town was small, and whenever one Jew quarrelled with another, he revenged himself generally upon all the rest by being absent from the synagogue. When, however, a Pole came to the town, there was always a full attendance; for the angry parties were ashamed of exhibiting their quarrel before so holy a man; therefore they came to their house of worship. The only time when the presence of a Pole was not needed, was on the occasion of Yohmkipur, or the great Day of Reconciliation; for upon this day every Jew forgives another, whatever his cause of quarrel may be. Nay, even, it is believed, that dead foes extend to each other their hands, and say "Scholaum," or Peace, and pardon one another, as they desire that God on this day should pardon them. But the next day, for the most part, the old disunion begins afresh.

At the time of which we are writing, hospitality was a beloved and holy duty. It was considered as a God-pleasing action to receive a stranger; to entertain him with the best that the house contained, and, for the time, to make him its master. But now that knowledge and enlightenment have increased, and the Jews, desirous of standing well with Christians, without entirely breaking with God, whenever they meet with a Pole at the synagogue, do not carry him off with them, as formerly. He is not, as used to be the case, conducted in triumph through the streets to their home; they give him not their best slippers to wear, after they have supplied him with stockings. On the contrary, they prefer paying for his entertainment at a Jewish restaurant. Restaurant! thou Upas-tree, in whose neighbourhood hospitality is poisoned and dies!

But at that time, and in the town of which we write, the Jews were sufficiently oppressed to feel that they were nothing but Jews; nor was it required from them to emulate any but those who were the most perfect Jews; therefore the old hospitality flourished amongst them, and a Pole coming to the place sold himself literally by auction; he went home with him who offered him most travelling-money, so that he would abide with him.

It is very true, nevertheless, that these Poles were not always the most agreeable guests for a cleanly housewife to entertain, nor were they always the most seemly. It happened thus that on one occasion, Philip Bendixen had a Pole for his guest, who was very fond of sour boiled fish. When Philip had emptied his plate, and was about to put it forward for more, the Pole took up the dish, and giving it to Jette, said, "My good Jette, set this aside for my supper!"

No one, however, was displeased with this, because they believed the greater inconvenience any one was put to by his guest, the greater satisfaction had God in his hospitality; and besides, the Pole had an inexhaustible store of witticisms and stories. These witticisms consisted for the most part in the peculiar style in which they were told, or they depended on a play of words, and would require a whole lexicon to make them intelligible. Thus they would tell a story of a Pole who was going to fight a duel. In the first place, however, it must be remarked that the Danish and German word *regel*, or rule, means in Hebrew, *foot*, the Hebrew for head being *rosch*. A Pole therefore, says the story, was challenged to fight, and it was arranged between the two adversaries that they should fight with swords. When the Pole had his weapon in hand, he was about to fall at once on his opponent, without troubling himself either about *tierce* or *quart*, of which he probably understood nothing. The seconds therefore ran between them, saying, "But, Mr. Ephraim, that is wholly against the rule *(regel).*" "How!" exclaimed the furious Pole; "Regel? I do not aim at the foot *(regel)*, I aim at the head *(rosch).*"

It was truly a holiday-time, those Friday evenings, when a Pole got into the story-telling vein, and one tale was begun almost before the other was ended. For even supposing that the story was known to the parents, it was then told especially for the child, the parents expressing themselves as quite pleased to hear it again. And so they were! And even if they—every one—could have told the story themselves, they listened to it again with as much zest as if it was quite new. It was not merely the bald narrative that they heard in the most frequently told religious stories; it was God's spirit which they recognised, and which was always new and interesting.

It was on one of these occasions that Jacob got his uncle to tell him about his being taken prisoner during the war in the disguise of a woman. A gourmand does not anticipate with more delight the savoury dish which is made ready for him, than Jacob, as he prepared himself to listen to his uncle's narrative.

"Our prince," began Isaac Bamberger, "was obliged, in concert with his neighbour, to send a man to the army; but as he and his neighbour were not on good terms, he would, for his part, only send one half, and therefore he chose my old blind father. Now, as a young, lively fellow is always of more value than an old blind man, I got leave to go in his stead. I was well-grown, almost as tall as I am now, but as smooth on my face as a girl.

"Whilst we were lying on the Belgian frontier, in the country town of Königsdorf, I fell in love with the daughter of a wealthy miller who lived close to the town. I met her in the town, for I dared never to go out to her because of her father, who kept a strict watch on account of the soldiers. One evening, however, having got leave of absence, I determined to go and see her. I therefore put on woman's clothes, and went as if to inquire after a place at the mill, and at all events obtain leave to stop there a little while. I was, however, received with open arms; I had offered my services when they were wanted, for two servant-girls had just run off with soldiers. What then, thought I to myself, can be more reasonable than that the soldiers should now in return become servant-girls?

"The wife, who found me so tall and strong, engaged me as milk-maid, and made me give her a solemn promise that I would not allow any of the soldiers to be making love to me; which I easily promised her, and with the determination to keep my word.

"In the evening, when supper was just over, there was suddenly heard a great commotion outside the mill, and the house was filled with a blaze of light. We rushed to the windows; a troop of French soldiers had surrounded the mill, and Königsdorf was in flames.

"'We must defend ourselves,' cried the miller, and called all his men-folk about him, while the women sought shelter in the garret.

"I remained with the men, and armed myself with a gun like the rest, and the miller could not sufficiently praise the brave young woman! Between every shot that he fired, he looked at me with admiration. Our defence was not of long continuance. The Frenchmen rushed into the house. A great big corporal snatched the gun out of my hand, with the exclamation, 'That is a wife for me!'

"'The Germans are coming!' cried the Frenchmen.

"It was so, and just as rapidly as they had come rode they off again, carrying with them no other booty than myself, whom the corporal held in his powerful arms. I made no opposition, being only too glad that my beloved had escaped their notice. The corporal took me on his horse before him; said the kindest things to me; and thus we rode through the burning Königsdorf. When we came to the French camp, the whole squadron laid claim to me; nor was the contest at an end until the corporal asserted energetically that it was his intention to make me his wife.

"'I have carried her off,' said he, 'in the fashion of a knight, and she is, all in all, just the wife for me. To-morrow the field-chaplain shall marry us!' With this all were contented.

"'Pierre Lasusse is going to be married!' cried they. 'Hurrah! the whole squadron is betrothed.'

"'My friends,' said Pierre Lasusse, 'I shall be a happy man—my wife measuring her sixty-four inches, and I myself seventy-two!'

"'Jacques,' said Pierre again, after a pause, and beckoning to a tall young fellow, 'if I should at any time chance to fall, thou must be her second, for thou art the tallest after me, and thou wilt be good to her.'

"I listened to this and a deal more that was said about me for a long time, determining if a favourable opportunity came, to make my sex known to them. I was not, however, without fear. The night was passed in the tent amid a deal of merry talk. In the morning, Pierre, accompanied by his friends, conducted me to the field-chaplain. In camp, people do not stand on ceremony. When the priest was about to begin the holy ceremony, I stopped him, and, as well as I could, tried to make myself intelligible.

"'What!' cried Pierre, who fancied that I merely wanted time, 'does the young woman want to consider whether she shall marry *me*, Pierre Lasusse, corporal in the Anjou regiment?'

"I began very earnestly to explain, but nobody understood me.

"Pierre inquired with impatience what I wanted—what scruples could I have?

"I screamed as loud as I could, 'I am not a young woman!' and snatching off my cap and opening my dress, I showed my short-cut military hair and my soldier's jacket.

"Pierre stood for some moments speechless; he then came up to me, slapped me on the back, and burst into a loud peal of laughter, in which he was joined by the whole squadron, and even by the priest himself."

Isaac Bamberger paused; and the mother, who was sensitive about such things, thought it was a pity to tell stories of this kind in the presence of the child; furthermore, she said, "It seems to me that thou toldest this story rather differently some years ago."

"Some years always make some difference," said Isaac, and he screwed his eyes together in a significant manner. "Thou, too, look'st somewhat different now to what thou didst some years ago."

"But a past event is not a living countenance; it stands in the memory as if hewn in stone," replied Jette, who obstinately pursued her object.

"No," said Isaac, somewhat impatiently, a story is not a law of Moses; a particle in it more or less does not invalidate a man's veracity. Besides, I have not told the most important part; how I was then arrested as a spy, but escaped, because the jailer in the morning, when he saw me laying my Tephilim, discovered that I was a Jew like himself. The boy may hear *that*, because from it he may know that God never forsakes a believing Jew who holds fast by his commandments, and carries his Tephilim always with him."

But now the Pole spoke in an authoritative manner. "Such a story," said he, "is not for a Friday evening. On the Sabbath people must do that which is right; sitting at a good table, they should keep in remembrance God's mercy towards those who keep his Sabbaths with honour. What I spend in keeping my Sabbaths may God give me two-fold, as he did to Joseph Manker Schabbas! This Joseph was poor, yet still he put by the half of each day's earnings wherewith to celebrate his

Sabbath; and when he, on the Friday morning, went out to make his purchases, he considered nothing too costly for the Lord's day of rest. Opposite to him lived a rich man named Eleazar, who did not trouble himself about the Sabbath, but laboured all days alike to increase his riches. He laughed at his poor neighbour who never could get on in the world, because he spent upon one day the half of the whole week's earnings. One day he met Joseph in the street, and laughed at him as usual, adding, 'You ought rather to think about laying something up for your old age, and as a marriage-portion for your daughter.'

"'Don't trouble yourself,' replied Joseph Mauker Schabbas; 'because God could give me all that you possess, if it pleased him to do so.'

"The rich Eleazar became troubled in his mind at these words, and by the bare possibility of the Lord being able to take his riches from him and give them to his poor neighbour.

"There happened about this time to come a great fortune-teller to the town, and Eleazar, who could not overcome his secret fear, went to him to know what awaited him in the future.

"'Be calm,' said the wise man, when he had examined his hand; 'your wealth shall neither be lost at sea, nor shall thieves steal it, nor fire consume it. You will be lucky in all your undertakings; yet still, in the end, the whole of your wealth shall only serve to purchase an agreeable Sabbath for Joseph Mauker Schabbas.'

"'Explain to me this contradiction!' exclaimed Eleazar.

"'I have spoken!' said the wise man, who could not be induced to say more.

"Eleazar was now full of anxiety, lest the fortune-teller's words should become true; and, in order to nullify them, he entered into the wildest speculations; but everything succeeded with him. He sent his ships to the farthest seas; but they returned in safety This anxiety increased more and more. On one occasion, a terrible fire, which raged in the town, approached his dwelling. He forbade that anything should be removed; and when the flames already lit up the gable of his house, he lifted up his eyes thankfully to heaven. At that moment, however, the wind changed; a heavy shower of rain passed over the town, and the fire ceased.

"On another occasion there was a dreadful storm at sea, just at the time several of Eleazar's ships were expected. A messenger approached him sorrowfully with the intelligence that one of them was just about to be stranded. Eleazar, full of joy, pressed a purse full of gold into his hand, and promised him double the amount when those tidings should be verified. The storm abated, and the next day his ship came safely into harbour.

"Eleazar's fear amounted almost to insanity. He let his warehouses and cellars stand open as a temptation to thieves. The thieves thronged thither; but the magistrates, who had expected it, thronged thither also, and thereby seized the whole gang. At length it was made known that Eleazar had suddenly sold all his possessions, and was gone to another town— no one knew where.

"In the meantime Joseph Mauker Schabbas continued, undisturbed, his accustomed way of life; and when, on Friday evenings, he sat at his well-provided table, and consecrated his bread and wine, nobody was happier than he in the whole land; nor could the king himself have made him rise up and leave the room.

"One Friday morning, when he went as usual out into the market to make his purchases, he saw a great crowd of people assembled before a booth. He went nearer, and discovered that the cause of the crowd was, that a fishmonger demanded a hundred gold pieces for one single fish. 'A hundred gold pieces! Did one ever hear such a thing!' exclaimed the people; 'From whom will you get it, good man? If it lies here eight days it will be somewhat cheaper!'

"Joseph could not but confess that he never had seen so beautiful a fish, neither that he had ever had a better opportunity of honouring his Sabbath.

"'A hundred gold pieces,' thought he; 'but it ts really dear! Nevertheless, our Lord has given me good earnings this last week, and for what other purpose than to celebrate his Sabbath! Go back, good people,' said he; 'the man is right; it is a fish worthy of a king's table. I will buy it for the honour of the Lord's Sabbath!'

"He paid the hundred gold pieces, and carried the fish home to his wife. 'It is too large for us alone,' said he; 'I will send a messenger and invite our friends to come to us in honour of the Sabbath.'

"His wife approved of his intention, and opened the fish. How great was her astonishment to find a lump within the fish which, on nearer inspection, proved to be a fragment of a human finger, encircled with a ring! Joseph took the ring and examined it.

"'Wife,' said he, 'I have made a grand bargain; the ring is worth above a thousand gold pieces!'

"He dried it carefully. 'Wife,' said he, 'this ring could not be purchased for a hundred thousand gold pieces!'

"At last, when it glittered before him in all its splendour, he cried, 'Wife! it could not be purchased with a kingdom!'

"The friends came, and Joseph showed them his prize; they congratulated him, and praised God, who had thus rewarded his piety.

"About that time it happened that the son of a neighbouring king was going to be married, and was inquiring after jewels and precious stones as presents for his bride. Joseph therefore set off and came to him; the ring pleased him, and he paid for it immediately a large sum of money, and the remainder he settled on him as an annuity.

"Joseph now could indulge the desire of his heart to the utmost in the keeping of his Sabbath, and could invite his friends and the poor to honour it with him; and often on these occasions, as he sat among his guests, he told the history of the ring. One evening, therefore, when, among others, having invited a stranger, a poor man with a dejected countenance, and only one hand, he related this story, the poor stranger, bursting into tears, exclaimed when it was ended,

"'Great God! Thus has thy soothsaying been fulfilled!'

"All inquired what these enigmatical words meant; whereupon the stranger, rising, said,

"'Have you, then, forgotten the rich Eleazar? I am he! Thus, according to the inevitable will of God has it befallen me. Behold! that which was foretold has come to pass. All my wealth has only served to obtain for Joseph Mauker Schabbas a Sabbath of gladness. You have all heard of the words of the fortune-teller, and how they became more and more verified? At last I could no longer bear it. I therefore made acquaintance with a foreign jeweller, who possessed a ring of inestimable value. I offered him for it all my possessions, which were also inestimable; he was persuaded to agree to the bargain, and I journeyed far, far away, from Joseph Mauker Schabbas. I was easy in my mind in the possession of this precious jewel, which I believed I could secure to myself.

"'One day, however, when I wished to refresh myself, I went to bathe in the sea, and whilst I was swimming for my own pleasure, I observed suddenly that a large fish had gradually approached me. I stretched out my hand in terror to defend myself; the fish caught it in his mouth, and, half unconscious, I was borne by the waves back to the shore. Judge of my horror and despair when I perceived that my finger had been bitten off,—precisely the very finger which wore the ring! I wandered about since that time, poor and helpless, and now I return to die in my native town; and now, also, I perceive how fully has that prediction regarding me been accomplished!'

All uttered exclamations of wonder, and all praised the greatness of God: Joseph, however, descended from the high seat on which he sat, and approaching the unfortunate Eleazar, he said,

"'I beseech of thee to remain for the future with me, and share all that I have; for the whole of it is thine!'

"And Eleazar accepted his invitation."

The long silence which prevailed after the Pole had finished, showed the attentive interest which his auditors had taken in the narrative.

At length Jette inquired whether these events had occurred in Canaan.

"I cannot tell with precision," replied the Pole; "but why do you ask?"

"Why," returned Jette, "I was thinking that if here a Jew were to go to the market to buy a fish, and were to say that he bought it in honour of his Lord's Sabbath, we should hear enough about it."

"Is there here much persecution?" asked the Pole.

"Oh, no—certainly not more than in other places," said Philip Bendixen. "We take care of ourselves, and keep ourselves to our own people; and if one hears anything unpleasant, one makes believe that one does not hear it."

"And if by chance it is said too loud for that," added Isaac Bamberger, "one is not afraid of showing that a Jew can fight his fellow."

"For God's sake!" exclaimed the Pole; "but that won't do.

Let the Jew only begin with the Christian! Better a thousand times be silent and bear everything! Whatever an individual Jew may do against the Christians, even if they themselves gave occasion for it, the whole body of Jews must suffer for. That was the way at Prague."

"When was it? What happened at Prague?" asked everyone.

"It is now about a hundred years since," said the Pole. "But there lived then in Prague a Jew named Lazarus Ovœiles, with his wife, Miriam; and they had a son of fourteen, who was called Simon. One Friday afternoon, a travelling Pole, such a one as myself, entered the house and asked Lazarus if he could help him on his journey. Lazarus was a good man, and would not allow the Pole to leave his house until he had shared his Sabbath meal; he showed him, therefore, into a chamber, prepared for him a bath, and conducted him to the synagogue. When they came home Miriam had lighted the Sabbath candles and spread the table, and they all cheerfully sat down to the savoury meal.

"After they had eaten, they began to speak among other things of the persecution which the Jews suffered from the Christians, and of the attempts which were made to seduce young men from the faith of their fathers. At that time the Christians had for some time enjoyed peace both among themselves and with the Turks; and when they are at peace, they always fall upon the Jews.

"Lazarus, who was a strong and powerful man, said mournfully, 'Alas! alas! it is a hard time! Our own children fall from us, and curse their fathers and their forefathers in the temples of the Christians. Thanks be to God, that I have yet my son, and can give the benediction of the Sabbath!'

"'I hear that within the last week two Jewish youths have abjured the faith of their fathers,' said Leib Löbel, the Pole.

"'Don't speak of it,' cried Lazarus, warmly; 'it spoils my Sabbath's peace. It is a cursed magic, against which we have no power.'

"'Why not speak of it?' asked Leib Löbel; 'the power which seems to you so dark, just as in magic, ought, I maintain, to be looked into. Yes, you perhaps will be amazed, when I tell you that in my wanderings in this country I have narrowly looked into this business, and I understand it. Look here! It is the Jesuits! And in order that they may accomplish their ends, and seduce the Jewish youth, they make use of sin—or, to speak plain out, of sinful women. They employ women who go to the Jew shops and buy goods, which they desire the young men to bring home to them. When once a poor lad has fallen into their snare, their first object is to persuade him to lay aside his Arbakamphoth—which is his sign of purity, his covenant with God. When this comes to the parents' knowledge, they severely chastise their son; and he, in dread of a yet severer punishment if he still continue in the path of error, mostly runs away from his home, and takes refuge with his supposed friend, who then gives him up to the Jesuits.'

"'If I had such a son I would flog him to death!' exclaimed Lazarus, trembling with rage at the bare thought.

"'Our Lord spare you in mercy from such a misfortune,' said Leib Löbel; 'but nevertheless be circumspect; for the holy fathers despise no means of obtaining their ends. Your son, too, is a handsome lad, and they like such to be servants in their church.'

"'Merciful God! I cannot bear to think of it,' exclaimed Lazarus, and held his hands before his eyes. 'My beloved Simon!' said he, turning towards his son, 'come and gladden thy father's eyes by showing me that I am a happy father, and that thou still wearest thy Arbakamphoth.'

"Simon, who sat opposite to him, rose, opened his dress, and turned about to approach his father, but as he passed the door to do so, suddenly opened it and disappeared.

"Lazarus continued sitting for some moments as if turned to stone, and then springing up furiously, hurried after his son.

"A breathless excitement prevailed at the table. After about a quarter of an hour's time, the voice of Lazarus was heard in contention in the passage. Pale and out of breath he returned and took his seat as before.

"'Will anybody take more?' asked he.

"No one replied.

"'Clear the table, then,' said he to the servant, 'let us pray.'

"'What hast thou done with thy child?' asked Miriam, full of terror.

"'My child!' shrieked Lazarus, 'I have no child! The bastard, who some minutes since sat opposite to me, shall be cursed in time and eternity; child, and child's children, shall be cursed; his name shall be rooted out from the earth, even as it is rooted out of my heart!'

"'My child!' lamented Miriam; 'thou hast murdered my Simon.'

"'Have courage!' said Leib Löbel; 'your husband has not found Simon. Do you think that a father would curse his son after he had murdered him?'

"Simon's flight caused a great commotion in the community. Until now they had been only the children of the poor who had been seduced; and who, after some little inquiry had been made after them, were soon forgotten by all excepting their own families. But Lazarus was the richest man in the whole Jews' quarter, and everybody talked of this misfortune as if it concerned themselves; besides which, it was soon understood that Lazarus would richly reward any one who would restore to him his son.

"After some time a young Jew of the name of Manasseh

came to Lazarus, and promised that he would have his son restored to him, in case he received the promised reward.

"'Yes that is all very well,' said Lazarus; 'but let me see some probability of it first.'

"'I can very easily do that,' said Manasseh; 'the thing will be done, only we must use circumspection. Your son is located in the house of the baptized Jew, Franz Kawka, and the maid-servant takes him every day to the Jesuits to be instructed. But as a matter of course, things do not go right with a baptized Jew; the maid-servant has robbed him; she has lately sold me two coverlets, on which is the name of Franz Kawka; I have told her that I will have her committed for theft, if she does not to-morrow bring your son to a place which I have named.'

"'That is another affair,' said Lazarus, glad to hear that Simon was still receiving instruction, and was not yet baptized. He immediately gave Manasseh ten gold pieces, and waited impatiently for the next day which would restore his son to the paternal home and the paternal faith.

"The following day Manasseh was punctual as to time and place. When Simon saw him approaching, he exclaimed to the girl, 'That man knows me; he will, perhaps, betray me.' But the girl held Simon fast. Manasseh sprang forward, threw the coverlets back to her, seized upon Simon, whose cries he prevented by holding his hand over his mouth, and bore him into the Jews' quarter.

"There a great crowd was immediately collected, who, amid shouts and curses, accompanied Simon and his conductor to the house of Lazarus.

"In the meantime Lazarus was walking impatiently up and down his chamber. Miriam and Löbel sat silent, in a state of dreadful expectation. Lazarus had declared his determination to send his son to his brother-in-law, Rabbi Feibel, of Fürth, that he might avoid the disgrace of his doing penance in the synagogue at Prague. Now, therefore, he awaited with fear and the utmost excitement the result of Manasseh's undertaking, and yet dreading once more to meet his deluded son.

"'Yes, it shall be so,' said he; 'he shall go to Fürth; Rabbi Feibel will be strict with him, and I will never more see him. But first, however, I will give him a severe chastisement for a remembrance.'

"'Wilt thou murder thy son in thy violence?' asked Miriam.

"'Have I not given Manasseh ten gold pieces? He has cost me sorrow and anxiety enough, to say nothing of the money that has been spent on him,' said the father.

"At length the united prayers of Miriam and Löbel obtained from him the promise that he would not see Simon, and that Löbel alone should receive him and conduct him to an adjoining apartment.

"When Simon was brought to the house, and Lazarus heard the loud voices of the crowd of Jews outside, he fancied that they were offering him their congratulations on the recovery of his son. The noise, however, continuing, he stepped out of the door, and asked the people, 'What will you, my friends?'

"'Chastisement!' cried many voices; 'that you should chastise your son!'

"The pride of the rich man was roused, and he said, 'What is it to you, whether I chastise my son or not?'

"With that the tumult still more increased, and a voice exclaimed, 'You have over-indulged your son; it is your own fault that he has been befooled, and is gone over to the Christians! Now you will not even punish him! Poor folks' children must do penance in the synagogue, so that every one who enters may smite them, and they must be thankful for it as a benefit; but you are going to send your son to Fürth: is he to do penance there? No; here he has disgraced our holy religion, and here it is that he shall do penance!'

"The crowd applauded by a loud shout, and some cried, 'If you will not chastise your son, we will!'

"Any one may conceive what that proud man suffered from these words, and all the more because he felt that it was with justice that he was thus humiliated.

"All his rage, however, turned against the one who had been the cause of this scandal; and the thought of Simon's folly awoke afresh a frenzy of rage.

"'Hold!' cried he, to the throng who were about to rush into the house; 'I will show you that I am as good a Jew as any among you!'

"With these words, he seized a stick, and rushed up-stairs to the room into which Simon had been conducted. Löbel heard him coming, and locked the door; but Lazarus burst it open with his foot, and sprang upon his son. In vain Löbel rushed between them, to hold him back. The furious man hurled him against the wall, so that he was stunned for the moment.

"'Bastard!' cried Lazarus, gnashing his teeth; 'why hast thou turned Christian?'

"'Dear father,' said the boy, mournfully, 'I will confess all, only do not kill me!'

"'Bastard! accursed bastard! confess why thou wouldst be a Christian?'

"'Because Dr. Mänzer, the rector of the University,' returned the boy, meekly, 'said that Jesus Christ, the crucified, is the Son of God and our Messiah.'

"These words, spoken in the fear of death, seemed to excite Lazarus beyond himself. He struck his son with the heavy stick, as he cried, 'There, that is for Jesus!'

"The son exclaimed, 'I am a Jew! Schema, Yisroel! Adaunoi Elauheinu, Audaunoi echoid!' (Hear, O Israel! the Lord thy God is the only eternal God!)

"But the father paid no attention. 'That is for Christ!

That is for the Crucified! That is for the Son of God! That is for the Messiah!'

"Here he paused, for Simon cried no longer, and the blood flowed abundantly. He raised him from the ground; he laid his hand on his breast, but it heaved not.

"At that moment the room was filled with a tumultuous throng of strangers. They were Christians, who, being aware of the disturbance in the Jews' quarter, had now thronged hither, and, still increasing in number, pressed into the house.

"When they saw Simon lying dead, they exclaimed, 'This was a Christianized child! The Jews have killed him!'

"With that they fell furiously, not alone on Lazarus, but on Löbel, and even poor Miriam, almost murdering them. After that they plundered the house, and lastly set fire to it. Then they entered the houses of the other Jews, plundering them and setting fire to them also, until the soldiers came and drove them away.

"A month afterwards, Lazarus, Löbel, and Manasseh were executed, with the most horrible tortures. Miriam, in the meantime, was dead, as well as her son. Thus was the curse of Lazarus fully accomplished, 'that his generation should be rooted out of the earth.'"

The Pole ceased to speak. A deep emotion was evident on every countenance.

"It is late," said Philip Bendixen, after a long pause; "let us pray!"

He requested his guest, to whom he wished to do all honour, to lead the prayers; and when these were ended, the whole family group retired to rest.

CHAPTER IX.

Strangers were very seldom seen in the house. With the exception of the Burgomaster and the Inspector of Excise,—who whenever they came to the shop were invited in,—the Bendixens received visits only from the few Jewish families who, besides themselves and uncle Bamberger, lived in the town, and that always upon the great Jewish feast-days.

The incessant little quarrels among the Jews prevented frequent social intercourse; and even when under apparently favourable circumstances they did meet, the social element had not sufficient intellectual and moral training to keep their tempers always under control. A little more pretence in one neighbour than in another; a little increase of splendour, by which one neighbour's wife cast another's into the shade, and so on, occasioned many a secret grudge, which only needed opportunity to make itself felt. Thus, for the greater part of the year, people looked askance at one another, spit before them in the street, depreciated the quality of their goods, and did each other as much mischief as possible.

It would be wrong, however, to deny but that there were etiquette and ceremonial enough when they did meet together; perhaps etiquette and unfriendliness are pretty nearly related. Nobody relinquished any of his dignity by going to visit a person more frequently than he visited in return: attention was paid to every word and look of either host or hostess. If they observed that more attention was paid to another than to themselves, if they were smiled upon more kindly, if more inquiries were made after their health, the observer became suddenly as silent as the dead, and after a little while rose up and went away with the firm determination never again to let his shadow darken their doors. But neither did this comprise all the dangers and difficulties of social intercourse, because the matron whose husband was rich expected to be received with more marks of respect than she whose husband was less rich; whilst the other, on her part, watched with jealous anxiety lest her rival should be preferred to her because of her larger amount of wealth; so that it seemed next to impossible that social intercourse should lead to anything but ill-will.

History relates that, whilst the Romans were besieging Jerusalem, party feuds raged with as much violence among the Jews themselves as against the enemy outside the walls.

Wonderful people! who in your exile present still the same picture! Was Jerusalem your mother, and have you sucked in discord with your mother's milk? You dwell scattered among foreign nations, who hate, envy, and despise you; and yet, instead of banding yourselves together, you hate, envy, and despise one another.

And what is the object of your mutual regard! Money! Money is the patent of your nobility, and you bow yourselves as humbly before him who is wealthy as the Christians bow before ribbons and stars. Ribbons and stars, however, any one may get; but money!—you are right! Of the two, you are most right! For is not gold your sword and your shield? Do not you buy with it the air you breathe, the life of your children, and the quiet of your grave? Have you not been commanded from times of old to bring money? Why, then, should people be angry that you seek after it?

And do not the Christians then love money, since they reproach you for getting it, and rejoicing over it? Are you alone infected by this infirmity; or does the worm gnaw the whole race alike? The misfortune is, that some of you have the bad habit of letting your eyes twinkle, and your finger convulsively clutch, if gold glimmers before you. Lay aside this ugly trick, and learn some pretty phrases about virtue and the dignity of human nature, and the filthiness of luere—but utter them without emphasis!

The New Year commenced with almost universal good-will in the town, so that nearly all the poor were invited to the house of Philip Bendixen. The men only went home from the synagogue to fetch their wives; and now, one after another, entered the large parlour, where Jette and her husband received them with the most exact attention. After many bows and curtseys on both sides, the company were seated in the room—all experiencing the agreeable influence of a holiday—a day of rest and solemnity.

Leib Essen, the last comer, rubbed his hands, and said, "To-day we had a regular gathering! Everything was so bright and beautiful, that I was quite delighted."

"So was I," said Philip Bendixen; "nor since I left Copenhagen have I heard any one blow the horn* so well as Rabbi Jokuff. He is a great master of the horn."

"Only think," said Mausehe Nyborg to his wife, Leib Essen presented me with the Mitzvo; I had Gelilo."†

---

* On the great feast-days, Satan presents himself as an accuser before the throne of God; therefore is a horn blown in the synagogue, every tone of which becomes an angel, which defends the congregation from the accusations of Satan.

† The worship of the Jews is based upon the principle that the people themselves should conduct it, and thus that a knowledge of the law and the ceremonies should not become the monopolised possession of a separate class. The priests, therefore—for the sacrifices have ceased since the fall of Jerusalem—have nothing to do with the ceremonial of worship, and might be wholly dispensed with. One of the congregation reads the prayers, if they have not a hired precentor. On Mondays and Tuesdays three, and on Saturdays eight por-

"Ho, but that was kind!" said his wife, and cast a friendly glance on Leib Essen.

"That was to strengthen our reconciliation," said Leib Essen, and offered his hand to Mausche Nyborg.

"I shall remember to pray for your Yohmkipur," said Mausche Nyborg's wife; "the blessed feast of reconciliation! it will be here in nine days. Dost thou keep this great feast?" inquired she of Jacob, as she drew him towards her.

---

tions of Thora, or the law of Moses, are read by the congregation themselves each portion being read by a different person.

The Thora is kept in the holy tabernacle, God's Spirit being throned therein. The ceremonial of the taking out of the book of the law, when it is to be read aloud, resembles, in pomp and etiquette, that in use at Christian courts. One person, bowing the while, reverently undraws the curtain, opens the tabernacle, takes the law therefrom, and delivers it to the precentor. When the law has been laid upon the reading-desk and opened, it is the office of another person to lift it up, and extend it towards the congregation, with the words, "The law of Moses is truth," which words are repeated aloud by the congregation. A third person then steps forward to close the book (Gelilo), and to wrap it in the mappo—a piece of cloth which resembles the swaddling-band of a child—and afterwards enclose it in its outer covering of velvet or silk, with the accompanying silver ornaments. This outer covering is presented to the synagogue by some wealthy person, in the same way as the Christian altar-cloths, &c. He who last reads from the Thora conveys it back to the tabernacle, and he who took it thence again receives it, replaces it, and, bowing, locks it in. Every one who touches Thora kisses it before he gives it from his hand, as well as the particular part of his fingers which have touched it, and which have thus been made holy.

All these various duties are regarded as God-pleasing acts (Mitzvaus), and are purchased by auction in the synagogue itself; the purchaser may, however, present them to another. He may give him the Mitzvo which he himself has purchased; and this is done when a person celebrates a household festival, or when one person wishes to show his goodwill to another. The money which is gained by these auction-sales belongs to the synagogue. In Copenhagen, where everything, since the erection of the new synagogue, is conducted in as aristocratic and absolute a manner as possible, democratic auctions are no longer permitted; nevertheless, these offices may be purchased there underhand the day before. This change gave occasion to various small revolts in the synagogue, before the new mode could be carried into effect. Those who made opposition, however, were turned out; and for this they easily consoled themselves, because the presence of ten Jews forms a congregation, and a synogogue in an upper room, or under the open heaven, is everywhere sufficient.

"Yes," said Jacob, proudly; "I fasted already half the day; and I fasted, too, half the day Tischebeaf."*

"Thou art indeed a fine lad," said Madame Nyborg, and gave Jacob a piece of orange.

The father and one of the company now discussed, in an under voice, the good qualities of Jacob; then there was a silence.

At length Schaul Bernburg remarked, "Certainly everything was very well conducted in the synagogue to day; but yet it was nothing to Copenhagen! What would I not give to hear again a regular Durhno!† It makes me ill with longing to think of it."

"Why did you not stay in Copenhagen, then?" asked the fat Wulf Wendel. "You are always talking about it. If I had been in your place I would have stopped there."

Schaul Bernburg had been obliged to leave Copenhagen on account of some unpleasant affair. He bit his lip and was silent, that it might not appear as if he understood the remark. But the others understood it; and the conversation was again at a stand-still.

In order to find something to talk about, Philip Bendixen walked up to the window, and looked out, as if for some particular object, and then remarked, "God knows why we have not the honour of Simon's Nasche's company to-day."

"He knew, probably, that he should meet me here," returned Wulf Wendel, with a malicious smile.

* The anniversary of the destruction of Jerusalem. This is a fast-day, and for the nine preceding days no flesh is eaten, in remembrance of the sorrows of Jerusalem.

† On the great feast-days, all the descendants of the race of the High Priests belonging to the congregation, standing on an elevated place in front of the tabernacle, and clothed from head to foot in white garments, pronounce, in a peculiar tone, and with mysterious, uniform gestures, a blessing upon all the assembled congregation. No one may dare to look at them, as they are supposed to represent the Godhead. This ceremony is called Durhno.

"Are you at variance?" asked Philip.

"At variance? The fellow stinks of pride, so that one cannot come near him," replied Wulf Wendel. "Now you shall hear. A few days ago he came into my shop; and as I had not anything to do just then, I chatted with him a little. He talked about the bad times, and about the loss—may it remain with him!—which he had some time ago, when the excise-inspector seized some of his goods; and he complained that he did not know how he should manage to pay the fine that was imposed. 'Now,' says I to him, 'I'll tell you what; don't let your wife wear such expensive silks for her dresses! Have not I justice in what I say? Such a scamp, to come and complain that you have hardly bread in the house; and yet, when one sees his wife, one might believe that she had married the richest man in the town?' 'What do you mean?' said he, and, spitting before me, he exclaimed, 'that will turn to no good, I can tell you! Take you care that the Lord does not punish your innocent children for your haughtiness! For the Lord, the God of Israel, is a righteous God, and he punishes the sins of the fathers.' More I did not hear, for I ran in to escape his bad words, and he went his way. Let the curse fall on him!"

"But you were really too hard on him, Wulf Wendel," said Philip. "Every one likes to see his wife well dressed. Does not Abba Hilkiah say that a man shall give his wife fair apparel, that she may make herself agreeable to him, so that he may not find pleasure in other women?"

"Listen, Philip Bendixen," cried Wulf Wendel, with a flushed countenance; "I don't want any admonition from you! You are not yet a priest. You think, perhaps, that because you have a few shillings more than me, that you are to lord it over me. The Lord is against the haughty."

His wife put her hand before his mouth, to prevent his uttering a word which should bring bad luck; but the exasperated Wulf Wendel rose to leave the house.

"Do not let this happy day be disturbed by dissension," said Philip Bendixen, taking his hand; "I did not mean to displease you."

Wulf Wendel allowed himself to be appeased, and resumed his seat.

"There goes old Martha," said Isaac Bamberger, and pointed out of the window, in order to divert the thoughts of the company from the foregoing painful scene.

Scarcely had this move been made, when a shrill voice was heard in the street below: "May you be rooted out! There you sit and feast, whilst a poor old woman like me cannot get even a *kuggel* to her *scholet** on the Sabbath. The Lord will not forget it!"

Isaac Bamberger opened the window, and replied good-humouredly,

"Well, then, come in and take some refreshment with us, and eat a piece of butter-cake, which has been saved for you from yesterday.

"Butter-cake have you, on Friday evening, whilst other children of Israel must be contented with dry bread and a bit of lean meat!" cried the old woman, and smote her hands together; "but I will not come into your house. I should only go as a beggar to the rich man; and you are no Boaz;—may your name be rooted out!"

Vexed at his unsuccessful attempt to restore cheerfulness to the company, Isaac closed the window; but still resolved to do his best, he smiled, and said to the guests,—

"I am no Boaz she says; neither is she a Ruth!"

* The Jews do not dare to cook on the Sabbath; on the Friday, therefore, they prepare a soup, which is kept hot over burning coals during Saturday. This is called *scholet*. A pudding, made of flour, sugar, and suet, is boiled in the soup; and this is the *kuggel*.

They laughed, and one of the women remarked,—

"Who troubles themselves about what old Martha says? If one were to strip oneself to clothe her, she would curse one because one would not give her one's skin also. Last evening she came to me for my customary Sabbath alms. I generally give her six skillings, but I had just then only four skillings in small change, and I gave them to her. What did she do? Why she threw the four skillings down upon the floor and said: 'If you have not the grace to give me six skillings, then I have the grace to give you as much!' And with that she put six skillings down on the table, and went out. Yet, what is one to do with such poor Jews!" continued the speaker, "if one gives a Christian begger one skilling, there is no end of the blessings he will heap on you; but as for a Jew, an alms is a claim, and he himself decides as to what amount you are to give him."

"If I had been in your place, Memmell, I should have done to Martha what I once did to black Ephraim, from Asia," said Isaac Bamberger; "you remember that he went about here collecting money because he had been burned out. He came to me too, and I was going to give him a gold piece. 'Pardon me, Mr. Bamberger,' said he, 'but your brother-in-law has given me two gold pieces.' I put my one piece into my pocket, and replied, 'Pardon me, Mr. Ephraim, then my brother-in-law has given for me also.'"

"God keep me from daring to do so with Martha," exclaimed Memmell, laughing. "But I can tell you, Jette Bendixen, that you may esteem yourself fortunate that Martha did not see the beautiful new gown you have got on to-day, or she would have cursed you all night," said she to Jette, looking somewhat enviously at her dress.

"It is not a new gown," replied Jette. "I have only had it cleaned, and made up again; one must help oneself as well as one can."

"That is another thing," said Memmell, reconciled to Jette's handsome appearance.

"As we are talking about Martha," began another woman, "have you heard how a little while ago she behaved to Schaule Essur? It was on a Friday, the day after he was a bankrupt, and she was going round for her Sabbath alms. When she was going to knock at his door, her daughter who was with her said, 'is it not better to excuse him his alms now, as he is a bankrupt?' 'Ei, what!' said Martha, angrily, 'who gives me anything?'"

"That's like her," said Memmell.

"I don't know why the poor of a congregation should demand more than they get," remarked Gidel, a plump little matron. "Is there not bread and meat distributed to them every Friday, and money besides? Don't they also, at the time of the Passover, have their passover-cake, and everybody remembers Purim with a gift? Is there any time of rejoicing without their having their share of its gladness? Do the Christians do as much for their poor?"

Old Rabbi Jacob now spoke; he was a little, grey-haired man, of a quiet and peaceful demeanour. He lived upon a little property of his own, and was much renowned for his learned writings, whence he was entitled Rabbi. "The merciful God." said he, looks upon the intention and not upon the gift. If thy brother asks thee for bread, thou must not give him a stone; but the unwilling mind converts the bread into a stone. You give alms to old Martha, and demand from her thanks. Do you not remember the time when she was rich? Then she was received with an affectionate Baruch habo (blessed be thy coming) when she entered your door, and the place of honour was given to her. She remembers that time when she receives alms at that very door. She does not look at the gift, but her ear and her heart wait in vain for the Baruch habo which she no longer receives. Let us praise Almighty God when we are saved from temptation."

The company sat silent and embarrassed.

"Tell me, Wulf Wendel," again begun the indefatigable Isaac Bamberger, "How is your lawsuit going on? He gives you a deal of trouble about your money, this chapman Jenson!"

"All the plagues on his head!" exclaimed Wulf Wendel. "If a Jew were to act in that way to a Christian, should not we hear about it? It is now half a year since I ought to have had my money, according to his written promise, and he has put off the payment all this time, on pretence that the goods were not worth as much. Did I compel him to buy my goods? And throughout the whole of his legal statement, he spoke of me as JEW Wendel. But, wait a little! The thing will soon be decided,—and if I sell his last bed from under him, I'll have my money! Every time he sees me, he grins a defiance at me. But only wait a little."

"There is no doubt but that you are in the right, Wulf Wendel," said Isaac; but this Jenson makes a horrible talk about it in the town. He spends all his time at the publichouse, and tells everybody that Jew Wendel will be his ruin, and leave him and his children nothing but straw to lie on."

"For God's sake!" cried many, anxiously, "don't drive it to that extremity; do you hear, Wulf Wendel?"

"What, am I to spend my money for nothing?" shrieked Wulf Wendel, in great exasperation. "Do I pick up my goods in the street? Did not I myself make the proposal that I would be satisfied with what three Christian shopkeepers should agree upon as the value of the goods?—and did not the fellow reject it? But now if it should cost me my life, I will have my money to the last farthing! Yes, *Jew* Wendel will leave him and his children lying on straw!" added he, gnashing his **teeth.**

It was impossible now to restore cheerfulness to the company. Many were filled with anxiety as to the consequences which this lawsuit would produce for all the Jews in the town, if Wulf Wendel prosecuted it with the enmity which he avowed.

Again the shrill voice of Martha was heard below the window, as she returned down the street; and with anything but agreeable feelings the company separated amid constrained compliments and expressions of friendship.

CHAPTER X.

AMONG the letters which Philip Bendixen received one morning by the post, was one which caused him to clasp his hands in fear and despair. It was from his brother in Copenhagen, and was as follows:

"DEAR BROTHER,

"When you receive this letter the news of the late dreadful events here may probably have reached you, and I now write that you may know that our lives are spared to us— blessed be the Lord. But what will be the end of it? Thus inquire we anxiously from each other, and none know how to make a consolatory reply; we look forward to the evening of every day with deathly fear.

"The Christians are as if they were gone mad, and break the windows of all the Jews; and woe to the Jew who dares to look out among them. Rabbi Jehudo, who was knocked down and trampled upon as he was going to his house, is dead; and many other pious Jews have been sorely mishandled. My father-in-law fell into the hands of two sailors, who vowed to kill him if he would not dance with them. What was the old man to do? They made him dance, and then they spit in his face, and said, 'There's for thee, thou Jew-smaus, because thou hast danced so badly!' They, however, led him uninjured home; but now he lies sick to death of pure fear. It is come here like a pestilence, from Hamburgh; and it spreads from one country to another. Would that it were merely the pestilence that they had got! Some days things are quiet again, and they have the windows mended. But it is their evening's amusement.

"We have thought of flying from this Gomorrah, and taking refuge with you; but the superintendent of police, old Haagen, has persuaded us to wait yet a few days. I went up to him to ask for a passport, and says he to me, in his way of talking, 'I remember you, in old by-gone days, when you came to our mother's house. Are you afraid, Marcus? Don't be afraid; we'll take care of you. Wait here a few days, until the king has sent in the soldiers; and leave all to me and my brave staffs!' I know, my Danish, better than that. Does the Lord put his strength in the staves of the police? However, if things don't soon alter, I and my wife and children shall leave the place; and hope that you will be able to receive us until all gets quiet again.

"Greet thy good wife and little son from us, and receive thyself the same affectionately from us all.

"Thy faithful Brother,
"Marcus."

Philip Bendixen hastened, in unspeakable sorrow of heart, over to his brother-in-law, to acquaint him with the fearful news. Here he met several Jews, who had already received similar letters, in some of which the unfortunate events were described in still stronger language. The soldiers had refused to serve, they said, and the burger-guard had taken part with the insurgents; the king was ready to sacrifice the Jews to save his crown; therefore every Jew throughout the kingdom was to be slain on a certain day, &c., &c.

A horrible fear of impending misfortune seized upon all present, and a deep pity for the faithful brethren who had already fallen under it. The men wept like children, and smote upon their breasts, in that bewilderment of grief which is incapable of reasoning. "Blessed are they who rest in the grave!" said they; "their eyes are closed in peace! We are as at the time of the Deluge; misfortune surrounds us, and there is no place for us to flee to! Woe, woe to us! The Lord has turned away his face from his people, and that which was written has come to pass, 'Your feasts shall be turned to sorrow, and your gladness to tears.'"

"What is the use of bewailing?" said Isaac Bamberger. "Our brethren at Copenhagen are in God's hand, and we cannot help them. But we can help ourselves, if we stand steadfastly together, and do not lose our courage."

"How can we?" asked they, eagerly.

"We are only a few," said Isaac Bamberger, stepping into their midst; "but we are sufficient to defend ourselves behind brick walls. I once saw a handful of Frenchmen defend themselves in a churchyard against a whole regiment, and they did not give up until cannon were brought against them. The Christians here have no cannon. Let us all assemble with our families, and defend ourselves to the last drop of blood. I offer you my house for this purpose."

"You talk very finely, Isaac Bamberger," cried Wulf Wendel. "But are we all to leave our houses and our property, and come and defend yours? And who says that we are all to be seized upon? Perhaps they will be satisfied with individuals, and spare the rest, the most powerful. But if we are all collected together, and are seized upon, then we shall all suffer."

"And why must we defend ourselves?" said another; "we are neither soldiers nor Frenchmen. It is all very well for people who have learned nothing else; but if I were to stand defending a house, and a crowd of people came up thronging and yelling, I should throw myself out of the window to them from very fear. I don't make myself out to be a greater hero than I am. Caleb was a warrior, but Aaron a man of peace."

"From the time of the destruction of Jerusalem," said a third, mournfully, "has it been the fate of Israel to suffer undefended. I will go home and await what the dear God will send us."

The rest were of the same mind; and, sadly dejected, each went his way.

Isaac Bamberger went over with Philip to comfort and encourage his wife.

In the meantime, later intelligence had also come to other inhabitants in the town, and people were assembled at various places to talk it over.

The magistrate and the inspector of excise were with the burgomaster. "I have given orders that every attempt shall be crushed in the bud," said the burgomaster; "let all trust to my management. God knows what I must do if a tumult actually breaks out! I have two police, one of whom was turned out of the excise because of his age and infirmity, and the other was put into the police because having in 1809 lost a leg, he had no other means of getting a livelihood. That is my whole force; but still I think that things will remain quiet here. I stand well with the townspeople, and a few sensible words, spoken at the right time, will do much."

"And even if the Jews did get such a fright that we for the time to come were free from them, we should have no such great loss," said the magistrate. "I am not intolerant, but I confess candidly that I am not very fond of these people of Moses. This repugnance to the Jews must have some deep ground,—it lies in the blood of us all."

"It lies rather in education," said the excise-inspector,—a kind-hearted, grey-haired man, in the decline of life. "They educate themselves, and we ourselves, in this feeling of dislike;

we suck in hard judgment of each other with our mother's milk."

"But they are, nevertheless, a money-griping, ignorant people," observed the magistrate; "and even the best among those who live in the town—for instance, Isaac Bamberger and his brother-in-law, Philip Bendixen—have a something disagreeable, a certain I don't know what about them. One feels someway as if one were in another atmosphere when one is among them; it is, perhaps, the onion-atmosphere," added he, with a short laugh.

"Bamberger and Bendixen are two clever and sensible men," said the inspector of excise; "and it would grieve me sincerely if any harm happened to them. And have you seen that handsome, sharp lad of Bendixen's? When I see that lad, I am regularly sorry to think he should be a Jew."

"Look you," exclaimed the magistrate, "you have just the same feelings as I have. If you see anything good among the Jews, you do not think it is suitable to them!"

"You misunderstand me; or perhaps I did not clearly express myself," said the inspector of excise, smiling and shaking his head.

"I will go out; I will go about among the Jews and put a good heart into them," said the burgomaster; "it will also produce a good effect upon the townspeople when they see that I go to the Jews."

The burgomaster put on his cap, and taking his Spanish cane in his hand, the three public officials walked down the street together.

At the public-house another assembly was occupied by the same subject. The room was almost full, and among the noise of billiard-balls and the ringing together of brandy-glasses might be heard the earnest voices of the speakers.

Larsen, the fat brandy-distiller, sat with his back against the open window, and began: "Yes," said he, and lifted his right hand, which held his large meerschaum pipe, "the Copenhageners are brisk folks. They don't stand shilly-shallying—they strike."

"The king will be in a dilemma," observed the barber, with an important and mysterious air; "they have sent him word that if he will let them do what they like to the Jews, he may sit quiet; but if not——"

"He may have the inconvenience of their fighting one another," interrupted the young Dr. Flor.

"You are always so full of your jokes, Mr. Dr.," said the barber, with suppressed vexation. "The Copenhageners are, however, nothing to jest at,"

"No, the Copenhageners are clever people," cried the brandy-distiller. "Hurrah for the Copenhageners!"

"Hurrah for the Copenhageners!" sounded in chorus.

"I should like to see the faces the Jews will make when they are down on their knees and are being cudgelled, and when they pray, 'Abraham, Isaac, and Jacob, come and help me!' and Abraham, Isaac, and Jacob take no notice!" exclaimed the young shopkeeper Peterson, laughing.

"The sight may not be so very far off," said Carstens the butcher, with a significant glance.

"And where would be the sin in killing a Jew?" exclaimed Green, the sexton; "they were Jews who killed Christ."

"And now they suck us Christians both bone and marrow," cried another.

"The raggamuffins that they are, and they reckon themselves too good to eat with other Christians," said the butcher; "I can kill for everybody else but the Jews. It is a shame that an ox should be demeaned by being eaten of them. What do the wretches do?"

"They lie brooding over the money which they have cheated

us Christians out of," exclaimed the landlord; "I serve wine and beer to the first men in the town, but never has a Jew asked me for as much as a glass of brandy. To the devil with them! What are they good for?"

It is not more than eight days," said Carpenter Hansen, "since that fat Wulf Wendel docked me of two rix-dollars for the work which I had done in his yard; one can't get dry bread by working for those folks!"

"Wulf Wendel!—why that was he who brought Jensen down to the poor-house?" said some one.

"Yes, he is a regular wretch!" cried another.

"They are all alike," cried a third.

"They ought to be taken as far as the barriers, and then sent off with a kick."

"They ought to be killed like mad dogs."

The drinkers and talkers at the public-house got no farther on this occasion than to say what "people ought to do." It was now noon, and one after another each went to his home.

Up at the poor-house, the former shopkeeper Jensen also was very active. It was now about two years since the termination of the unhappy lawsuit with Wulf Wendel. He was become miserably thin, and it was easy to see that a deep consumption was wasting his life's strength. Now, however, his otherwise dull blue eyes were lit up by a strange fire, and a red spot came and went upon his pale sunken cheeks.

It was as if a frenzy had seized upon him at the prospect of what he had regarded hitherto as his unattainable vengeance being at hand. He ran about with strange gestures, like shapes that are at times seen in dreams, and that appear to the dreamer to converse rather by action than by words. He went from his work-place first to one and then to another, touched them on the arm, and whispered, "The king has commanded that all the Jews should be killed to-morrow. Only think! to-morrow we shall plunder the rich Jews, and kill them. Hast thou seen the king's command? To-morrow I shall pay off Wulf Wendel. We have summoned the peasants; they will help us to plunder and to kill!"

His state of mind seemed magnetically, as it were, to communicate itself to the others, and only increased in excitement under the restraint which the presence of the superintendent compelled them to put on their feelings. When the hours of work were over, they all went into the street, thence into the market, where they found many peasants. Jensen again ran from one to another.

"Hast thou not heard of the king's command," said he, in a low, earnest voice, "that all the Jews should be killed? Come here to-morrow with flails and scythes, and we'll kill the Jews, and take their money."

"Nay, is it really so?" said the peasants; "yes, we have heard rumours about it all day. Yes, if the king commands, we will do his bidding."

"Yes; come to-morrow morning and make your sales, as usual, and to-morrow evening, towards dusk, we will kill the Jews."

"Who is that fellow?" asked some of the peasants.

"He is one Jensen, who was formerly a shopkeeper," answered another; "he is a clever fellow; he knows what he is about."

"In Copenhagen the Jews are killed; to-morrow they will be killed here, and we shall get their money;" continued Jensen to say to them, until the last had left the town.

From the market he returned homeward; but whenever he passed the house of a Jew, he stopped and exclaimed, "Wait till to-morrow!" and they who were with him joined in the hoarse cry, "Wait till to-morrow!"

In the evening he sat alone with his wife in their miserable little room. "To-morrow!" said he, "I'll settle my account with Wulf Wendel. I was sure that God would not let me die without doing so, even though he performed a miracle."

"In Christ's name!" said his wife—"and yet he was the death of our two little ones! Poor little things, they died of want and wretchedness!"—and she wept.

"To-morrow!" said he again; "then will I gladly die. I know that thou will soon follow me: is it not so, mother?"

The wife wept in silence.

He continued, "We had only been married three years, when I took thee to the poor-house."

The woman sobbed.

"And now for two long years, day out and day in, have I seen thee in this coarse dress, whilst *his* wife has gone in her silks and velvets! But to-morrow we'll have a reckoning, Wulf Wendel!"

"Yet, nevertheless, he offered to leave it to reference," said his wife; impelled by that feeling of justice which women so often have in a higher degree than men.

"Did he not know very well that I could not pay? How could I, so ill as I was? and what were the two hundred thalers to a rich man?—to me, they were everything. They cost me my health, my happiness, and my two children. They were a dear pennyworth, Wulf Wendel! But to-morrow we'll settle accounts."

"Let us sing a hymn, mother," said he, after a pause; "it is a long time since we have sung one together."

He took up the hymn-book, opened it, and began to sing the first hymn that met his eye; and now they who were without heard the husband and wife singing with their weak voices the 404th hymn:—

"I know that towards the grave I speed,
   That life by death is seal'd;
But *when*, O God! thou hast decreed,
   And not to me reveal'd.
That, that alone is known to Thee;
Thou in thy world hast placed me,
   And all my days hast number'd."

The sounds died away; and all became still in the dark, dismal abode.

CHAPTER XI.

Early the next morning, Isaac Bamberger came over to the house of his brother-in-law.

"Philip," said he, gravely, "we have now lived many years with one another as brothers—dost thou wish, as I do, that we should continue the same to the last?"

Philip pressed his hand in silence.

Isaac continued:—"The burgomaster has proposed that we should keep open our shops till evening, as if nothing out of the common way was likely to occur. I will do so. But as soon as it begins to get dusk I shall lock up, bring over my most valuable things, and I and my wife shall remain here. Thou hast more to defend than I have, brother—thou hast a son!"

"My son! my poor child!" said Philip; and tears filled his eyes.

"We will defend him," cried Isaac, with a strong voice, "so long as I can wield an axe no one shall come near him."

"My poor lad!" again said Philip.

"Be a man, Philip!" cried Isaac, and grasped him by the arm; "it helps nothing to be down-hearted. Defend the lad, don't cry about him."

"Oh, Isaac," said Philip, "thou dost not know what it is to defend a child. Every stroke given by an enemy seems to fall twofold on the parent's heart."

Isaac passed the back of his hand over his eyes, and returned to his own home.

Never had salesmen been more reluctant to sell, nor customers more eager to buy, than upon this day. The Jews thought to drive away the peasants, who thronged their shops, by asking exorbitant prices for their goods; but the peasants paid whatever they asked, and saw the money go into the till, with an expression of countenance which seemed to say, we shall have it back again, however, to-night.

Peasants swarmed over the town, and were especially lively; nobody, however, anticipated the catastrophe which was prepared for the evening—a strange scene, which could scarcely have found its parallel amongst any people, excepting the grave Danish peasantry. The peasants fancied that they were quite sure of the Jews, and now played with them, as the cat plays with the mouse. Jews would gladly have been mice, merely that they might have crept into holes.

As soon as it began to get dusk, all the Jews locked their shops, and the peasants collected in the market-place. Paupers from the poor-houses, working men, schoolboys, and here and there a townsman, joined them; and now, forming themselves into regular procession, they advanced in perfect silence towards the house of Wulf Wendel.

At the beginning the crowd seemed to be awed by the deep silence which prevailed; but as soon as they perceived that no opposition was about to be made to their proceedings, they burst open the door and rushed into the shop. In a moment the drawers and shelves were emptied into bags, which they had brought with them, and the unwearied Jensen led onward the assailants into the house itself. When they had burst open the door of the innermost room, they beheld Wulf Wendel standing before his wife, his grown-up daughter, and his money-box.

The women were pale as death, and could scarcely stand upright. Wulf Wendel trembled; but his fear was a convulsive frenzy at sight of the danger which threatened his beloved wealth. Scarcely, however, as much time passed as has been required to describe his condition, when the two enemies stood face to face.

Without a word they rushed at each other. Wulf Wendel's powerful fist struck a blow on the weak chest of his foe, while a heavy stroke from Jensen's cudgel fell on Wendel's head, and the two mortal enemies lay side by side like brothers.

This scene involuntarily excited the peasants, as every energetic outbreak of human passion excites the feeling of the spectator; a volcano is seen to open, the fellow to which every one seems to bear within himself. Some occupied themselves with Jensen; others carried Wulf Wendel, together with the fainting women, out of the house, and consigned them to the nearest neighbours, Simon Nasche's, whose door they broke open. As if his house were already sanctified by the presence of their victim, they proceeded onward without doing further mischief.

The next house they came to was Philip Bendixen's. The doors were broken open, and the family retreated slowly from room to room, until at last they were compelled to seek shelter in the cellar, where their most valuable goods had already been conveyed. The assailants, who heard the cellar-door hastily closed and secured, paused a little, to reflect before they ventured in pursuit along the vaulted subterranean passage.

"I know the way," at length cried a stout peasant, and put himself at their head; "I was a servant in this house."

They rushed forward, but came again to a standstill at a corner.

"Only follow me!" cried the peasant, and hastened before the rest.

A faint glimmer was seen; a suppressed cry was heard, and the peasant rushed back with a loud shriek.

"What is it?" cried many voices.

"It is the God of the Jews who sits there!" cried the fellow, almost beside himself with terror and pain. "Did you not see something? There he is again!"

Seized by a panic terror he fled, and all followed him to the passage.

Arrived in the house once more, they encountered the burgomaster. He was attired in his scarlet coat, armed with his staff and sword, and accompanied by his two police servants, who, at all events, might figure as supernumeraries.

"What are you about here?" inquired he, sternly, from the men who were entering.

Nobody answered.

"And what is amiss with you?" asked he, as he saw the bleeding peasant who was staggering forward. "You have been wounded; but it has been your own doing," added he. "I arrest you in the king's name!"

He laid his hand upon the fellow, who, from loss of blood and terror, sank fainting to the ground.

The words, "In the king's name," operated on the peasants like thunder.

"In the king's name!" again exclaimed the burgomaster, sternly, "I command every one to disperse and return home; whosoever I again meet will be punished as an insurgent and a disturber of his majesty's peace. Do you understand me?"

The peasants stole away, leaving behind them the full sacks of plunder.

In the meantime the family had listened, in breathless fear, to the simultaneously advancing mob, and then, with silent prayers thanked God when they perceived it again receding.

"Jacob! where art thou?" at length said the anxious mother, and felt about with her hands for him in the dark.

"Where art thou, Jacob?" cried she, louder, when she did not find him;—"Where is the lad? Did I not put him before me into the cellar? Where is he? Where art thou my son—my Jacob!" cried she, with the anguish of a bereaved mother.

"He must have crept into some corner," said the uncle; perhaps he has fainted with terror. I recollect that he was born amid the terror of war and uproar."

They sought for him in every corner, but he was nowhere to be found.

"Schema Yisroel! they have found him and carried him off with them!" cried the mother, in unspeakable despair. They have murdered him, therefore he is so quiet."

"Look out, Isaac, and keep thy promise!" exclaimed Philip Bendixen; and, bursting open the cellar door, he rushed out with an axe in his hand.

"Father!" said a low voice, when he had gone a few paces.

"Jacob! God in heaven! Is it thou?" cried the father, and let fall the axe.

The boy sat upon a stone step, and held his dagger in his hand. It was covered with blood to the hilt. The feeble light which fell into the passage showed to the father and uncle the pale, agitated countenance of the boy, and his bloody weapon. At a glance they guessed what had happened.

With a strange emotion of terror and admiration the father bowed over his child, who fainted in his arms.

The uncle said, "Now is there blood between him and the Christians!"

The burgomaster came to seek for the family, and led them in triumph back to their dwelling-rooms. He took the fainting boy from his father, and brought him tenderly to consciousness, scolding the servant girl the while, because she was slow in arranging the pillows of the sofa. After this he took Isaac Bamberger aside, and whispered to him, with a significant glance, "A peasant has been stabbed with a knife down there. It a matter of indifference to me who has done it; he has nobody to thank but himself. Of course you know nothing about it, Mr. Bamberger."

Isaac thought it was best to strengthen the burgomaster in his belief by silence, than by denying it to occasion any inquiry.

The burgomaster turned to the others: "And now," said he, "open your shops to-morrow morning, as usual. I will be responsible for there being no further annoyance to you. Do not be alarmed any longer, Madame Bamberger, nor you, dear Madame Bendixen! Good recovery to the little one! Good night!" He shook hands with the men, and left the house.

Their feelings, however, were somewhat different to what the burgomaster believed. They were silent, but they felt that they could not yet separate. There was something between them which they shunned to speak about; yet all knew that the other's thoughts were occupied upon it. There was a secret, not to the world, but among themselves; they are afraid of lifting the veil, as if to avoid seeing more. They felt as if the mystery would come out, if they spoke of it; but that with silence it would rest in oblivion.

When the boy opened his eyes, his mother asked him if he would have anything to eat. He said yes, and partook of the offered food with avidity.

They looked at each other with lightened hearts, and somewhat later all went to rest.*

---

* This extraordinary outbreak against the Jews—"The Jews' Feud," as it is called—occurred in September, 1819. It took place almost simultaneously in various towns and capitals, and originated from causes yet unexplained.—*Trans.*

CHAPTER XII.

The waves after a storm do not immediately sink into a calm. It requires some time, also, before excited temperaments regain their accustomed equilibrium; at all events, the sight of every Christian countenance awoke in the mind of the Jew the remembrance of the hatred of which he was the object, and of which he lately had been made so conscious. The more educated class of Christians, who by word or deed had taken part in this Jew-persecution, were now secretly ashamed when they saw a Jew, and then were angry with themselves because they had been obliged to be ashamed before a Jew. The more ignorant class of the town's-people, especially such as owed the Jews money, came to them immediately after this disturbance with the most friendly countenances, and assured every one, with an appearance of sincerity, that they had taken no part in the outbreak.

There are in the world much fewer romantic incidents than we read of in novels, but many more than we believe in daily life. The countenance upon which inanity or stupidity seems to have set its seal may serve especially to conceal many a crafty thought which has stolen into the mind. How much indifference can it assume when it is most prudent not to show sympathy!—how kindly can it smile upon an enemy who is too strong, or to whom it is best to yield!—and, above all, how many comedies do we not play one with another, almost without knowing it, or without feeling any unwillingness!

When are two individuals ever perfectly candid with each

other, even when they sit down to talk most open-heartedly to each other? How many families are there in which there are not one or more little mysteries—sometimes also great ones? When you sit together at table, apparently merely occupied with each other, or with the little world within your four walls, if each one were suddenly to tell the other what his or her thoughts were—if the wife should tell her husband, or the husband his wife; the daughter her mother; the lover his betrothed—if circumspection were no longer to keep watch at the door of the heart—it would be more than we could bear; it would be as if the white skin should be removed from the muscles and fibres; as if we should see the heart throb within the breast. Let it be closed! *hanc veniam damus petimusque vicissim.*

An interval of a year has now passed in its accustomed quietness, and our attention will now first be directed to Jacob, who, on a Saturday morning, in the summer of 1821, might be seen walking by his father's side towards the house in which the synagogue was held. Both were clad in holiday attire, and Jacob, for the first time in his life, wore the coat, hat, and other habiliments of a man. This, in fact, was his Barmitzvah, or the first Sabbath after he had completed his thirteenth year, the important day on which, under the blessing of the law, he was to be received into the community of men.

The tabernacle, in which the book of the law was preserved, was concealed by the new silk curtain which Philip Bendixen had presented to the synagogue on this occasion; two large yellow wax candles burned upon the reading-desk, from which the law would be delivered; chandeliers were lighted, and the whole of the little community were clad in their best.

As soon as they had entered, and respectfully bowed themselves before the tabernacle, the father took a piece of the finest woollen cloth, embroidered all round, and in the corners with crimson, and with a broad edging of gold, and laid it upon the shoulders of his son. This done, each took his seat in silence, and repeated in a low voice the prescribed prayers, which the precentor read aloud.

Next followed the reading of the law. Such of the community as had purchased the right of this privilege advanced, singing, towards the tabernacle, drew apart the curtains, and took thence the law, the rest of the community repeating prayers aloud. If a stranger had heard the loud voice of the assembly, without understanding the ceremonial, he would have imagined that the choir was about to make an onslaught, from which the others would deter them by warnings.

The precentor received the law, and laid it, amid general silence, upon the reading-desk. He opened at the place where the reading for the day should begin, extended his silver staff, and said, "Stand forward, Mr. Jacob, son of Mr. Philip, a Levite."

The father whispered a blessing, but made no attempt to conduct his son forward, for freely and independently must the youth make the appointed vows. With still more anxiety than he felt when, somewhat later, he made his examination, Jacob passed, with a pale countenance and trembling knees, through the thick crowd of Jews, and mounted the steps. He touched, as he had been carefully instructed to do, the book of the law with the Tsitsis (embroidered corners of his Thalis, or new woollen garment), kissed them, and then repeated, in a peculiarly singing tone, which belongs to the formula of benediction, "Blessed be thou, O God! Ruler of the world! who hast blessed us above all other people, and hast given to us the law." Having said these words, he proceeded to read, in an artificial, rhythmical manner, that particular verse of the law which chance had appointed him; whilst stern and merciless judges stood round, and listened for the slightest mistake that by any possibility he might make.

The Jews believe that if there is any good thing promised in the verse which is read on this day, it is a prophecy for their future lives; if there is anything evil, they regard it as a pure accident. Jacob read:

"And the Lord God said unto the serpent, 'Cursed be thou above all the beasts of the field: upon thy belly shalt thou go, and dust shalt thou eat all the days of thy life. And I will put enmity between thy seed and the woman's; he shall bruise thy head, and thou shalt wound his heel.'"

Again having touched the law with the corners of his garment, kissed them, and repeated the blessing, he turned to descend the steps; but in his confusion he made a mistake, and was about to come down by the same side that he had ascended, which is never done, so that the precentor was obliged to take him by the arm and put him right. People involuntarily cast down their eyes, that they might not observe this unusual mistake; and as soon as Jacob stepped from the lowest stair, he received the congratulations of his father and the community. The old Rabbi Jokub pinched his cheek, and said, "A brave, good youth!" adding, in a lower voice, and lifting his eyes towards heaven, "God keep thy good children, when they are in the world!"

When the rest of the service of the day was over, all who had congratulated him were invited home by his father to dinner.

Jacob was so confused that he hardly knew how he got home. Later, however, all seemed to become clear to him, and he could recal almost every face which had gazed from the windows at the home-going procession; he remembered how everybody had been dressed in the synagogue, and fancied that he could accurately give even the length of the flame of the tall waxcandles, which he had, in fact, scarcely observed while in the place. And although his heart had often, in later years, throbbed high with pride—although the time came when strong, passionate, blissful feelings drove the blood impetuously through his veins—yet there was no day, no hour, which remained in his remembrance with such a dreamy, magical glory as this.

In the afternoon, when the guests were gone, the father and uncle sat together on the sofa. Jacob stood with his mother at the window, and was looking silently into the street.

His father, who seemed to have difficulty in tearing himself from his thoughts, at length addressed him in a voice of unusual tenderness. "Come here, my dear son," said he, "that I may speak with thee."

Jacob approached. His father laid his hand upon his head, and said, "Now, my son, thou art a man—a Jew. Thou art no longer a twig upon my branch; thou art thyself a tree."

"A beautiful tall tree!" interrupted the uncle, and held his hand flat about a yard above the ground.

The father continued: "Hitherto I have been responsible to God for thee; for the future, thou thyself must bear thy sins before God. Thou art now a grown man."

"And canst get married, if thou wilt," again interrupted the uncle; and, taking him from his father, set him on his knee.

The father continued: "When I was Barmitzvah, my mother said to me, 'Go, and earn thy own bread;' but I will part mine with thee, my Jacob, as long as I have anything for myself."

"A virtue of pure necessity!" exclaimed the uncle; "let thy father only attempt to say, 'Go, and earn thy own bread.' He would soon see that two words went to that bargain!"

Jacob's eyes wandered from his uncle's merry countenance to his father's kind, but grave one, and his own feelings wavered between smiles and tears. The more jocular his uncle was, the more sad became the tender, affectionate earnestness of his father. He felt as if his throat was closed—as if he himself could not utter a word; he was so infinitely happy, yet at the same time so infinitely sad. His mother just then came up, took him in her arms, and kissed him; and this silent assurance that she also would share all with him—that she never would forsake him—seemed to release the convulsive tension of his feelings, and he burst into tears.

His uncle looked at him with amazement.

"What the deuce is amiss with the lad?" said he; "Is he ill? Who has vexed him? Have I vexed thee, Jacob?" and he clasped him in his arms.

"No, uncle," replied he, trying to repress his tears; "but thy words were so strange."

"Nay, that one can see," said Isaac Bamberger, in a tone of vexation. "I did not wish that any one to-day should talk solemnly to the lad, and therefore I talked cheerfully; and so he cries, because of my cheerfulness! That is good! We shall soon have enough to do with him."

These words made Jacob cry all the more; the father, too, was affected, and was silent for some moments, and then said:

"Don't cry, Jacob; don't be childish. To-day thou art become a man, and it is my duty to speak seriously to thee. In a few days thou wilt leave my house, where I have cared for thee and brought thee up, as was my duty, as an upright Jew. When the angel of accusation stands before the throne of God, and I submissively await my doom, thou wilt stand forward, and bear this testimony for me—wilt thou not, Jacob?"

"Yes," sobbed he.

The father again spoke: "Before thou leavest me, I will give thee the best advice that I can. Let thy ears be open to receive my fatherly words."

Jacob dried his eyes, and looked attentively upon his father. The father drew him closer to him, and continued:

"My soul is anxious for thee. God grant that when thou leavest my side, thou mayest not take the wrong path!

"Preserve the good counsel thou hast received from thy father, thy mother, and thy uncle. It was given with the best heart, and was spoken for thy good.

"Christians will teach thee many things which are new and good, but for that reason thou must not forget the old. Use every morning thy Jewish prayer, and forget not thy Tephilim; the day is begun well which begins with God.

"Give heed that thy Tsitsis (corners of the robe) be not defiled; for the eye of God rests upon the bond of purity.

"Pray every evening; so that God's Spirit may keep thee through the night, when thy father is far from thee.

"Go on holidays to the synagogue; what thou losest thereby in the school thou wilt easily get up again; for God strengthens the mind on holidays.

"Be gentle with thy companions and associates; it is better to suffer than to do wrong.

"Show respect to older Jews; it will obtain for thee a good name, and a good name is the best inheritance.

"For the rest, may God Almighty bless thee!"

With these words he clasped his son to his heart, kissed him, and mingled his tears with his.

Late in the evening Philip Bendixen stood alone in his counting-house examining papers.

"If I have said A," remarked he, "I can also say B. Will he be a student, and not a trader? Ha! in one respect my son need not be a Jew!"

He sealed the papers, and inscribed them, "My son's inheritance."

At that moment he heard a knocking at the window, which he cautiously approached. When he had undone the shutter, he saw his brother-in-law.

"Open the window," said Isaac Bamberger.

When this was done, a purse came in sight, which sounded heavy as Isaac set it down upon the sill within the open casement.

"As I was sitting across the road," said Isaac, "it troubled me to think that I had caused the lad to cry to-day, and then I bethought me that I had not made him any present on his Barmitzvah. Now do thou take charge of this money for him —before I take it again."

"Isaac!" said Philip, with emotion.

"Take charge of the money," exclaimed Isaac, almost sternly; and then added, in a sort of a jest, "If the money is left standing here all night, I will not be answerable for it."

When Jacob, a few days afterwards, stood with his father on the deck of the vessel which conveyed him to Zealand, and, somewhat depressed by the pain of parting, gazed upon the receding shore, upon the very spot where he had fought his first fight, a long forgotten picture rose up before his imagination. It was the countenance of the boy with whom he had then striven so furiously. His mind instinctively, as it were, riveted itself upon this scene, that it might be diverted from longing thoughts of home, and thus the image of his earliest enemy accompanied him, until pain and weariness sent him to his bed.

CHAPTER XIII.

It was lucky that in selecting the school which was nearest to uncle Marcus's house, and where Latin was well taught, they hit upon the best school in Copenhagen.

The head master of this school combined with the energy and strictness of the teacher a warm interest in his occupation. Unlike many of the school directors of the present day, whose consciences are satisfied by merely enforcing the discipline prescribed by the university, as regards learning, and who trouble themselves only about good conduct within the limits of the school, he endeavoured not alone to operate upon the *minds*, but upon the *souls*, of his pupils; he did not desire to rule over them alone as the teacher of the hour, but to stand beside them as their guide and their educator; still these endeavours, while, as there was then, and still is, among Christians so great a difference between the educator and the teacher, could only be occasional, or by way of exception. The most nobly zealous master is generally obliged to satisfy himself with the oversight which the other teachers can give; and any really familiar intercourse between himself and his pupils is hardly possible.

Jacob, who was so far from home, and who was especially recommended to his kind attention by his father, was still only present at the school during his school hours, as he lodged in the house of his uncle, and, therefore, as regarded the head master, it was rather attention and general oversight which would be looked for than any direct moral influence.

"When I see," said this excellent man one day to some of the under masters, a short time after Jacob's entrance in the school, —"when I see that boy, with his oriental countenance, sitting low down on the bench among the dull, heavy-headed scholars, it seems to me as if they were all a collection of domestic animals, amongst whom had come a young tame panther. I only hope the whelps will be kind to the panther cub, so that its nature may not be roused."

These words were as much spoken in jest as in earnest, but to his surprise he soon saw that they were quite correct.

At the beginning, Jacob was enraptured by his new position. But, although his intellect had been developed by the subtleties of his Talmudic studies, and his memory crammed with fragments of knowledge gathered from innumerable sources, yet he was now come to school without knowing a single school-book; he was like a person who can play, but who knows not a note. He was examined as the other boys were, but he could not answer a word. When, however, he began to participate in the instruction, and thereby, so to speak, the compass of his mind seemed to extend beyond that which had hitherto filled it, and he himself became conscious of what he needed, he made amazing progress.

And what a delight it was to him to sit upon a bench among other boys! To be considered as good as they—sometimes even to be preferred before them—not to feel any difference excepting that which industry and natural abilities occasioned! How industrious he was! and how he longed every evening for the next day, when he might recommence this glorious strife!

What a delight it was to sit upon a bench among other boys! But it was thus only during the hours when the boys were, like soldiers, under the restraint of strict discipline. Scarcely were the school hours over before Jacob heard that he was a Jew. True, it was no longer necessary for him immediately to leave his playmates, and for him to stand as much aloof as if a wooden fence had separated them. As long as he was unaccustomed to school life, and the strife of emulation with his fellows had all the attractions of novelty, he did not so much mind this new persecution; his whole soul was taken up with the school hours, and with the objects that occupied them. But after some time, when the youthful enthusiasm had somewhat abated, his mind became more sensitively alive to the other boys' ridicule. When the whole class would swarm around him laughing and shouting "Jew!" or "Ach wai mir!" or "Hep, hep!" he felt almost stupified by it; it was as if he heard the whole world shouting at him, and as if he must bow himself before their voices.

If, however, a single boy dared to approach him, and taunt him with the exclamation of "Be off with thee, Jew!" or such like, it seemed to him immediately much more of a personal affront, and, like a wounded tiger, he bent his fine flexible limbs, and sprang upon his enemy. The end always was the same; a crowd rushed on against him, and Jacob was beaten.

One evening, the man whose duty it was to sweep out the rooms found a boy lying insensible on one of the floors, with marks on his body of having been severely handled. His head was cut, and blood flowed from the wound; and in this state of insensibility he was conveyed home.

The next morning a command was issued that all the scholars should assemble in the great hall, where the masters already sat in conclave.

The rector ascended the elevated seat, and related the occurrence of the foregoing evening, adding, "There is, I am afraid, very little hope of the boy who has been guilty of this outrage convicting himself; and probably the wounded boy himself, when he recovers, may conceal his name, from a feeling of schoolboy-honour. But let the guilty one be whoever he may, he will bear with him the consciousness that his teachers and every right-thinking schoolfellow regard his conduct with the deepest displeasure. And this I expect from every one among you who has the honour of the school at heart, that he will not conceal, from a mistaken sense of honour, anything that he may know regarding this affair; so that the guilty one, if possible, may be discovered, in order that suspicion may not rest on the innocent."

The rector cast a keen, penetrating glance round the assembly; but all were silent.

The next moment, Jacob Bendixen rose and said:

"It was I who did it."

"How!" exclaimed the head-master, and stepped back in astonishment; "you, Bendixen! the best-behaved and the most quiet of all the boys in the school! I cannot believe it!"

"It is as I say," continued Jacob, immoveably.

"But what insanity could have possessed you—for you could not possibly do it intentionally?"

"Yes, I did it intentionally," said Jacob, in the same tone. "He was always the one who taunted me most with being a Jew, and yet he always managed to conceal himself behind the others. Yesterday we happened to be the last in the school; and when I was going, he ran after me, and shouted, 'Get out of the way, Jew!' and struck me against the door, so that I hurt my knee. On that, I struck him, and left him as he was found. I know very well," added he, coming forward a step or two, "that they all think of me as he did, and call me a Jew; but yet they none of them do it when we are alone!"

Jacob's lips quivered, and his cheeks were pale as marble. A death-like stillness prevailed through the hall. The rector gazed fixedly upon him; the masters gathered round his chair; and after some moments' whispering together, they all went out. When they had closed the door after them, one single boy said, in a suppressed tone, "Now, Jew, thou'lt catch it!"

The others were all silent, and several minutes passed in breathless expectation. Jacob remained standing, immoveable, and heard nothing. At length the masters returned; and, amid deep silence, the rector reascended the high chair.

"Jacob Bendixen!" said he, addressing him, "the insults of which you have been the object are so low and despicable, and I feel so sensibly the effect which, if they were allowed to continue, must be produced on your mind, that I cannot consider myself as justified in punishing you." The rector paused, with his eyes still fixed on Jacob, who stood as if transfixed; and then, turning to the other scholars, he said, in a stern voice, "And you others, pay attention to what I say! If the ennobling and humanizing sentiments which it is the purpose of the school to instil into your hearts are not sufficient to raise you above the vices of the mob, then you may expect the severest punishment whenever any instances of this kind come again to my knowledge. And now I hope, Bendixen," said he, again turning to Jacob, "that you will have sufficient confidence in me—never in the future to think of avenging yourself, however much you may be affronted. Remember what you owe to the school, and come to me for justice. Now, go all of you quietly to the playground, and wait till the next hour begins. I trust that this hour, although it may not be devoted to books, will not be lost."

When all the boys, and amongst them Jacob, were gone, one of the masters said to the rector, "Would it not have been better to have kept Bendixen up here, than to let him go down among them?"

"On the contrary," said the rector. "Should we, at the very moment when we endeavour to reconcile them to him, separate him from them? If he were separated from them at this moment, reconciliation would not be so easy in the future.

A wound may be closed whilst it is fresh, if it will close at all. And even if it should be unpleasant to him at this moment, it will do him no harm to suffer a little."

"I never should have expected such energetic character in a child of his nation," remarked one of the masters. "In some other schools where I have taught there were also Jew-boys, but they took blows and insults as mere matters of course. I used to be regularly provoked at their patient submission; one has not need, however, to be provoked on that score in this case."

"I shall not soon forget the scene we have had," said the rector; "I candidly confess that I was very much impressed when Bendixen said, 'On that I struck him, and left him as he was found.' I felt at that moment that the boy must not be punished,—I felt clearly that it was not a mere schoolboy's quarrel; it was the old national quarrel; and I am convinced that nothing is to be done with such a character, excepting through kindness."

"And you may be sure that they will have another fight," said a second master; "I assure you I was quite afraid to see them go down together. He strikes hard, the little Satan! as we have seen."

"Yes. What desperation there must have been in the boy's soul!" resumed the master. "He believed that he stood alone among nothing but enemies, and that he now should be wholly overcome. Such a boy must be treated with gentleness."

"You were a sort of prophet when you, a few months since, compared him to a panther's cub. Do you remember?"

"Yes, unluckily, a better prophet than I believed."

The lessons were resumed and continued as if nothing had happened. In the evening, when the school hours were over, the rector called Jacob into his room.

After he had seated himself and made Jacob also sit, he said to him, "Now tell me what you do in an evening when you go from school."

Jacob, who expected that he had been brought here for punishment, answered, in a low voice, "I do my lessons."

"And when you have done them, what then?"

"I read other things to pass on the time."

"Do you never go out walking with any of your schoolfellows?"

"No," replied Jacob, and involuntarily cast down his eyes.

The good rector felt that he was about to touch the old wound, and asked further—

"But your uncle has children, has he not? Don't you play or walk with them?"

"He has two sons," replied Jacob; "one of whom is about my age, the other somewhat older. But the one is apprenticed with a silk-mercer and draper, the other with a grocer, and they seldom come home except on Friday evenings."

"Has he no daughters?"

"Yes, three; but one is quite little, and sometimes I teach her to read; and the two older think me very silly, because I wish to be a student. They say that I ought rather to be an officer, for that officers are much finer fellows than students. But I am determined to be a student."

The rector smiled inwardly at having had, thus unawares, this glimpse afforded him into the hearts of Jewish girls.

"But when you are tired of reading, what do you do then?" asked he.

Jacob hesitated to reply.

The rector was made curious by this hesitation, and asked, "Do you then amuse yourself with nothing?"

"Yes," replied Jacob, and looked on the ground.

"Nay, how is that?" persisted the rector. "What is there to look so frightened about?"

"When I am tired of reading," at length said he, still hesitating as if ashamed; "then I fancy that there comes a little bird, and carries me home to my parents and my uncle, and so I am at home all the rest of the evening."

"And is that all your amusement?" asked the rector, touched by the boy's artless words.

"Oh, but then I am so happy," said Jacob, and a faint crimson tinged his cheeks. "I seem to gather flowers in the garden, and the wild sea-grasses on the shore; and I can hear my mother sing quite low, and I can see my father and my uncle, though they cannot see me. But sometimes it makes me cry, and so I go to bed."

The rector looked at him a long time in silence. At length he rose, and took down a volume of the poems of Oehlenschläger, which were just then published, and gave it to Jacob.

"Read this," said he, "then again will come a little bird and carry you away, though not exactly to your parents—but, in any case, it is a good thing to see something of the world; and, as you have so much time to spare, what do you think of coming to me sometimes and reading a little more than you learn in school? You will be all the cleverer student for it."

Jacob thanked him, with a deep sense of his kindness, and the rector then let him go home.

CHAPTER XIV.

The school-life went on; but it is difficult to say whether Jacob had more reason to be satisfied with his position among his school-fellows now than formerly. He was in time freed from the insulting shouts and words of opprobrium, as well as the rude crowd that had hitherto at times pursued him; but the profound silence and the coldness that had succeeded, were to him almost more painful, because he very well knew what they betokened. This silence spoke loudly; but what objection could he take against it? These glances and gestures—he understood their meaning perfectly well, but he did not dare to seem to understand them, lest he should make himself ridiculous. He often felt as people do in the night when they fear something, and wish that the unknown something would present itself, that an end might be put to their uncertain terror.

With the cunning peculiar to school-boys, and which is almost juridical, his comrades knew how to say the most unpleasant things to him, without his being able to charge them with saying any thing of the kind. One of them, for instance, would begin, as if accidentally, to speak of a great (*smaus*) entertainment, which they had had at home, and about all the (*flöde*) cream, sauce and again flöde (cream), so that the whole was a confused play of words ending in *aus* and *öde;* in the midst of which, another would interrupt him very gravely, "Now, take care what you are doing! You are talking about *smaus*, and Bendixen is listening."

"I am not talking about *smaus*," replied the narrator, with equal gravity.

"Yes, but you were; you said *Jöde*, (Jew) too; I'll go and tell the rector."

"Now what a lie that is! Did I talk about a *Jöde*, you other fellows there?"

"Yes, you did," the others would say; "you called Bendixen a *Jöde-smaus*—we heard you! Bendixen, do you go and tell the rector."

Young as Jacob was, necessity had already taught him so much self-command that he could now sit still and apparently not hear such things when they were said. He would gladly have fallen on any one of them; but which was the guilty individual?—besides, the kindness which he had received from the rector would have enabled him to bear calmly more even than this.

After a few months the boy, whom Jacob had beaten so sadly, returned to school, and took his place again as if nothing had happened. There was no trace of a desire for vengeance on his part towards Jacob; it was as if the two had never known each other. That want of energy is peculiar to the Danish character; it lacks energy to act, energy to love, and, above all, energy to hate. Among the peasantry it is no unusual thing to see a man cured of his enmity as soon as he has received a box on the ear from the hand of his adversary. It is a purely homœopathic remedy. With a more inflammable people, a conflict like that between Jacob and his companion would have produced an enmity, which, from the school, would have extended through the whole life; but the Christian boy, on the contrary, seemed to have overcome, in great measure, his former ill-will against Jacob. Jacob, who drew inferences from his own nature, and who was struck by the unexpected placidity and forbearance which the boy exhibited towards him, now began to feel very sorry for what he had done. One day, as the boy stood at the table, and was turning over the leaves of a book, Jacob, who was near him, remarked his pale, sickly countenance, and a deep sentiment of pity, almost affection, warmed his heart; he stole nearer to him, and with sincere emotion seized his hand, and gazed at him with tears in his eyes. The boy, however, snatched away his hand, exclaiming, "Nay, will you strike me again, Jew!"

Jacob's full heart contracted itself again, and he thought to himself, "Now, however, we are quits."

Thus time sped on, week succeeded week, month succeeded month; Jacob went to school, and visited the rector regularly, according to his invitation; was taught by him, and became, without being conscious of it, the object of his attention and regard. Sometimes, on a holiday, he spent the whole day with him, from morning till night; and, on one occasion, was introduced by him to his family.

Jacob could easily perceive from the kindness which was shown to him, that the rector had said something in his favour beforehand; and he fancied also that he could see how careful everybody was in the opinions which they expressed, and how they avoided every allusion to Jews or Judaism; but, more than all, was he interested in the domestic and social life of the family, and which now, for the first time, he saw as it existed among Christians. The lively, witty conversation of the ladies and gentlemen—conversation, of which the unmistakeable element was a refined, cultivated intellect; the gaiety at the table, and even the arrangement of the table itself, and the various dishes, many of which were, to Jacob, forbidden meats, yet which were, from that very cause only, apparently the more enticing; and, lastly, after dinner, music and song and a little improvised dance. All this was to him a strange mixture of rapture and sickness of heart; it was a realization of the wild and wonderful phantom world in which he had dreamed and lived in his earlier childhood, and from which he now seemed to be more distantly removed than ever, because he did not understand how to participate in it. These people seemed all to belong to a highly-favoured caste; to have learned a mysterious art, by which, out of nothing, they could create such an amount of pleasure. He was seized by a painful longing; he wished that he had been born of this caste.

One holiday, in consequence of an appointment with the rector, he came early to him in the morning. He was not up when Jacob arrived, and he had to wait for him in his library. Before long he made his appearance, half-dressed, in his shirt sleeves, and with his dressing-gown over his arm. He walked to the open window, cast a cheerful glance towards heaven, inhaled a full draught of fresh spring-morning air, and then seated himself with a happy countenance at the breakfast-table.

Every one of his movements was an object of attention to Jacob. This mode of performing the morning prayer, by a cheerful salutation to God, was so easy and unencumbered in comparison with his own form of morning worship; laying the Tephilim, and the half parrot-like repetition of long, and for the most part, unintelligible Hebrew prayers; whilst the rector's contented countenance showed evidently that it might be done with a good conscience. When, also, the rector this morning read with Jacob that chapter of Herodotus, in which it is related of the Spartans at Thermopylæ, that they anointed themselves, and placed garlands upon their heads before they went into battle, Jacob noticed, for the first time, that neither had his heroic, almost worshipped, Spartans laid the Tephilim.

The next morning, for the first time in his life, he omitted his accustomed ceremonial of worship, and, like a criminal, stole past the silk bag in which the Tephilim was contained, and so out of the house. But when the day, and the whole evening, had passed without the skies falling, or any other terrific event occurring, he again became calm, and resolved to try it yet once more, and to pray as the rector had done. He tried it again, and yet again, and at length it became his accustomed mode.

The faith, which is either composed of ceremonies and superstitions, or is purely spiritual, is not like a building out of which one stone may be taken and another put in its place. As soon as doubts are let into the mind regarding it, the whole structure totters and tumbles to pieces, nor can the materials be made use of to build with anew. Doubts attack religious faith, not like rust, which eats into iron slowly; but like some subtle poison, which needs only to touch the human tongue, and straightway it is diffused through the system.

Jacob had read Oehlenschläger with profound attention, and lived with him in the northern heroic age—the old times of paganism. The only thing in which he could not fully take part with the old warriors was, in their feasts in Valhalla, where they ate so much pork. In a while, however, he took courage to ask himself whether God would be displeased, if the flesh of this or that animal touched his lips. Is it probable, reasoned he, that various kinds of food passing at different times into my stomach can be any breach of the divine moral law? Would God, dwelling aloft in heaven, concern himself whether I, after having eaten butter, allow an exact hour to pass before I eat flesh meat? It cannot be! And he ventured at the rector's table to eat bread and butter with meat, and found no inconvenience therefrom.

He had read of the Turks who came to Scanderbeg's grave, and who hung themselves round with his bones, as amulets to defend them against danger, and had smiled at their superstition. They were nothing but the bones of a dead man—what power could there be in them? All at once he suddenly perceived that he himself wore an amulet, his arbakamphoth. It was only a piece of woollen cloth—what strength could there be in it? And he laid aside his arbakamphoth, which he had worn since his seventh year,—a token of the covenant between himself and the God of the Jews.

Amid such mortal combats, and such inquiries, which, however, were unknown to the whole world, Jacob passed a long time.

In certain moments a dark, anxious thought would arise within his mind—that the rector, who had given the first occasion to these new ideas, might, perhaps, be one of those dangerous seducers of the young who had drawn the youthful Simon of Prague into their snare; but he soon felt an inward conviction that it was a higher spirit which he himself had evoked which had operated upon him. Yet he dreamed, for a long time, almost every night, that he sat at the Sabbath-board, and that his father said to him, as Larazus said to his son,— "Let me see thy arbakamphoth, my son!" and that he, too ashamed and terrified, had stolen to the door and fled from his father.

But it was only in the darkness of night that the old mystical remembrances arose threateningly before him,—as stories of elfin maidens and nixes haunt the wanderer in the gloomy wood. When the light of day again shone around him the phantoms vanished, and he lived in the clear and free light of the spirit.

It was now the Jews' day of the Passover; and it was necessary for Jacob to remain away from school several days, in order to celebrate this solemn festival duly.

In the morning Jacob accompanied his uncle to the synagogue. It was with strange feelings that he now, after a long interval of time, found himself once more in this place. For a moment there seemed such an inexplicable vacuum in his being.

He had despoiled his God of so many attributes, and now what remained of him seemed almost nothing. But, beyond this old divinity, their seemed to hover a loftier ethereal existence,—as the belief of the Al-father in the pagan Scandinavian mind hovered over even As-Odin,—and with passionate intensity of feeling he turned himself to this lofty being in prayer.

"Thou good, great God! Thou it was who didst lead the Jews out of the land of their enemies! I will belong to thee! I will trust in thee! but forgive me that I cannot believe everything—that I no longer believe!"

And he joined the loud cry of the congregation, which now uttered its—" Hear, oh Israel! the Lord thy God is one eternal existence!"

Strengthened by this simple outpouring of spirit, he omitted to repeat the other Hebrew prayers; and saw, with a mixture of pride and melancholy, the rest of the congregation praying in simplicity and sincerity. But when the moment came that the law should be unwrapped from its coverings, and the people thronged forward to kiss the parchment-roll, or merely to touch it with their finger, which they kissed instead, he said to himself, —" See, these men kiss the dead parchment, and the dead writing inscribed upon it, and believe that these are the living spirit."

When all the members of the family assembled at noon to enjoy in peace and joy the festal meal, Jacob felt a certain uneasiness,—as if he were undeserving to participate in this general joy, when he had not participated in the general devotion. He well remembered the time when he too, with feelings of equally religious ardour, had entered the comfortable room, and with contentment, equal to theirs, had seated himself at the decorated table; and though his understanding now told him that he was right, still there was in his heart a secret pain and lamentation.

But they came to his help without knowing it, in this silent conflict. During dinner the wife began to cut up a fowl, and the husband took up a little piece from the dish to taste it.

"Thou mayst think," said she, "what a regular fright I had when I was drawing the fowl to find a pin in its craw."

The husband turned deadly pale, and took in haste the piece of meat from his mouth.

"And why didst thou not tell me before?" exclaimed he, in terror, "art thou mad, wife? Wilt thou make the whole house unclean?"

"Nay, compose thyself," replied the wife, and continued to carve the fowl; "I sent it to the priest, and let him see the craw with the pin in it, and he said that we might eat the hen without hesitation; but that we must, in the first place, bury the craw."

But the husband had no longer any fancy for the fowl.

"It is remarkable," said Jacob, "that the hen should become clean because the craw was buried. One would think that the craw must have made the hen already unclean, and that it could not be of much benefit then to bury the craw. It was just as if one should put the antidote in the poison-bottle, after a man had drunk the poison!"

"Don't be sinful, Jacob," said Marcus Bendixen; "the priest must know best. There are many mysterious things which a man may believe without being able to explain them. What is, indeed, the Tekufo?"

"Yes, what is the Tekufo?" asked Jacob.

"The Tekufo falls from heaven four times a year," replied Marcus; "it is a drop of blood: where it comes from nobody can tell; but no one must speak of it to children. And if it falls on butter or meat, or anything of that kind, and if anyone eats of that whereon the Tekufo has fallen, he will die. Therefore, every pious housewife upon these days lays a nail by the side of such victuals as she has in the house, and there the Tekufo falls not!"

"A nail!" said Jacob; "can a lifeless object actually have the power to resist the will of God?"

"Does not the conductor turn aside the lightning?" replied the uncle.

"Yes, but the lightning is a power of Nature which is thus turned aside by another natural power. God has not laid his will in either of these. But is it likely that he requires a nail, as a sign to him who is pious and who is not? Is not He himself acquainted with the heart of man?"

"The Lord requires a sign from men, that he may know who is well inclined to him and remembers him. Did not God command that the Jews should sprinkle their door-posts with the blood of the paschal lamb, that his angel might distinguish their houses from those of the Egyptians?"

"God is almighty," began the eldest of the cousins—speaking with Rabbinical unction; "but sometimes he does not exert his whole power. He might have created man out of nothing, but yet he fashioned him from the earth. Why did not Adam live to be a thousand years old? It had been determined that Adam should live to be a thousand years old, and David should be still-born. But the Lord, as a gift to the Jews, took seventy years from the life of Adam and gave them to David. Might not the Lord just as easily have created seventy years alone for David?"

"But such things belong to mythology!" exclaimed Jacob; "it is not necessary to believe them, any more than the story of Saturn who ate his own children."

The uncle replied, sternly; "Nothing of what is written about the Jews belongs to ——; what didst thou call it—Jacob? What sort of a word is it that the Christians have been teaching thee? Nothing that ever was written about the Jews is not to be believed! Perhaps, if we were to examine into the matter, there is no need for us to believe in Yohmkipur (the Feast of Reconciliation) :.there is no need for us to fast or to pray, or to confess our sins. Is it not so?"

"Yes!" exclaimed Jacob—and he gave himself up with his whole soul to images which the very mention of this feast-day called up; "yes, Yohmkipur is a beautiful, a poetical festival! —for its sake alone it was worth while being a Jew! When the whole congregation stand in their white linen shrouds; when Hrasan and the two elders arise and stand before the Book of the Law to exculpate the assembly, 'before the judgment-seat of the higher and the lower regions; in the name of God, and in the name of the community,' in case any unrepentant sinner should be among them; when the Thallis is consecrated and the congregation veil themselves; when the priest reads aloud the vow, and at the word Kaureim (they knelt) all throw themselves upon their knees; when the white figures call upon the names of the dead, and wish them a blessed repose; when the Levites bring the holy water to Kaunim, and then after they have sprinkled themselves, distribute to all the sanctifying gift; when the horn is blown, and enemy offers his hand to enemy—then I believe, and pray as well as any one; them am I proud of being a Jew!"

"Yeschkauach!" (thanks) said the uncle—"who is not proud of Yohmkipur? What Jew is not proud of his whole religion?"

"Yes, truly!" continued Jacob, "there is a deal that is beautiful in it. But," added he, in a somewhat lower voice, "there is at the same time a deal of absurd superstition."

"Jacob!" exclaimed his uncle, "dare thou say so under my roof? Name to me the very smallest thing that is absurd! Let me hear! Now, tell me!"

"Well," said Jacob with a little smile, "that is not so very difficult to do; for example, the extreme care with which thou every Friday evening cutt'st thy nails; then collecting the clippings, cutt'st a little chip of wood from the table or the window-sill, and burnst them altogether."

"What the deuce?" cried the uncle, "don't I do it, that I may not, at the day of judgment, when the Lord calls, have to go about collecting the clippings of my nails? Are not the little chips of wood my witnesses that I have burned the nails? Don't, another time, make fun of what thou dost not understand. Take care that thou, at the day of judgment, hast not to remain on the earth seeking for that which thou hast lost!"

With these words he turned round with an air of annoyance, and said to the others:

"Rebbausai!—we will pray, and thus all farther disputes shall be ended."

Jacob seemed to breathe with difficulty. The atmosphere of the room appeared to him oppressive, and as if heavy with superstition. He longed after the fresh air of the school; nay even, he longed for his schoolfellows—for Christians; his imprisoned spirit yearned after those who understood it, even as a solitary captive pines after intercourse with human beings, though it were with his foes.

The evening and the night seemed wearisomely long, and like a released bird he hastened the next day to school. As he took his place in the class, he felt so inconceivably happy that he could have embraced all his schoolfellows for joy of seeing them once more. It occurs not to the inexperienced to doubt but that the feelings which fill their hearts almost to bursting, are filling the hearts likewise of all around them.

With a cheerful and affectionate glance, therefore, poor Jacob seemed to enclasp them all, as he exclaimed, "Well, how have you all been while I've been away?"

But the boys had in nowise changed in the few days of his absence, and one of them replied:

"Very well, thank you, Bendixen, but not so well off as you've been, for you've been up among the Jew-priests, and been made much of and had cake, because you cut such a fine figure in the synagogue!"

A roar of laughter, much more the result of boyish thoughtlessness than malice, succeeded these words. But Jacob's enthusiastic feelings rushed back with a quick revulsion to his heart, and he suddenly rememberd that he was a Jew, and these were Christians. An inward anguish seized upon his soul, as he darkly felt that he had left the shore on which was his home; that he had been, and ever should be, repulsed from the other, and that he now must be borne out alone into the stream.

"The Jew must have lost his wits," said the other boys.

CHAPTER XII.

When Jacob returned home from school to his uncle's house, it seemed to him as if he went to a prison, and when he then thought that he should have to go back again to school, a feeling of repugnance came over him. The weather was dull and uninviting, and it seemed to him as if even the heavens themselves hung oppressively over him, and merely vaulted his passage from one prison to another. Almost ill from depression of mind, Jacob one evening, soon after his time, on returning to his room, found a letter from his father. The letter treated of many small matters which were interesting to him, and ended by saying that as soon as the school-examination was over, they hoped to see him at home.

Home, and the thought of again seeing it, produced at this moment a most beneficial effect on Jacob's mind: there was then, thought he to himself, a peaceful haven to which he could flee. His soul gave itself up to first one pleasing anticipation and then another, with the same ease that the lottery-devotee throws aside the old number and takes up another.

He calculated how many hours the long months contained; he deducted from them the number which would be passed in sleep, and rejoiced to think how much he could shorten those that remained by reading. With every day that closed, he reckoned how much the time of his captivity was still farther reduced.

At length it came — the so long anticipated day of his departure, and he travelled with a peasant to Korsoer. When he had passed the first public-house, which the man stopped at to bait his horses, Jacob went on beforehand; and as soon as he had gone so far on the road as to suppose himself unseen of any human eye, he rushed into a meadow, threw himself on the ground, and rolled over in the grass, uttering inarticulate cries —cries of gladness, which would have made any spectator who knew the cause weep for pity. The youth rejoiced like a wild animal which has escaped from man.

His father met him at Nyborg, and accompanied him home. When the carriage stopped at the door, his mother rushed out, caught her son in her arms, and almost carried him into the house, clasping him to her heart and weeping over him.

The uncle came from across the street; and while he, in his usual way, held Jacob by the ear, said to him, "Nay, then, he is here, is he? What is he come here for?" and ended by kissing him, and pinching his ear more violently than ever.

Jacob almost sunk under all the affection that was lavished on him. Overcome by the excess of his happiness, he forgot that he ought to behave like a man, and express himself in a manly way, and that it was unbecoming to show his feelings. He was conquered by his own true nature; the emotions which were born with him and developed by his education burst forth, and uttering a scream of joy, he flung his arms round his uncle's neck.

Both father and mother felt a moment's jealousy, because he had shown greater affection for his uncle than for themselves; they knew not that it was precisely to his uncle that he could show his affection, because it was less in degree; for them it was too strong—at this moment, at least, he could not express it. As he threw himself on his uncle's breast, he himself felt annoyed that he seemed to show him this preference, and this very annoyance of feeling seemed to add to the outward coolness with which he met his parents.

A few days passed on, and the deep impressions which his reception at home made upon him, gradually gave way to other feelings which crowded upon his soul.

He went to that particular spot in the garden, to which the most beloved images of his childhood were attached,—the summer-house, where the family during the Feast of the Tabernacles arranged their leafy tent. Here it was that he had imagined his wonderful adventures; had fancied himself wandering with his people in the wilderness, seeking shade from the burning sun beneath its shadow; here he had in his childish ambition fancied himself the leader of his people, like a holy, inspired prophet. He was once more on this spot; and once more, stretching himself on a bench, he closed his eyes that he might again behold the beloved visions. But they came not, or if they came they were no longer tangible; for his ambition now was of another kind—it was to make a brilliant *examen artium*, and in the *tableau* of the future, the shadowy forms from the desert of Sinai would not consort.

Jacob left the spot with that slight pain with which, when one wakes, one gives up the hope of continuing the beautiful dream from which one has been awoke.

He remembered the peace which formerly had rested over the garden on Sabbath mornings, and when he had regarded every ripe berry as holy, because on the Sabbath it was forbidden to him to gather any fruit. He wished again to experience these gentle feelings, and the first Sabbath after his arrival at home hastened early into the garden. But neither the garden nor the fruit seemed any longer holy, because he was not able any longer to regard them as such. He could not arouse the sweet memory into a living existence, because he no longer regarded it as a greater sin to gather a cherry on the

Saturday than on any other day. He smiled, however, at his former superstition; but while returning from the garden into the house with a smile on his lips, a sad feeling had taken possession of his heart.

He had been endeavouring to rid himself from the thraldom of ceremonies, or to bring them into harmony with reason. That he at meal times should wash his hands, appeared to him a. cleanly habit; that the bread should be broken whilst a blessing was asked upon it, was poetically beautiful; it seemed beautiful to him, also, that the hat should be placed upon the head when a blessing was pronounced at the table, and in the supposed presence of God. Did not the grandees of Spain cover their heads in the presence of their king?

One morning, after he had been at home some little time, his father took him aside, with a grave countenance, and said,

"Jacob, it appears to me that thou hast laid aside thy Tephilim?"

"Yes, father, I have done so," replied Jacob, with inward terror of the scene which he knew was about to follow.

"Hast thou forgotten them at Copenhagen? If so, I can furnish thee with others," continued his father.

"Thou must not be angry, father," replied Jacob, in a tremulous voice, "but I pray to God every morning without Tephilim."

"What?" exclaimed his father, in a voice at once expressive of pain and anger, "dost thou no longer use Tephilim? Jacob, my son, couldst thou make me thus unhappy?"

"Father," said he, "I cannot convince myself that it is so well-pleasing to God that I should bind one leathern strap nine times round my arm, and another leathern strap round my forehead. God of a truth looks merely into the heart; if that is good and pure, he does not require Tephilim."

"Leathern strap, Jacob! Dost thou then regard Tephilim

merely as a leathern strap? Is the synagogue to thee nothing but a building of stone? Is it the leather we worship, or God's holy Word, which it preserves? Is it not written in our most sacred law, Schema Yisroel, that we should lay these words upon our head, upon our heart, and upon our hands?"

"Yes, father, but that certainly has a figurative meaning," replied Jacob, with a voice of pleading rather than argument; "I seek to lay the words of my God, but not the parchment on which they are written, upon my heart."

"And thy Arbakamphoth, Jacob?" as if he would drain the cup of sorrow to the dregs; "hast thou also put away thy Arbakamphoth?"

"Yes," said he, almost in a whisper, so terrible was the growing expression in his father's face.

The father raised himself from his bowed attitude, and stretching forth his hand, said,

"The Jew Philip, son of Rabbi Bendixen, has no longer a son! The son that he once had—is dead! By the grave of the Jew Philip will no one say Kadisch; no one will pray that his dust may rest in peace. His race will be forgotten by the Jewish people, and before the throne of God he will accuse himself, because he has given a son into the world."

With these words he left the room.

Jacob stood for a moment, as if annihilated by the dreadful words, and by the awful manner in which this, otherwise so gentle a father, had uttered a curse upon himself. The next moment, however, when he remembered the cause, in his own eyes so unimportant, which had occasioned this solemn denunciation, it would have appeared almost comic to him, if he had loved his father less. It was hardly possible for him livingly to recal the immense value which only three years before even he himself had attached to the duly laying of Tephilim and to the Arbakamphoth, as the symbols of Judaism.

He had not, however, much time for reflection of any kind, for his father and uncle now entered the room together—the first with an expression of resignation and pain in his countenance, the last in a state of the most violent agitation of mind.

"Thou no longer lay'st Tephilim," began the uncle, immediately, "nor wearest any longer thy Arbakamphoth! Thou art, indeed, a precious youth!—one has a deal of satisfaction in thee! Perhaps thou hast eaten of unclean meats. Do they taste good? Answer me, boy; hast thou eaten pork?"

Jacob's knees trembled; but he replied, "Yes!"

A violent box on the ear from the hand of his uncle instantly followed this confession. Jacob reeled, and was almost unconscious; a moment passed before he recovered the full use of his senses.

It was the first time in his life that he had received corporal punishment. His eye involuntarily flashed round the room, as if in search of a weapon. But in the next moment he had taken his determination; he left the room, the house, and the town, and walked hastily along the high-road. With his teeth closely set, and his whole mind in a chaotic confusion, he still continued to walk on.

For some little time after he had left the house, both his uncle and father felt too much exasperated to trouble themselves about his departure. Before long, however, his uncle walked to the window, and looked down into the street.

When he did not see Jacob there, he turned round to Philip and said, "It was a good thing that he ran away, or else perhaps I might have murdered him."

"Where can he have gone to?" asked Philip.

"Very likely he is gone down to the sea-side, and will not venture to come back again before we send after him. But, as for me, he may go to the world's end! He may as well disgrace himself once for all."

"That was a hard blow of thine," remarked the father, after a little while.

"Perhaps," returned Isaac Bamberger, sarcastically, "I ought to have taken him on my knee and caressed him, and said, 'God will bless thee, my lad! Thou hast forsaken the faith of thy fathers; thou hast eaten of the unclean thing—thou hast tasted pork, thou thick, thick head! hast eaten that of which it is said in the law of Moses that if a Jew eats he shall be cursed in eternity; still, nevertheless, thou art my own little Jacob!' Is it thus that I ought to have spoken?"

Philip held his hands before his face, and wept silently. At length, he said,—

"What am I to do with the lad? How am I to answer to God, if he goes on as he has begun?"

"He has been confirmed," replied Isaac Bamberger; "thou art not responsible, if both good words and chastisement are fruitless."

"Where can he be?" again asked the father, as if of himself.

"Oh, he is, as I said, gone into the garden, or else to the shore," replied he, as if with perfect indifference.

"I will let Benjamin go and see after him," said the father.

He called Benjamin. Benjamin, however, informed them that he himself had seen Jacob some time before leave the town by the East-gate.

The mother now came in.

"Where is Jacob?" inquired she. "Is it true that he has set off because you have beaten him?"

"The cursed fellow!" said the uncle; "he shall have as many blows as can be laid upon him."

"Have done with thy violence," said Philip; "thou mayst drive him out into bad company. Besides, it will get talked of that he has run away, and why he has done so. What will our relations say? It is better that I let him come here, and quietly send him back to Copenhagen. Let him thus, in God's name, take care of himself. I wash my hands of the business. I have given him a careful Jewish education; I have done my best."

"But it has been thy doing, in so far as thou hast consented to this cursed studying!" exclaimed Isaac, as he went towards the door. "Benjamin," then said he, addressing the servant, "do thou go over the way and order the horses to be put in my carriage, and let it be brought to the door immediately."

Jacob had already gone several miles when his father and uncle came driving posthaste in pursuit of him. When they came up with him, his father said, speaking mildly, "Jacob, take thy seat, and return home with us."

"Thou hast said that I am no longer thy son; let me go and take care of myself," replied Jacob.

"Don't be childish, Jacob!" exclaimed his uncle, peremptorily. "Come back with us; all will be forgotten."

"It is very easy for thee to forget," returned Jacob; "thou—thou who has struck me, Isaac Bamberger!"

"I was too hasty, Jacob," said his uncle; "come back with us."

"No!" continued Jacob, speaking with a sad but firm voice. "Show me only this one kindness—let me never see thy face again; thou hast struck me!"

"Boy!" exclaimed the uncle, with emotion, "thy old uncle has asked for forgiveness from thee; is not that sufficient for thy obstinate temper?"

Jacob saw that he might concede with honour,—but still, with a feeling of defiance and wounded pride, he made as if he would still continue on his way; but his father said, "Wilt thou, then, never see thy mother again?—nor me? Let us at least take leave of each other before we part, my son!"

Jacob could bear no more,—he burst into tears; and taking his seat in the carriage, they drove back to the town.

Jacob was once more under the roof of his father; not another word was said on the subject of their differences; but no disharmony in a family is worse than that of which the subject is never alluded to.

Jacob soon observed that he was like a stranger in the family. Meat and drink, and all that was requisite for his convenience, was supplied to him; he was like a beloved guest, but nothing more; he was no longer included in the bond of confidence which embraced his mother, his father, and his uncle. How painful it was to feel, if there had been nothing else, that when he entered the room, they mostly ceased to speak on the subject which had occupied them before.

Jacob saw that his father was full of sorrow; yet it was not in his power to lessen or assuage it,—because he had already eaten of forbidden meats. And even if he were again to resume the use of the neglected Tephilim, nobody would believe that it was done from sincerity.

To his mother he felt that he could still open his soul; for love to her child cannot be annihilated in the mother's heart. He ventured, therefore, one evening, when he sat with her in the twilight, to speak to her about the painful state of things between his father and himself.

"Thy father," said his mother, mournfully, "will never cease to be an affectionate parent to thee; he will do everything that lies in his power for thee. But the sight of thee will always be distressing to him, because he knows that when he and I stand before the Lord, we shall in vain seek for thee."

"Do not weep, Jacob," continued she, seeing him shed tears, "I shall be the first who goes, and I will intercede with the good God for thee."

Jacob's tears flowed faster than ever.

Soon after this his father entered the room, and Jacob observed that his mother's hand, which had tenderly wound itself in his locks, was involuntarily drawn back at his approach. He dried his tears, and an unspeakably bitter feeling stole into his heart.

When the time of his departure came, all seemed to feel as if a stone was lifted from their hearts. The separation was painful, but their continuance together would have been still more so.

As Jacob stood on the deck of the vessel which conveyed him back to the shore of Zealand, he felt that he was more homeless than the sea-gulls which the storm drove around the ship.

CHAPTER XIII.

On the evening of the 28th of October, 182—, the house of the rich Jewish merchant, Israelsen, in Copenhagen, was splendidly lighted up. His son had become a student, and a great entertainment was given on this occasion. Wax lights burned in the many silver branch-candlesticks, and light flashed from the massive silver service and the brilliant glass which covered the table. Besides the merchant's family, the company consisted of several Christians, two young men who had become students the same day—an elder Jewish student, and, lastly, Jacob Bendixen.

When they were seated at table, and the Jewish hospitality had shown itself in the number of dishes that were served, and in the often-repeated request that the guests would help themselves as freely as if they were at home, the merchant rose, filled his glass, and said,

"We will drink my son's health, on the occasion of his having become, happily, this day a student."

All joined in the hurrah, which the young Mr. Israelsen himself commenced.

Shortly after one of the guests—Wilhelm Fangel, a Christian —rose and said,

"I crave permission to propose the health of one of our young student-friends now present, who well deserves it, as he has passed his examination, and has been mentioned with honour—the health of Jacob Bendixen!"

It was the first time that anybody had ever shown any personal honour to Jacob. It is true that, that same day, his name had been mentioned in the Regent's Church with distinction, by the rector magnificus, but that had been merely in accordance with the requirements of the law, in consequence of the high-class character obtained at his examination—a distinction which would have been just as much his own even if the rector magnificus had not repeated the usual formula in his cold voice. But this, on the contrary, was a personal freewill offering of respect; and the pride and ambition which existed in his character awoke now within him for the first time a sense of delight.

As he rose to ring his glass against all those which were immediately extended towards him, he cast a strange, rapid glance at Fangel's countenance—a glance which seemed to express that he would instantly prevent himself from ever forgetting that young man.

"*Mentioned!*" said the merchant, when they had resumed their seats; "what does that mean?"

"It means," replied one of the guests, "that Bendixen has become a student with distinction; that he has gained more than a first-class character."

"Aaron," said the merchant, turning to his son very gravely, "what is the reason that you have not been mentioned? Have not I spent as much money over you as Bendixen's father over him? Why, then, have I not as much advantage of my money?"

"No!" replied the son, and looked vexed; "but Bendixen has had nothing else to do but read."

"And what more have you had to do than to read, you stupid fellow?" said the father.

"I have not been stupid," replied the son, extremely mortified and annoyed at the little restraint which his father put upon his temper.

"You do your son an injustice, Mr. Merchant," said Fangel, interposing; he too has certainly been very industrious—but everybody is not gifted alike."

"That is true, Mr. Fangel," said the father, mollified; "you are a reasonable young man. But then tell me what is the exact meaning of this distinction which you speak of in Bendixen's case?"

"They who get more than six *præ's*, and not a single *haud, non*, or *nul*, are expressly mentioned by the rector of the university as the cleverest students."

"And were there many besides Bendixen who received this distinction?"

"No—he was the only one."

The merchant's eyes sparkled, and he said, "He was the only one who made himself distinguished—and he is a Jew!"

He rose and said to Bendixen, "Now I will drink your health —I would you were my son. My young friends," added he, after a short pause, and turning towards the Christian students, "it is mark of great respect when an old man stands before a young one. You have seen that I rise up before Bendixen!"

There was something in the old merchant's manner which was very affecting, and tears came to Jacob's eyes.

Wilhelm Fangel started up and exclaimed, "Mr. Merchant! here's to you as rector magnificus! you distribute honours nobly! Rector Merchant Israelsen, hurrah!"

All the company rose and joined in chorus, hurrah! and all rung their glasses together amid general animation.

"Have you lately been at the play?" asked the merchant's eldest daughter Rose, addressing her neighbour, one of the students.

"No, so much the worse! I have not been able during the examination," replied he.

"Then you have not seen Blanca?"

"No, I have not."

"Oh, that is very nice!" said she.

"Then neither have you seen her?" remarked he.

"No; I'll tell you how it is. I have only a quarter of a seat, and so I have not managed to see the piece."

"A quarter of a seat!" repeated the young man, and measured the young lady's full figure with his eye; "in that case it must be difficult enough."

"Yes; that is to say, we four sisters take it by turn to go to the one seat. But it is a shame, father, that you will only take one place for us at the theatre," said she, with a beseeching glance at her father.

"One place costs money enough," replied the merchant. "Let me see; four marks, and nine months—how much is four times nine?" asked he of his youngest son, that he might accustom him to reckoning in his head.

"Four times nine, father?—two marks and four!"

Some of the company laughed; but the father turned with a satisfied smile to his neighbour, and whispered, "What a head for business there is on that lad's shoulders! With God's help he'll turn out something to be proud of! He shall not study, and waste the Lord's time and my money; he shall be distinguished as a merchant. But none of you are either eating or drinking. Help yourselves from what you like; everything is made to be eaten! Bendixen, eat and drink; a clever student can't do without eating and drinking. You must often come and see me, Bendixen."

Jacob thanked him heartily for this invitation.

"How is your father in health?" asked the merchant; "I remember him very well. I have often been at your grandfather's."

"I thank you, he is well," said Jacob, curtly.

"And your mother? Was not she a daughter of old Rabbi Nathan, and of Gidel, a sister of Philip Herz's wife?" asked the merchant.

"My mother is dead," replied Jacob, and bent over his plate to conceal his emotion.

The merchant's countenance changed from cheerfulness to the deepest sympathy. He covered his head, and murmured softly the formula, "Boruch dajon emmes" ("Blessed be the righteous Judge!") and the whole company looked with compassion on Jacob.

"When did she die, the poor thing?" inquired the merchant.

"Three months since," replied Jacob, and put a firm restraint upon himself, to keep from weeping.

"Poor young man!" said the merchant; "and what did she die of?"

Jacob could contain himself no longer. Fortunately one of the guests pushed his chair from the table, and the merchant, with this, remembered that it was time to end the meal. They all rose, and said, "Blessed be the time of meals!" shook hands, and went into another room.

Jacob was not at all at his ease. The merchant's son was out of humour, and the merchant himself out of spirits. A Jew feels himself personally interested, when he hears of the death of a Jew. He regards himself and his people as God's elect; but there is, nevertheless, one fearful foe, whom the Lord, in consequence of the laws of the world, will not destroy—and that is Death! This enemy has been into the congregation, and carried off his victim; the Angel of Death has been into the circle of the Jews—perhaps, even then, hovers above his head. When will his own fatherless children rend their clothes? When will he, under the guidance of that dark power, be conducted through the grave to that mysterious life which exists beyond it? For there is a life beyond. Have not the dead been heard praying together in their coffins, as the hour approached for a good man's burial? And has not, also, the noise as of angry voices been heard, when one who has lived evilly has been about to be laid to rest among the faithful? Yes, there is a life beyond; and it is this mysterious life in death which the Jew regards with reverent awe. But you Christians believe in this also; for it is not quiet, immoveable death which terrifies you at night in the churchyard; is it not rather the life in death which gives tho fullest effect to your ghost-stories?

The company separated soon after; and when Jacob had gone through several streets, he found himself alone with a Jewish student, who had been nearly the whole of the evening a silent participator of the feast. His name was Levy Martin.

"This merchant Israelsen is somewhat coarse in his manner," remarked Martin, "but his dinners are excellently cooked."

"Yes; one can see that he is a good-natured man," replied Jacob.

"Did you take notice of his wife?" asked Martin; "she did not say a single word all the evening. When she had eaten, she sat and twirled her thumbs with almost a human look."

"I dare say she is not accustomed to be in company with Christians," said Jacob.

"And what four graces of daughters!" laughed Martin, "the one fatter than the other."

"Mr. Martin," exclaimed Jacob, "I cannot bear to talk ill of any man at whose table I have sat."

"Nay, I don't mean any harm; you know very well that we Jews always backbite one another a little," said Martin. "Besides, I have been sitting silent almost all the evening—I must have a little compensation."

"Yes, you were very silent; but why were you so?"

"But do you tell me first: are you in any way connected with

Israelsen's family?" asked Martin; "and are you so zealous a Jew that you always applaud the Jews?"

"Not in the least," returned Jacob; "it is the first time I ever was in Israelsen's house. I don't, indeed, even know how I came to be invited; I only know the son quite casually. And as regards the Jews, I only wish that I liked them better than I do."

"I merely wanted to know, that I might not by any chance knock against you," said Martin. "You see, the whole time I sat upon thorns, for I did not know but that any moment some offence might be given to the Christians by some little want of tact. You saw how the father scolded the son, and you heard about the great genius for trade! But what I was most afraid of was, that before leaving the table, the merchant would put on his hat, and exclaim, 'We will pray!'—and it is really wonderful that he did not do so. What should such Jews as those bring Christians among them for? In its present condition, Judaism is incompatible with Christianity. In a mixed company like that, I never feel at my ease. There are strong lines of demarcation between those two social spheres; there is no common spirit to unite them, and under the influence of which both parties can move together. What is understood by one party is unintelligible to the other. No; I would much rather be with all Jews, or all Christians: I can get on capitally with either of them alone. We Jew students are a sort of amphibious creatures; we can live both with Jews and with Christians."

Youth always imagines that the experience which it has had is an education of which no one else knows anything. Jacob was astonished to hear another speak of Jews and Christians in a manner so similar to his own mode of thinking and feeling regarding them. After a moment or two, he remarked:

"Did you say that we Jew students were amphibious creatures? It seems to me that we are exactly the opposite—that we have forsaken the element in which we are at home, and have betaken ourselves to one which does not agree with us."

"Oh! that is imagination," exclaimed Martin; "that is only till one gets used to the life of the two spheres. When one has an easy mind, and now and then can close one's ears, it immediately becomes pleasant to exist alternately in the two opposite elements; now one is a bird, now a fish, just as one has a fancy for it."

"You certainly must be of a happy temperament," said Jacob.

"Oh, yes! You must come and see me sometimes; we shall entertain one another very well," said Martin.

"You must come and see me, too; I live here."

"Done!" said Martin. "To-morrow I shall come and smoke my morning pipe with you, before I go to the Hospital. Now, good night. Thanks for this evening."

"Good night, Martin. Thanks!"

CHAPTER XIV

Some days afterwards, quite early in the morning, one of Jacob's cousins rushed into the room, without giving himself time to knock or to say, "Good day!" He was out of breath, and exclaimed,—

"You must come to father; the priest has sent a messenger after him and you."

"What should I do with the priest?" asked Jacob; "I have nothing to do with him."

"What pride!" exclaimed the cousin; "you have nothing to do with the priest? But he has something to do with you! He wishes to see you."

Jacob knew that he ought to be flattered by this invitation, which showed what attention it had excited among the Jews that a Jewish youth from the provinces had passed a brilliant examination; but either from youthful presumption, or else to surprise his cousin, he satisfied himself by saying,—

"Very well, I'll come."

"And in the evening you are to go to Merchant Bernbaum's. They sent to us because they did not know where you lived," added the cousin.

"Am I?" asked Jacob.

"How conceited you are, since you have become a bit of a student!" said the cousin; "who does not receive with a low bow an invitation from the wealthy Bernbaum? But whether you go or not does not matter to me."

With these words, the cousin ran off again. When he reached home, he popped his head in at the door, and exclaimed, "He'll come directly, though he stinks with pride!" and then continued his way to his shop in Östergade.

When Jacob reached his uncle Marcus's, he found his aunt busy folding a large white cravat; this she tied round Jacob's neck, and stuck into it his uncle's large diamond breast-pin. She accompanied him to the door, and brushed every grain of dust from his clothes.

Marcus walked with an unusually proud air; he participated with his nephew in the honour of having been sent for to the priest's, and took to himself, in thought, the larger share.

"How the other Jews will stare on Friday afternoon, when they hear that I have been invited to the priest's," thought he to himself.

Jacob also walked in silence, and was thinking to himself what could the priest have to say to him. The nearer he came to the place, the more he felt agitated by fear and awe; it seemed to him almost as if conscience were about to hear and sit in judgment over the ceremonies which he had disregarded.

When they had mounted the flight of rickety stairs in the old, tumble-down house of the priest, they were received in an anteroom by his servant,—a learned and pious man, who took high rank among the Jews, something like a king's chamberlain. By him they were softly conducted into the room where the priest sat reading in his *Hrumisch.**

It was a long time before the priest looked up; and during the respectful silence that prevailed, Jacob summoned courage enough calmly to observe his priest.

Over the pale countenance, with its white beard,—over the old man's whole exterior,—over all that surrounded him, how-

* The Five Books of Moses in print. Thora, or the Law, is written on parchment.

ever old and faded it might be,—seemed to brood a peaceful repose, which involuntarily awoke in Jacob a deep, melancholy longing, as if, amid the tempesting of the sea, he was looking upon a calm light on land. Here he could see that doubt had never been nourished; here prevailed an eternal Sabbath; alone, in company with his God! separated by ceremonies from the whole of the Christian world, lived this man in a spiritual Canaan.

"If one could but be a Jew like him!" thought Jacob, with a low sigh.

At length the servant ventured to approach his priest, and whispered to him that the invited guests had arrived. The old man bowed himself reverentially over his volume before he turned from it, and then bade his guests a friendly Baruch habo (Welcome)! They advanced nearer to him, and received from him the laying on of hands and a benediction. He then desired them to be seated; and when they each had taken a seat, he set himself steadfastly to examine Jacob. He fixed his eyes on him, but it was evident that he was embarrassed to find a subject on which to speak. He had not duly considered with himself beforehand for what reason it was that he really wanted to see the young Jew whom the Christians had so greatly distinguished; and now that he stood before him he seemed to be filled with an instinctive sense of a foreign element in the young man, which he himself could neither comprehend nor value. The old man continued to stare at Jacob, who, in his turn, looked full of expectation. The uncle sat as upon thorns, the priest's servant stood in reverential silence at the door. At length the old man rose, fetched a large rosy-cheeked apple, and gave it to Jacob, saying,—

"Do not forget to lay thy Tephilim."

He seated himself again before his printed Books of Moses, and the audience was at an end.

The whole scene with its deep silence had been so extraordinary, that it it made an almost romantic impression upon Jacob. When the priest riveted those clear, unimpassioned eyes upon him, it seemed to him as if he could see into his heart. But the longer he continued to gaze, the expression of the eyes became more and more unintelligible; it seemed as if the priest and himself receded from each other, with an ever-increasing separation. When the door closed after them, and the old servant who attended them to the stairs had said his last "Seid Mauchel" (adieu), and softly glided back again, it seemed to him as if himself and Judaism had had an interview, and after a fruitless endeavour to become intelligible to each other had now parted, and each gone on his own separate path.

He was interrupted in his visionary thoughts by his uncle, who, with anger which he could with difficulty repress, said, "Was that, then, the way in which you talk to the priest?"

Jacob replied, mildly, "I did not say a word, uncle!"

"That was exactly the misfortune," exclaimed his uncle; "people don't sit staring their priest in the face without speaking a word."

"But what could I say to him, uncle? Only tell me!" said Jacob, somewhat annoyed.

At these words Marcus grew angry, stopped and turned to Jacob, and setting a hand on either hip, looked fixedly at him; "Am I to teach thee," said he, "what thou shouldst say to thy priest? For what purpose has thy father let thee study, and spent his money over thee? For what?—Answer me!"

"Nay, my father did not send me to study for that purpose!" replied Jacob; and pursued his way.

"Jacob! Jacob!" said his uncle, now following him, "thou art making a fool of me into the bargain. Thou troublest thyself neither about the priest nor thy uncle; nor, perhaps, about thy father either. Thou art become an alien; thou wilt get into trouble at last—though; but why do I vex myself about thee? Thou art not my son, thank God!"

"Hear uncle," said Jacob, "I will not be anything but friends with thee. I have lived in thy house; and thou hast treated me very kindly, therefore I will not be offended with thy words. But, now, do be just towards me. What could I have said to the priest? Was it not my place to wait until he spoke to me?"

"It is all one, now," replied his uncle,—"but thou art become an alien! I have seen it for some time, but I would not say anything. What does it matter to me? Thou art *barmitzvah* —thou art responsible for thyself, and I have no power over thee. But this I advise thee, for thy own sake: stop before it is too late. No good can ever come of forsaking the God of Israel, that I can assure thee! Do not give cause of offence. Now, this very evening thou art going, for the first time, to visit with the wealthy Bernbaums', who are well-bred and good people. Take care of thyself!—Anything but friendly with me? Why should we be anything but friends? Thou art my brother's son; thou art as welcome to my house as ever. Wilt thou come in now?"

"No, thank you, uncle; I am afraid that my aunt will scold also when she hears of our visit. There, take thy breast-pin! and many thanks for the loan."

"The poor breast-pin!" said the uncle, looking at it; "when it was stuck in thy cravat, nobody thought how the visit would turn out."

"No, uncle,—but it has no cause of complain; it went with us to be seen, not to talk!"

"How you are joking!" said the uncle, unable to repress a smile; and went into the house.

In the evening, Jacob, considerably out of spirits and somewhat anxious, betook himself to the house of the wealthy Bernbaums.

When he entered the drawing-room, in which was assembled a considerable number of people, the lady of the house rose, came forward to receive him, saying, " Welcome, Mr. Bendixen ; it delights me to see you in my house, the doors of which stand open to every intellectual man, whether young or old. You will see here many persons whom I shall afterwards have the pleasure of making you acquainted with. Be so good as to take a seat; we are now reading."

Jacob bowed, and took a seat near the table. Around it sat the lady, her four daughters, and two sons, besides two young Jew students, who, once a week, were privileged to dine with the family, together with the merchant's clerk, who was the reader. The merchant himself sat by the stove and slept. By the window stood three Jew students; and somewhat later Martin arrived.

"Where was it that we left off?" asked the lady.

"At 'Ha!'" replied the reader; I set my finger over the 'Ha!'"

"Who says Ha?" asked she.

"Noureddin," replied the young man.

"Yes, now I remember; well, read on."

The young man was reading "Aladdin," by Oehlenschläger; but he read it as if it had been the merchants cash-book, and with a strong Jewish accent. Jacob, however, was so occupied by his feelings as a guest and with respect for the hospitable family, that he involuntarily endeavoured to see everything in as beautiful and excellent a point of view as possible, and before long he followed the reading with interest, attending merely to the subject and not listening with critical ears. The three students at the window, on the contrary, stood with their heads together, and laughed.

The reading went on for some time uninterruptedly; at length, they came to the point where Noureddin wishes to part with the new copper-lamp for an old one; and the reader, desiring to give effect by change of tone, uttered the words—

"Who will give their worn-out copper lamps for new ones?"

in precisely the same tone with which the lower class of Jews cry their wares in the streets and markets.

At this extraordinary cry the merchant woke, rubbed his eyes, and said, "That was a very queer trade! What crazy book have you got reading there?"

"Do not interrupt our æsthetic enjoyment," said the lady, somewhat tartly,—"read on!"

The reading proceeded; it rumbled on, like wheels over a rough road.

The merchant made some vain attempts to fall again into a nap, and at length, wearied by want of success, raised himself upright in his chair and looked at his wife; presently he addressed her.

"What dost thou think, Rebecca? Refoel Leibmann has been overturned to-day. What a dreadful house there will be with all those little children."

"Lord have mercy!" cried the lady; where did it happen?"

"On Knipple's-bridge; I heard of it on 'Change; but I did not like to tell thee directly."

The lady dropped into silence; and it was evident from her countenance that her thoughts were more occupied by the poor unhappy family than by the reading. She did not regain her spirits, until she had whispered something to one of her daughters, who immediately left the room, no doubt to send some relief to the afflicted family. This done, the lady again gave herself up to the reading.

"Shall we not soon have tea?" inquired the merchant.

"We shall have finished directly;" returned the lady; "Aaron, read a little faster."

One of the students said, half aloud, "Ge-up!"

The reading now advanced from a round trot to a gallop; and when Aaron came to the last word he stopped so suddenly that it was as if a carriage-wheel had run against a tree. Everybody seemed to feel a shock.

Tea, and other refreshments, were now handed round to the company.

"It is really a beautiful work!—quite classical!" remarked the lady.

"Pardon me, Madam," said one of the students—a lawyer—advancing towards the table; "but still there are great faults in it. If it were not the fashion to pronounce Aladdin classical and divine, sensible people would meet with an audience; I will, however, only call your attention to a few little things, and I think you will say that I am right. What I first and foremost require in a poet is truth and nature. By this I mean, for example, that a sailor should talk like a sailor, and not like a professor; a shepherd like a shepherd, and not like a merchant or a sea-captain; is not that right?"

"Yes, very right," said the lady.

"And, further, I require," continued the young lawyer, "that an Oriental should converse like Orientals; that we should not —a—I must borrow the book—Aladdin should not speak of 'tearing a slit in his breeches-knees,' which is not Oriental, because in the East they do not wear small-clothes; neither should he talk of playing at 'toss-farthing' and 'trap-ball,' which is Copenhagenish, not Oriental. Still more inconsistent is it that he talks of measuring a young lady across the bust, for this is not permitted in Oriental harems. All these things the poet might have avoided if he had given himself the trouble to read something about the East, of which many books of travels give most accurate accounts. Above all, was it absurd to make the favourite dish of a poor tailor-boy be pheasant—"

"Yes; but in the East, Mr. Isaksen," said the lady.

"Well, let the pheasants pass; but flesh-soup, which Aladdin orders the Spirit of the Lamp to bring him, that is not Oriental?"

"Are you quite sure of that, Isaksen?" asked Martin; "all mankind have come from Lower Asia—who knows but that flesh-soup has come from the same point?"

"I have no wish to inquire after that now," said Isaksen; "what I here say is my serious opinion. I regret that such oversights, which are apparent to every one of sound understanding, have not been corrected. No one can be carried out of himself by this work; one's understanding every moment is appealed to unpleasantly. Mustapha, Morgiane, Noureddin, Aladdin, and so on—every one of them are constantly losing their characters as Orientals, and talk like Copenhageners. For example, at page 66, he speaks of the Nacker's Pit—in Ispahan; page 186, of a Tea-urn—at Ispahan; at page 324, the Fairies sing *hymns*, and pray Allah to reward Fatima. It is disgusting. There is one place especially, about which a few days ago I was disputing with one of my acquaintance; it is at page 48. The poet makes the Spirit of the Lamp say:

> 'A new Prometheus will again convey
> That noble light of life unto mankind;
> A second Odin, from the mountain-rock,
> Through Gunlöd's love obtain the holy draught.'

"That the Spirit of the Lamp should be acquainted with both the Grecian and the Northern mythology may be admitted certainly, in one point of view—namely, that the Spirit of the Lamp has a universal knowledge. But, poetically taken, the Spirit of the Lamp is Oriental, and an Oriental spirit and atmosphere should be diffused through the whole story of the lamp. It is Oehlenschläger who speaks here with his mythological knowledge, and thus rends every illusion from our minds. It is a jumble of Grecian and Northern mythology, and quite provokes me. What is your opinion, Mr. Bendixen? Am not I right?"

Jacob hesitated in his reply—"I have really not seen the faults you speak of," he said; "just as I only know that there are specks on the sun because astronomers tell me so."

"Do you study astronomy?" asked the lady of the house, quickly.

Two students began to laugh; she turned round to them with tears in her eyes, and exclaimed, "Good heavens! what have I said which makes you laugh at me?"

The faces of the two young men flushed crimson, and they protested that they had not laughed at her.

She turned from them with a lightened heart, and said to Isaksen, "There may very likely be in Aladdin all the faults which you have mentioned. Aaron reads so confusedly that one may easily overlook the faults. Aaron, you must study style more in reading. But for the rest, you are of my opinion with regard to Oehlenschläger—that he is a great man. He is sometimes, it is true, a little over-strained; and he, perhaps, had better not meddle with Persian stories: he should confine himself to the Danish and Roman."

"Yes," said Isaksen, "there is, for example, the legend of Cupid and Psyche; I should like to see him treat that."

"Cupid and Pyske?" said Madame Bernbaum, "it seems to me that that was spoken of lately."

"Pardon me, madam," said Isaksen, "but it is not called Pyske, but Psyche."

"It is really shocking, how you dictate to me this evening!" said she, angrily. "P, y, s, does not spell Pyz?"

"No; it is pronounced Psy, madam."

"Don't come here to teach me that!" exclaimed she; "you shall not dispute me out of my sound understanding! What does P, y, s, c, h, e, spell, Aaron?"

"I have always pronounced that name Pyske," replied Aaron.

"I assure you it is pronounced Psyche, my good lady," persisted the student.

"You are uncivil, Mr. Isaksen," said she; "it is not handsome of you in my own house! You think because you are a student, that you possess the wisdom of all the world! Nay, nay!"

"And you, Madame Bernbaum, because you have more wealth than my parents, think that you can treat me thus!" said Isaksen, and took up his hat. "I shall not very often trouble you. But if it were the last word I had to speak, I should say that it is pronounced Psyche. Good night!"

There was nobody present who could knit together the two broken threads of social intercourse, or obviate the disagreeable effect which this scene had caused. A few disconnected remarks as to wind and weather were made, and soon afterwards people began to take leave."

When Martin and Bendixen had walked a short distance together, the latter remarked, "There was something queer about this evening party; it was pretty much as one might fancy King Christopher and his negroes holding a court in Hayti. I have read how one will go with a pair of general's epaulettes on his otherwise naked shoulders; another in a pair of cavalry-boots and a coat, but without trousers, whilst a third will content himself with nothing but spurs on his heels. In this fashion do our friends present themselves as regards their æsthetic attainments. Isaksen has prosaic common-sense in all its naked barrenness; Madame Bernbaum has the most entire want of common sense, while her sons and daughters are possessed of, just as it may happen to be, either nothing at all, or only a pair of spurs on the heel."

"That is a very good picture!" said Martin, smiling; "things did go a little queerly! But," continued he, more seriously, " true intellectual and moral development cannot make their way into Jewish family life, until we, who are a sort of pioneers, have ourselves cultivated a family life."

"I could almost wish," said Jacob, "that I had not been present at Bernbaum's this evening. It always produces a great depression of mind in me to see Jews conduct themselves as they did. What would Christians think of us, if they were witnesses of such scenes as those between Madame Bernbaum and the students?"

"On the contrary, it was very amusing to me," said Martin, and burst into a loud laugh. "And it is comic enough," continued he, seeing Jacob look at him with astonishment, "it is almost absurd to think, that we immediately begin to talk seriously and profoundly about our nation! A couple of Christian students going from an evening party, would talk about wine, L'ombre, or the ladies, like respectable, rational, and well-behaved young fellows! And yet," continued he, the next moment, " this very circumstance is precisely a sign that things are not so hopeless among the Jews. Individuals never stand intellectually in a state of isolation; they are the children of their time and their circumstances. Our very anxiety about the Jews is a proof that a new spirit is beginning to move among our people. Only give time, and the Jews will not be behind the age. Our present intellectual state is a building erected in haste; whilst it is being outwardly adorned, much is going on within it. In twenty or thirty years, when the influences which are now operating upon us shall have fermented and cleared themselves, we shall compel the Christians to respect us."

"God grant that it may be so!" said Jacob; "all that I wish is, to be able to obtain for myself a position in which I may gain their esteem."

"An ambition not of the highest order," said Martin.

"And yet it may be found a sufficiently difficult one to achieve," said Jacob, with a sigh.

"Nay, now we are getting too deep in the subject," exclaimed Martin, "to-night, at all events, let us be gay and contented; come, let us go into a coffee-house."

CHAPTER XV.

One day Martin entered Jacob's room with the air of a man who had cast off a heavy burden and now treads on air.

"Ah! good day to you; let me have a pipe," exclaimed he. "I have got an eight days' leave of absence from the Hospital to study anatomy. But I will, in the first place, have an afternoon's holiday; therefore am I come to you—firstly, for a little amusement; and secondly, that we may go out somewhere together. Where shall we go to? But what the deuce is that for a face! Many a time have I seen you look out of sorts, but never so thoroughly melancholiously out of sorts as to-day. Your stomach must be out of order, or else you are bilious; perhaps we have an affection of the liver to contend with! Or, let me see,—we had yesterday an interesting case of curvature of the spine; I shall be extremely happy to give you the benefit of my newly-acquired experience. Do you feel thirst? Allow me to see your tongue?"

"Get your pipe, Martin!" returned Jacob,—"get your pipe, and don't be so full of your jokes! I really am not in a joking mood to-day."

"Have you really met with anything unpleasant, though— has anything happened?" asked his friend, gravely.

"I might tell you, Martin, for you could understand me," said Jacob. "Yes; some time I will tell you."

"Good Heavens! what is it?" exclaimed Martin; "is it some unhappy love affair?"

"Yes, it is in one sense a love affair," said Jacob, with bitterness; "but the misfortune is, that there is so much hatred mixed up with the love. Oh, yes, it may very well be called an unhappy love affair! My whole mind, my soul, my devotion, belongs to the Christians; and I could wish myself at the head of an army which I might lead out against them, with which I might besiege Copenhagen, so that I might win their love in return."

"This is a method, however, which has not come within the range of my practice!" observed the young surgeon.

"Don't make fun of me, even if I do make myself ridiculous in your eyes," said Jacob; "I am too much excited just now to weigh my words."

"But, in Heaven's name, what have they done to you? And who is it that has wounded you so deeply?"

"It is no new wound which I have received; it is an old wound, which has been torn open afresh," said Jacob. "Yes, it is an old wound; I fancy that I must have received it at my birth. It is that Jewish persecution which I suffered from elsewhere, and which now meets me anew. That which the school-boys commenced, the students have continued. Between hours at the college, the students amuse themselves in any way they like,—to-day it was by pelting one another with paper balls; and though I did not take any part in the amusement, yet a great number were aimed at me. In the first instance, I took it all in sport; but before long, I heard one and another say, 'Give it to the Jew!' I pretended not to hear, and took it all quietly. At last, however, a large piece of wood was aimed at me which struck me on the back. With that I rose up, and seizing the piece of wood, hurled it back among them, striking one such a blow on the head as made him for the future keep out of the way. It is all extremely disagreeable; and now I feel a most unconquerable disinclination to go back to the college. They even close the university against me—against Jews. And in what have I deserved this persecution? Are they not grown men? have they not understanding enough to perceive that knowledge is our common mother—that we are brothers?"

"Yes, but brothers throw pieces of wood at one another sometimes," said Martin.

"Do not ridicule me," said Jacob. "If you cannot understand my feelings, and share in my indignation, tell me so, and I will say no more."

"I do understand them," returned Martin. "Speak out openly; not that you are going to be driven from the college by a few thoughtless lads; you should march up to them, and defy them!"

"Ah, Martin! you don't comprehend of how much more importance this is to me. You, perhaps, suppose that all the pain which I suffer is merely from the piece of wood that was thrown at me. No; that is a very insignificant thing; but it reminds me of all the misery which presses upon me, and upon you also, Martin—in being a Jew! Why did you not continue to be, like your father before you, a butcher?* why did not I remain behind my father's desk? Why did our spirits forsake the homes where affection extended its arms to enfold us, and seek an 'elective affinity' with the Christian mind, which despises us, and which repels us from it? We are and remain to be Jews, even as the negro slave is and remains to be black, although he may emancipate himself. Like him, we become emancipated only to understand a freedom and equality which is death to us. Do they ever forget the Jew in the human being? Does not *the Jew* always stand before their thoughts as a line of demarcation? They do not, when in society, speak

* Butchers, among the Jews, rank much higher than among the Christians, for with them a butcher must be a very good man.

of Lutheran Peterson, Catholic Jenson, and so on; but they say, the Jew Bendixen, even though it may not be spoken aloud. When people would be very civil, they speak of *the Hebrews, or your people;* and when one is dining with them, if, for example, ham is on the table, one's neighbour never forgets, in offering one a slice, to inquire, 'But do you eat it? may I venture to offer you some?' Jew! Jew! One might suppose that we bore that name branded upon our foreheads, for they never avoid reminding us of it!"

"It is all true what you say," returned Martin; "but, either I am used to it, or I am less sensitive on this subject than you are, but it no longer annoys me. If any one offers me ham, and expresses any doubt about my ability to eat it, why, then, I eat it at once."

Jacob, wearied and dispirited, made no reply, and a silence ensued.

"Hear, Bendixen!" at length exclaimed his friend—and a certain twitching of the muscles of his countenance showed that at this moment he was agitated by deep feeling—"I see plainly enough that there is a great difference between us two. I am poor; and the necessity of looking forwards towards my future and of providing for myself, has overcome that sensitive delicacy of feeling which at one time existed in my soul, though to a less extent than in yours. Besides that, I am of an easy temper, and regard many things with indifference; whilst you are more choleric and visionary; and beyond this, you are wealthy, and anxiety about the means of life does not, therefore, swallow up other troubles. You must make a resolve, an energetic resolve; you cannot, as I do, belong to both classes; you must choose either the one or the other. Be, then, a Jew; unite yourself to the Jews; study Judaic theology, and become a Rabbi."

"It is impossible!" exclaimed Jacob, warmly. "Are not the

greater part of the Jewish ceremonies opposed to my convictions? Shall I erect the whole of my future life on hypocrisy and falsehood? Besides which, I cannot unite myself to the Jews. The first condition of a happy life-long union is accordance in moral and intellectual feeling and culture. Just as well might you advise me to live in a little country town among shoemakers and tailors—however kind and good-natured they might be. My blood is kindred with the Jews; by nature I love them; but my mind cannot exist amongst them. It is a Christian mind, and it seeks its kind with instinctive violence."

"Then become a Christian!—be baptized!" urged Martin.

"Martin, you cannot mean that seriously," exclaimed Jacob. "Be baptized! deny my past life, my childhood, my whole present life! Be baptized! like a coward, flee from the conflict, —for this I feel, and I never have felt it more forcibly than at the present moment that it is a conflict, and a nobler conflict than as regards my own insignificant, individual self; it has reference to my people—to my poor, subjected people—the race of my dead mother. If we, who in moral and intellectual training are superior to our people, abandon them, there will at last remain nothing but mere froth left behind; and thus the arrogance of the Christians will be strengthened, and their persecution of us justified. No; I will combat against the Christians until they acknowledge the man in me, spite of the Jew. Even though I should fall in the struggle, I dedicate myself to it. Besides," resumed he, after a pause, and speaking with a still deeper voice,—" besides, I do not acknowledge the Christian religion. Judaism is indeed coming out of bondage through the influence of civilization; the minds among her who are in advance are already freed from their fetters. A worm gnaws at the root of our present condition, and we are rent asunder because we are in a transition state. But the

Christendom of the present day is tottering also; men's minds no longer place their reliance on creeds; anxiously, almost despairingly, they seek for a new Christianity. The worm gnaws the whole race; despair rules over it! When they sing the songs of their highest rejoicing, I seem to hear a secret consuming pain amid their melody. They do not know that as their exultation ascends, despair raises alike her demoniacally derisive voice. When I, on such occasions, sit among them, I seem to see, with a secret horror, that Samson has shaken the pillars of the temple, and that we shall all be buried together."

Martin looked at him in silence.

He continued: "And it has been a consolation to me in this long subjection that misery broods over us all."

"Bendixen! Bendixen!" exclaimed his friend, "there is something frightful in your state of mind."

"Oh!" said Jacob, "I feel at this moment truly how much I hate them. Let me now make a clean breast. I have regarded it as an honour, as a condescension, when one of them has crossed over the street to me! Is there hatred enough in the world to outweigh this humiliation?"

"And I have heard Christian students reproach you for being proud, inflexible, and reserved!" exclaimed Martin.

"Because I, in my humility, was afraid of approaching them," said he; "because I have waited for a friendly advance on their side with the same timid longing that a slave waits for a kind glance from his master."

"But cannot you also see," argued Martin, "that on your side too there may have been fault, when people, who may have wished to make advances, yet could not do it."

"I was the subjected party," said Jacob, "and it became them to make the advances to me."

"But do you then really imagine that every Christian always

keeps in his mind the subjection of the Jew, just as you in your most sensitive mind never can lose the remembrance of it?"

Jacob was silent.

"Now do not be unjust," resumed Martin. "I propose to you one of two alternatives. You may, just as well as me, have intercourse with Christians; only overcome your extreme sensitiveness of mind. Why will you not associate with such young fellows as really like you? Wilhelm Fangel, for instance, he always speaks of you with the greatest kindness; he is disposed to be a good friend to you. Why will you not meet his advances? You will do battle for the Jews, you say. How will you do it? Are there any other weapons than self-control? Are there any other means than by advancing towards the Christians when the Christians advance towards you? We Jewish students should lead the battle, that is true; we should go in advance against the Christians, and in our own persons teach them what is good among the Jews. Now for it then. Let us go. Take your hat, and we will go to the Academy of Surgery, where we shall find Fangel and several others. I will be your physician, as well as your apothecary and sick nurse; I will not alone prescribe medicines, but I will prepare and administer them. Come now!"

Jacob hesitated.

"Bendixen," said Martin, "now it is my turn to be grave To-day I open to you the door to mankind. Perhaps we two may never again be in the same state of mind that we are to-day; I may perhaps never again feel the same desire to stand by you that I feel at this moment. Avail yourself of this moment, or else I shall close the door."

Jacob took up his hat, and accompanied him from the house.

CHAPTER XVI.

Of all the students in the University of Copenhagen, the students of medicine are not only the gayest, but those who hold the most liberal opinions. They see in the human being only the better or the worse man; perhaps, indeed, only the better or worse human body. When a Jew must be treated for typhus according to the same method as a Christian; when a Jewish limb is not more difficult to amputate than that of a Christian; when, finally, the muscles and nerves are placed in the same order in the Jew as in the Christian, they do not see any reason to make any difference between a Christian and a Jew. The nature of their studies brings them into closer intimacy with each other than that of any other students; therefore, and at the same time, because they become familiar in seeing life and death, suffering and convalescence, balanced as it were, there is more youthful recklessness, more social hilarity among these medical students than among any others.

Jacob was soon at home among these young men; and in the numerous meetings at the various hospitals, where scientific disputes alternated with the most lively jests, he found himself a participator in that student life which had always appeared to him so delightful. It was the sociality, however, rather than the merriment which was so invigorating to him; it was the feeling that now, at length, he was among companions, which produced so beneficial an effect upon him.

Thus wore away the first twelve months of his student life. He passed his second examination, and, as might be expected, chose the study of medicine for the profession of his life. In proportion as his mind became more cheerful, he lost something of his extreme sensitiveness, and began to smile at the idea that a curse hung over him, or, at all events, to hope that if it did brood over his childhood and youth, it had now disappeared like a storm-cloud from the horizon.

Jacob was now twenty; and after having heard so much said about him, some of our young-lady readers, at all events, will wish to know what was his outward appearance. He looked like a Jew, but by no means a common one. A highly cultivated mind, and tender and refined feelings, had ennobled the expression of what might by many have been considered too strongly marked a Jewish physiognomy. For knowledge passes through the soul with a purifying effect, and the soul labours and labours until it converts the outward being into something like a suitable dwelling for itself—until the countenance, so to say, becomes its outward type.

Jacob is now twenty; and the narrative at this point hastily leaps over a few years of his life. And why so? Because no human life is in reality a succession of events which deserve to be chronicled. One must now and then give the hero time to breathe a little.

Still, in the same manner that we receive an occasional letter from an absent friend, which gives us a general idea of his journey, will we take an occasional episode from this period of his life, by which we may gain a general idea of the years which we pass over.

CHAPTER XVII.

A TRIP INTO THE COUNTRY.

"How fresh and pleasant the air is, after the rain which fell last night," said a student one morning, looking from the window into the green court of the college, as they were waiting for the clinical professor.

"I have half a mind to go into the country to-day," said another, glancing up to the clear blue sky; "has anybody a mind to go with me?"

"Yes, let us all have a trip into the country to-day!" exclaimed the first speaker.

"I cannot; I must read." "I must go to my grinder." "I must go to a party to-night," said deploring voices on all sides.

"By heaven! we'll get up a rebellion," said Martin; "but, after all, the hospital will be reasonable. You must, you say, go to your grinder; you must read; and you must—heaven knows what! All these very causes which prevent your going into the country, are the precise reasons why you should go! I am pretty sure that nobody troubles themselves about college or hospital, but that all will go into the country."

"When a thing is once proposed, it ought never to be given up!" exclaimed Fangel; "for the honour of the hospital a carriage-full of us, at least, ought to go. First let us know who are the volunteers; the rest must draw lots. They who are volunteers—stand forward!"

All came forward.

"I like that," continued Fangel; "and now we should send deputations to the Fever and General Hospitals."

"We should do like Saul," said Martin, "who slew an ox, and sent the bloody fragments round the country, with the command to march out against the enemy, and with the information that thus should it be done to every one who did not accompany Saul and Samuel."

"Bravo!" cried Fangel, "Gröndal, slay Martin, and run with the emphatic fragments through all Israel."

"Ah!" replied Martin, "they are right, who say that in our days is the world turned upside down. However, I bow to the spirit of the age, and present my neck to Gröndal and Fangel!"

"A good answer to a poor witticism!" exclaimed Fangel; "the trip to the country begins well. *Allons!* Let us send every one on a journey into eternity who opposes our trip into the country!"

"But where is Bendixen?" asked somebody. "He is as good as a thermometer or a safety-valve. When the others are merry, he is grave; when we are grave, he is extravagant and wild. He, on such occasions, may be compared to the cylinder in Watt's steam-engine, which lets water into the boiler when there is too little; and stops it when there is too much."

"Here comes the thermometer, the safety-valve, the cylinder, and so on!" exclaimed Fangel, pointing towards the door, which was that moment opened by Bendixen.

"Bendixen, will you go with us into the country?"

"Yes, of course. Who is going there?"

"All of us."

"That is charming! When are you going?"

"At four o'clock we all meet here, go out, and take a carriage."

At this moment the professor entered, and the lecture began.

"How delightful it is to be at liberty, to get out of the city, where one cannot breathe freely for walls and houses! I inhale the fresh air, as the parched earth drinks in the shower, and feel as if I could never have enough. If one could only for a moment ascend up into the air and lose oneself in a whirlwind, or, better still, in a mass of glorious cloud; if one could descend on light wings down to the sea and then rise up again towards the sun! It is a melancholy lot, this of mankind; even in death they are not released, but are screwed up in a close fitting box, and laid in the earth. It would be better if the body were burned, and the ashes, like the blessed Pugatschews, scattered to all the winds."

This long outbreak proceeded from Bendixen, as the carriage rolled along the shore; and the Sound, with its scattered white sails, lay outstretched before the eye.

Gröndal, who sat beside him, thus replied to this outpouring of his feelings:

"I think, too, that it would be better if the body were burned; then people would not be so nervous about their dead being intact under ground; one should then sometimes get a regular subject."

"Oh, you never think about anything but *subjects!*" exclaimed Bendixen. "I think if ever you should meet with a lady suffering from an interesting incurable disease, you would marry her merely to obtain the corpse."

"That may be," replied Gröndal.

König, who sat behind them, joined in the conversation:

"It is an acknowledged fact," said he, "and can be logically proved that Gröndal will never go to heaven."

"How so?" asked Jacob.

"Why, if the Creator himself would be most truly merciful to Gröndal, he would not place him in heaven, because heaven would not be heaven to him, inasmuch as no bodies are to be found there. Gröndal's kingdom of heaven would be the lower regions, where he could study every imaginable contortion of the muscles in the different kinds of fire to which sinners were subjected."

"That is an extremely illogical proof," said Gröndal; "for if patients take their bodies with them into the lower regions, why may they not do the same in the kingdom of heaven?"

"Listen to him!" exclaimed König; "he has abandoned the expression *men*, and uses instead, *patients!*"

"Well," said Gröndal, "does anybody arrive in the other world in any character but that of a patient? Does not every one suffer at last from the most incurable, the most acute of diseases—that of death? As for the rest, it is a matter of indifference to me where the breath which I have breathed forth goes to when I am dead."

"So, then, you do not at all believe in a soul, and the immortality of the soul!" exclaimed König.

"Bah!" replied Gröndal, and puffed far out the smoke of his cigar, while his countenance assumed a more earnest thoughtful expression; "your immortality is too massive for me. Whatever I do in thought or action, in conflict with the world or with my ownself, is my immortal part. When the ink is exhausted in the pen, it can write no longer; but that which it has written, and that which remains to all time, is neither the ink nor the pen; it is the spirit which was in that which was written."

Several of the young men joined in the dispute, and every one, as is always the case on such occasions, tried to bring the rest to his opinion of immortality and life beyond the grave.

At last Bendixen, gazing thoughtfully to the distance where the sea and the horizon met, observed, "It is wonderful how every one's ideas of immortality and the future life are formed according to their own wishes, and how all endeavour to make the rest lay down the same rules to God—as if our future life was to be constituted according to a majority of votes! Immortality! what is it but the whole poetry of human life; the spring from which every poetical emotion proceeds. When poetry dies in me, my soul will die, even though my body should remain alive. There is no immortality, except for him who believes in it, and he who believes in it does not need it, his life has been beautiful enough; he has had the reward of his belief. I believe in eternal poetry and in eternal life!"

"You are no Jew, Bendixen!" said Gröndal.

"That may very well be," replied he; "but neither am I a Christian."

"Bendixen! have you lately seen that little Clara who came out last week?" asked some one from the hind seat.

"No, I have not," replied he, in a tone of vexation.

"But she always cast kind looks at you. You know where she lives, only you won't tell."

"Oh, I think nothing of kind looks," said Bendixen; "eyes often promise more than they mean."

"What nonsense is that! Do you want to make yourself out for a pattern of virtue?"

"I do not pretend to be a pattern of virtue," returned he, "but I appeal to yourself; such glances may fill the soul with the hope of unknown, indescribable happiness; but is the promised hope ever fulfilled? Have you found it so?"

"One goes farther and still continues to seek; life is an unceasing conflict and endeavour," replied some one, gaily.

"I do not enjoy the heart-ache which the coquettish glance of beautiful eyes too often causes. I would much rather be free from the fickle delusion, from the ever-unsatisfied longing."

"Heart-ache! Bendixen is sentimental!" exclaimed they, and laughed.

Jacob was silent, and the conversation took another turn. Shortly after the carriage drove into Klampenborg.

The house was full of noisy guests, who demanded attention; shouted and laughed; called for every possible thing, and when it came forgot that they had called for it. After considerable thought and consultation, our party of students at length decided upon what each would have, and ordered it, and then, while it was preparing, divided themselves into parties and wandered out.

König and Jacob came by chance together to the eating-room window, where Jacob noticed a quantity of forget-me-not, standing in a jug.

"May I take one of these flowers?" asked he, from the young servant-maid, who stood within the room.

"Yes, be so good," replied the handsome young woman, in the kindest manner.

"What is it?" asked König, and came nearer. Oh, forget-me-not! Young lady, will you give me one to keep in remembrance of you?"

"Yes, gladly," said she smiling, and gave him two stems of the flower.

With the rapidity of lightening Jacob had made an observation which awoke a feeling of humiliation, pain, and mortification, in his heart.

"When I asked for these flowers," said he to himself, "it was not for the sake of the flowers, the pretty girl gave their value, and I asked them for her sake, and yet I said, 'May I take them?' Whilst he, the lucky fellow, born of Christian folk, and penetrated, without knowing it, by the spirit of romance, immediately finds the right word, and says, 'Will you give me them?' Ah, these Christians are fortunate fellows!"

They both walked away. König placed the flowers in his button-hole, and in half an hour's time forgot all about them.

Jacob laid them in his memorandum-book. They all wandered about, amusing themselves with any idle fancy that presented itself; but still there was an uneasy dissatisfaction in Jacob's soul; he was almost ready to look upon the others as if made of a better material than himself.

At length their refreshments were ready.

A large table was spread for them in the garden, in a lonely spot, whence was a view over the blue sea and the wood. The sun had sunk low in the heavens, and a cool refreshing breeze softly fanned the thick foliage of the branches, while in the distance glided the little fishing-boats with their red sails. The table was covered with a white cloth, the various dishes smoked, the wine sparkled in the glasses, and every countenance beamed with youthful life's enjoyment. Jacob glanced over the whole scene; the feeling of the beauty and delightfulness of the moment filled his heart to overflowing; the affluent wholesome life of youth glowed in his veins, whilst that silent nameless yearning clung yet closer to his soul. He seized his glass, and exclaimed—

"The first glass I offer to the gods of the lower world; to pain and sorrow, and to death, which brings us so many tears. Their shadowy forms lurk around us mortals when the bright spirits of day are with us, well knowing that there comes a night and a darkness when it is their turn to work. But I defy you, ye gloomy powers, for the light in my soul shall not be quenched! Still, if I can win your friendship by a glass of wine, I will do it,—there drink it up!"

And with these words he emptied his glass upon the ground; and the whole company followed his example, with shouts of exultation.

Fangel now filled his glass, and said—

"I am no Bendixen; I cannot begin my speech upon stilts, and end it in my stockings; therefore I content myself by saying that I offer my second glass to—myself! Whilst the gods of the lower world seize upon their share of the earth, I drink my glass like a man, and drink it to the last drop—Skaal!"

"I drink with you! I drink with you!" exclaimed all; and the glasses were drained to the dregs.

"Something was said, just now," remarked Gröndal to his neighbour, "about heart-ache caused by the eyes of a woman. Now that has come under my praxis. When I was quite a youngster, there were a pair of eyes which, whenever they glanced upon me, set my heart into the strangest agitation of unhappy woe, just according to Bendixen's diagnosis. I did not understand anything about it until about a year afterwards, when she drowned herself. It is exactly eight years this evening since. The eyes were beautiful, and I empty a glass to each of them."

He emptied two glasses in haste.

"Ah, Gröndal," whispered König, " that's the reason why you run out to see any drowned woman that is mentioned in the newspaper. I used to fancy it was for the sake of the body but I now understand it."

After a pause, Jacob said,—

"Sometimes one hears something said for the first time, and yet there comes a consciousness over one as if one had heard the same thing before in some extraordinary dim antiquity. I remember perfectly that an occurrence such as Gröndal has just related, stands in uncertain outline before my mind's eye, as if my soul had had a presentiment that some time or other it would hear of it. It was one evening in the Östergade (East-street), I was walking along wrapped in my own thoughts, when a young lady passed me. I saw through her veil that very glance which has just been mentioned. I trembled inwardly; it was as if the beams of those eyes having warmed me, I had suddenly again come into the cold. An officer quickly followed the lady,—spoke to her; and when they reached the King's New-market, she took his arm. I turned round with an inexpressibly bitter feeling in my heart. It seemed to me as if the officer would seduce to ruin an innocent girl whom I loved. I laughed at myself for my own folly; but I could not get rid of this feeling. I have hated all officers since that evening!"

"*All* officers? that is severe!" said one of the company. " Who knows that all were equally guilty with this one?"

"Yes, all officers," continued Jacob, with warmth,—"that is to say, all young officers. They are a set of men who pass the greater part of their time in the pursuit of women,—they are sensual,—nothing else; and, at length, they cannot regard women with a pure sentiment. They are altogether unlike the old knights, whose place they have taken!"

Martin bent towards Jacob, and whispered to him,—

" And who form a corps into which no Jew is admissible;— is it not so?"

Jacob crimsoned, and was silent.

" Let us have a song?" cried one.

"Let the song go round," cried another.

One after another struck up a well-known song, and the rest all joined in chorus.

This was in the good old times,—in the childhood of clubs, æsthetic and political. In those days there were neither liberals nor illiberals, constitutionalists nor radicals. The people had not then eaten of the journalist-tree of knowledge, nor discovered that they were unclothed. It was in the good old time, when the genial dithyrambics of Rahbek and Colleger lived in the heart of the people, and were sung by their lips. Then there was no need of singing societies; song came with the wine just as easy and naturally as political talk comes now.

Now a different class of song, interrupted with joke and laughter, sounds across the silent sea.

"It is now Jacob's turn," said they.

He considered with himself for a few seconds, and then, quickly raising his head, he struck up one of Wilhelm Müller's German Greek songs. These songs are forgotten by the present generation, just as they have forgotten the wild struggles for freedom which called them forth. Perhaps a few of those now living may remember the deep pain and the glowing inspiration of Hellenic antiquity and Hellenic freedom which breathes in many of these songs. Jacob sang one of them with his beautiful voice,—and, as he ceased, the whole company sat silent and grave.

"See," said he, after a pause, "the sun is now setting, and those same crimson beams which add beauty to our gaiety, may, perhaps, be shining on Greek corpses, or down into the prisons of the German students who sought to be free; let us remember them before we forget ourselves in drink."

"That was against the rule," cried one; "you should have sung a song in the chorus of which we could all have joined."

"That was no fault of mine," replied Jacob; "why did you not join? Strange enough is it," continued he, "that I, the son of an enslaved people, must remind you of freedom! Although looking at it correctly, it is as it should be,—for the Jews stand in much closer connection with freedom than you do!"

"Capital! capital!" exclaimed his hearers. "Now for a good proof of that, Bendixen."

"Well, you see, the Jews are the pipe-head of freedom. When the others inhale the animating fumes, the essence sinks down to them. When the people of Germany and Denmark will have liberty, the burden presses more heavily on the Jews. As soon as there is freedom in the air, the Jews feel it,—just as the gouty patient feels every change in the atmosphere. I therefore, *ex-officio*, must talk to you of freedom. The little circumstance of my loving freedom, instead of fearing it, makes no difference in the matter."

"I drink to the proof," said Gröndal, filling his glass; "and for the Greeks and Missalonghi I am ready to drink with you altogether,—in proof whereof I throw down my glove, figuratively of course."

"Yes,—hurrah for Hellas, and for Hellenic liberty!" exclaimed Fangel. "Properly I only know the country by the caning I got for Homer when at school, and that perhaps is precisely the reason why I cherish an otherwise inexplicable tenderness for that country. Now, then, hurrah for Father Homer! πόντος οἰνόεις! Is he not right! Does not the sea at this moment look like splendid Bordeaux wine? Who would not swim in this glorious St. Julien?"

"I protest against the use of wine for any outward purposes," said Gröndal; "but as we are drinking to the freedom of Greece, let us also empty a glass to the freedom of Denmark! which, in truth, lies nearer to us."

"Oh, yes!" said Jacob, whose blood was now excited, and who was no longer under his own control; "I empty my glass to this toast. In truth I think most of Denmark."

"The deuce you do!" exclaimed Gröndal; "one might think that it was your fatherland as well as ours. Were you not born and bred in Funen? Can you deny that?"

"No," replied Jacob; but then Denmark cannot be my fatherland to so full an extent as it is yours, because I am not treated as a son to so full an extent as you are. Do you actually believe that any Jew who arrives at the consciousness of his own worth as a human being, does not keenly feel the difference with which the state treats him and his Christian fellow-citizens? People reproach the Jew because he has not a fatherland; why do they not give him one?"

"But the difference of treatment is a mere nothing," remarked one of the company. "There are only a few things in which the Jewish disabilities present themselves."

"True freedom acknowledges no disabilities where the man has moral and intellectual worth!" exclaimed Jacob, "the very smallest disability converts freedom into oppression."

"I know next to nothing in which a Jew has the disadvantage of a Christian," exclaimed König. "Did you, Jacob, come off any the worse in your examinations, because you were a Jew?"

"Next to nothing, do you say!" replied Jacob. "I will not speak of opinion, although it, perhaps, is the most important of all, and operates more than all the laws and canons put together. But tell me, can a Jew hold any office under government?—Can he become even a watchman?—Can he be an officer in the army? and even when he serves in the burgher-guard, and it comes to his turn to be captain, what must he do? He must resign! I said that I would say nothing about opinion, but still I will mention a characteristic fact or two. There are many guilds, the ironmongers' guild for instance, which exclude the Jews, and prevent any Jew-boy from being taken as apprentice. A Jew cannot bear the petty annoyances of the rifle brigade; and when a dramatic author does not know what else to write about, he brings a Jew into his piece and gets a clown to play the part. The national character is never hit, nor is the dialect even correct; but the rabble laughs, and the rabble—it is such an ass, the greater part of the public!"

"You are too severe, Bendixen," cried Fangel; "I have amused myself gloriously at the theatre over a Jew; but, God knows, I do not despise the Jews."

"That also is severe enough," remarked Jacob coldly; "that any one should have to say, 'I do not despise the Jews.'"

"What would you have, Bendixen?" shouted Fangel.

"Would you have me cry hurrah for the Jews?—Hurrah for the Jews!"

"Hurrah for the Jews!" shouted the whole company.

"I would," said Jacob, without paying any attention to the toast; "I would have you to tell me why I, who sit here among you, am not as good, am not as fully entitled to every liberty, to every advantage, to every office, as any of you. I would" added he, in a tone in which bitterness and some degree of temper were blended, "I would have you to tell me why I might not, just as well as any of you, be even a watchman?"

"You shall be a watchman! Bendixen shall be a watchman!" exclaimed they all in full clamour; "Hurrah for Bendixen the watchman!"

Jacob was tired of his own earnestness, and he felt a certain degree of shame in having given way to his feelings so much. He was silent.

Gröndal, in the meantime, had gone into the kitchen to brew a bowl of punch, "according to his own receipe," and now, accompanied by the servant, returned, bearing the steaming bowl in triumph. Triumphantly was he received by his companions, who soon, Jacob as well as the rest, forgot the important questions of liberty and Jewish rights over the glowing liquor.

CHAPTER XVIII.

THE INVITATION TO THE BALL.

One winter afteroon Jacob sat with his friend König. They were studying botany together, and König had collected with much care an excellent herbarium, which he thankfully saw increased and enjoyed by his college associates. The two were in the middle of an animated dispute about a rare plant of which König had not a specimen, when a messenger came in from a woman in the neighbourhood to beg that the doctor would immediately go over to her house, as her husband had fallen down in the street and broken his leg.

"The blessed streets of Copenhagen!" said König, when the messenger had gone; and throwing off his house-coat, he had put on another, which rendered his appearance more suitable for out of doors. "These blessed streets, they furnish, in the winter season, a young medical student with a tolerable practice! Do you stop here, Bendixen, till I come back! the whole thing won't take me long."

König lived with his family; and the door which opened between his room and the family sitting-room now stood ajar, and hence it was that Jacob very soon after his friend was gone, became the involuntary auditor of the following dialogue:—

Mother. "Don't spend all thy time in looking out of the window at the sledges. Thou wilt never get thy dress ready.

Thou wilt drive it all to the last minute, and then thou wilt have to sew at night, and that, I promise thee, I will not allow."

Louise. "I can't help it, dear mother. When I hear the sledge-bells ringing, I have no power over my eyes. Dost thou know what I think? I sit and fancy to myself, 'Now, suppose that was somebody come in a handsome sledge to fetch me!' I know, very well, that there is nobody coming, but yet I can't help looking out to see if by any chance the adventure should really happen."

Mother. "What a simpleton thou art! Thou hadst a deal better be thinking that without a dress thou canst not be at the ball."

"Oh, yes, the ball!" exclaimed Louise—and, springing up, she danced round the room.

Mother. "Now, do be sensible, Louise! How silly it is for a girl of thy age to behave in this way."

Henriette (the elder sister). "But what gentlemen are, after all, to be invited? Only think, there are already eighteen ladies invited, and when there are too many ladies, the gentlemen are so full of themselves."

Louise. "We two, at all events, shall have partners enough, because we are the daughters of the house."

Mother. "That is not very hospitable towards our guests, my child. But there will be gentlemen enough. There are your two brothers, and the two lieutenants, and Gröndal and Bendixen, and—"

Louise (interrupting her). "But, will you ask the Jew?"

Mother. "I think so, especially as you complain of the want of gentlemen; but you can leave him out, if you like."

Jacob heard no more. The young girl's remark had gone like a dagger through him. He had felt a sort of attachment to her; her cheerful, genial demeanour had interested him, she had often conversed with him in the most friendly, nay, even cordial manner, and now she had spoken so disparagingly of him when he was mentioned with others—and that because he was a Jew. He was not prepared to receive calmly a blow from this quarter. He rose involuntarily, and left the room.

After a while König returned; and as he supposed that Bendixen had gone into the other room to sit with his family, he, too, went in to inquire after him.

"Where is Bendixen?" asked he, when he perceived that he was not in the room.

"Bendixen? He has not been here!"

"Has he not been here?" said König, half incredulously; "I desired him to wait for me when I went out."

"Oh, Heavens! then he must have heard what I said!" exclaimed Louise; "I remember, now, thinking that I heard the door shut, and then I fancied I was mistaken."

"What hast thou said, then?" asked the brother; "and how could you be so thoughtless as to talk of people when the door of my room stood ajar, and you did not know who might be there?"

"We heard thee go out; and never imagined that any one was left in the room."

"But, what have you been saying that you are so afraid of his having heard?"

"Oh," said Louise, "mother was talking about who was to be invited to the ball, and I said, 'But will you ask the Jew?' And then mother answered, 'You can leave him out if you like.'"

"Nay, that would be quite enough for Bendixen! But what in the world could induce a girl, who makes a pretence to refinement and good breeding, to forget herself to that degree, even in thought!" exclaimed König very much annoyed. "Bendixen is my friend, and that ought to have been sufficient for my sister not to have disparaged him. But thou must make an apology to him, or if thou wilt not, then I will do it in thy presence."

"Ludvig!" said Louisie, turning towards him, with a certain degree of maidenly dignity; "thou wilt well consider it, before thou humiliatest thy sister. For the rest, it may, perhaps, serve as a little excuse for me, when I tell thee the true cause of my remark. It was a sort of coquetry, or what you will. Henriette is always teazing me about him, and I now pretended a greater indifference about him than I really feel, and I did not know any better way of showing it than this. I hope that this confession is punishment enough for my involuntary fault, and that thou thyself wilt put this matter straight without humiliating me."

"Yes, it is all very well for thee to get out of the mess by throwing everything upon me!" retorted König. "But this I do require, as a mere act of justice, that he is invited to the ball."

With these words he went out to seek for his friend.

In the meantime, the irritated feelings of Jacob had had time to cool. He now reasoned with himself somewhat in this way: "What right had I to hear these words? They were not intended for me; if they had known that I was near they would never have said them. But, why does this girl think only of me as the *Jew* Bendixen? Bah, if all comes to all, am I not the Jew Bendixen? Good Heavens! I wish that foolish girl had only shut the door before she began to talk!"

Whilst these thoughts were uneasily passing through his mind, a knock was heard at his door, and König entered. The one was almost too much embarrassed to observe the other's embarrassment in this meeting. Each gave the other his hand mechanically; Jacob assumed the external self-possession which he felt was necessary, and said, in a perfectly natural voice,—

"Pardon me, that I ran away before your return; but I recollected a letter which wanted posting."

Poor König was very near jumping for joy; he believed that the words were unheard; and involuntarily he exclaimed, "Thank God!" and then suddenly stopped, fearing that this exclamation might betray him in some way.

But there was no need for apprehension: Jacob seemed to find nothing remarkable in the exclamation. On the contrary, he said, "Thank God!" to himself.

The two friends sat down with minds greatly relieved, and with very cordial feelings towards each other. Never before had Jacob with more politeness and genuine good-will filled a pipe for König, and never had König so busied himself to save his friend the trouble. The conversation passed with great animation from one subject to another, perhaps because the one was afraid of the other having time to reflect on what had fallen from them in the first instance, and for the same cause they parted only when it was quite late.

Nevertheless, before parting König, as if it were a mere matter of course, presented the invitation to the ball; and Jacob on his side, as if that also were a matter of course, accepted it with many thanks.

"You do dance, then?" asked König.

"Yes, I learned to dance at school," returned Jacob; "but still I have never yet been to a regular ball."

"Oh," said König, "what is a ball otherwise than just to dance."

And with these words they said "good night," and parted; each feeling happy because no impediment now stood between their friendship.

CHAPTER XIX.

THE BALL.

WHEN any one, with a shiver of cold and anxiety, notices a ball-room before the dance begins, he sees the groups of ladies in their various coloured dresses; he see the walls, the mirrors, the chandelier; he has even eyes for the drawn-down roller-blinds, and perhaps also for the ornaments of the ceiling. He meets with his friends and acquaintances, but he hardly recognises them; they speak another language than common, and their thoughts are turned to other things. He feels himself solitary, and is not at all at his ease, because he fancies that the askance-looking and whispering young ladies are privately making themselves merry at his expense; yet he dare not approach them, although that is the very thing that they are wishing for. Modern fashion, with all its etiquette and formality, extends its cold sceptre over the room; people do not move themselves like human beings with warm, crimson blood in their hearts, but like statues.

It is not till the first touch of the violins is heard that a beam of light is diffused over all countenances. People then begin to approach one another; they place themselves in line, and here and there a bright smile bursts forth like a warm sunbeam.

Suddenly the full gush of music is heard, and close-embracing couples whirl with beaming countenances round the room.

Where is now the apartment, with its ornamented ceiling, with its chandelier, and its roller-blinds? It is at once become a temple, an Ionic temple in which Aphrodite is enthroned, and where her winged son amuses himself by shooting off his arrows. He need not strike very hard in order to pierce the uncovered bosom, but into the heart which fancies itself secure behind its white silk waistcoat and black coat, he may send his most cruel arrow with all his might.

In the midst of modern Christian cities rear themselves tall, and glittering with lights, these Ionic temples, wherein rules the Olympian deities; and where men worship beauty and forget their catechisms; hence is it that Christian priests have always been zealous against dancing.

Yet all men are not of the faithful in these temples. There are some who walk about in fine black coats, stiff satin cravats, and eye-glasses stuck in one eye. They pronounce one lady's foot as too large, the figure of another inelegant; find fault with the lemonade of the hostess, and discover that several of the violins are a note too high; they dance only very little, but eat all the more. Others there are who are very pitiable to look at; they are afraid of falling in love; because, what do you meet with at a ball, say they; a pretty face, a pretty figure, a pair of pretty feet,—but household virtues, the beautiful household and womanly virtues, which can alone make a husband happy, they are not to be found here. These men are either theological candidates, or army-surgeons, and neither of these are needed on Mount Ida.

But when a man with a fresh and healthy heart enters a ball-room for the first time, the divinities smile upon him as they smiled in the days of their first prosperity, when mankind offered sacrifice upon the Cyprian hill; they fling an oblivion of all earthly care over his mind, and he listens to the melody of half-forgotten, never before heard myths.

Jacob listened to them for a moment, while the music was

joyously sounding; lovely women floating past him, and he himself holding a beautiful girl in his arms. His soul stood still, as if to recollect and take hold upon itself. Then suddenly recognised he again the scene. Here were the blue eyes and bright locks of his mother's songs; the beautiful ideal world of his childhood was realised; one of the shapes which had peopled it was it was in his embrace. The locks, it is true, were no longer of a golden yellow, they were much darker, but that had come with years.

It was Fangel's sister Thora. She was only just returned from Holstein, and Jacob saw her for the first time this evening, as Wilhelm introduced him to her. She was then standing in a group of ladies, and not a word was said; a low bow, and an almost imperceptible courtesy was the whole presentation. As her glance hastily surveyed Jacob, it seemed to him as if there was a double depth in her eye; she did not look at him, and yet she saw him. There was an expression in that glance which for a moment uneasily agitated his imagination. Now, on the contrary, when she with the joyousness of a child, quickly glanced on those around her, then as quickly at him, as if she expected to hear him speak, there was no trace of that unintelligible, glassy gaze in her eye, and he wondered how he ever could have seen such an expression in it. She was so beautiful, such a grace seemed to involop her,—there was so much elegance and harmony diffused over her whole being, that he almost feared to touch her; and, lost in rapturous emotion, knew not how to find words in which to speak.

At length he said, "And now I see you, the Lady Thora, of whom so much has been said."

"Yes," replied she gaily, "here you behold the celebrated Church of Frondhjem," &c., &c., &c.

"And if anyone asks whether fame has spoken truly, I answer boldly, yes!" replied Jacob.

"He is not so stupid then, after all, when he once makes a beginning," thought Thora.

"Thora!" continued he, thoughtfully. "It is a beautiful name. From my earliest youth I was taught to love this name."

"My German cousin," said she, "also found something significant in the name; it is the feminine of Thor, our Scandinavian god, the son of Odin."

"Yes, in Danish," said Jacob; "for it is that Sif, with the golden hair and gentle glance, who was the wife of the god."

Thora seemed less to hear the words than the tone in which they were spoken. She was silent; and seemed to measure him with a mysterious glance, as if she had seen him incorrectly. Jacob, however, was almost provoked with himself for what he had said; for his feelings were much more intense,—much more beautiful.

When another gentleman led Thora to her place in the next dance, and began a conversation with her, she turned her head involuntarily, as if she was seeking for something; her eyes met Bendixen's at the far end of the room; she blushed, and cast them down.

"May I have the pleasure of introducing my two friends to each other," said König, as he, in company with a young officer, came up to Jacob. "Lieutenant Engborg,—Candidate Bendixen!"

"I believe that Mr. Bendixen and I are old acquaintances from Funen," said the lieutenant; "you, perhaps do not remember me."

But Jacob had already recognised him; it was the countenance of his first enemy. It was the boy with whom he had fought, in mortal hatred, on the shore. And now to meet here, on this evening! It produced an effect upon him such as when, on a summer's day, a dark cloud passes before the sun, and reminds one of night.

And the lieutenant was handsome, and had an attractive, elegant exterior.

From this moment, Jacob was conscious of an involuntary dread of some coming evil. A fierce, yet undefined desire of combat seemed to urge him against some undefined foe. Then, again, his soul seemed buoyed up above these dark apprehensions by a fervent, rapturous bliss, when he once more stood by the side of Thora.

They stood by the window, somewhat apart from the dancers. He said,—

"What wonderful happiness a human being is capable of enjoying! It is as if in this very room I seized upon happiness herself with my hands, and as if I almost feared her being too near me. I almost could fancy that the human organization is too weak to bear too close a proximity with happiness. One feels as if it were the best to enjoy it, like the mariner, when the land breeze bears out to him at sea the odour from the spice isles."

"Are you fond of dancing?" asked Thora.

"Dancing? No, one does not dance at a ball."

"What? don't you dance?" exclaimed she; "have you not danced with me this very moment?"

"Yes, I danced with *you!*" said he.

Thora felt that this was no common ball-room compliment: the voice was too heartfelt and emphatic for that.

"It is related in old legends," continued he, after a pause, "that when any one will seek at midnight for some buried treasure in the earth, he must be silent; but when he seeks the treasure of life, then he must speak,—if one had but the magical word!"

"Oh, as far as I can observe, you will not fail of it," said she, as gaily as possible.

"Yes," said he, turning almost pale as he spoke, "if I had the word which breaks down the barriers of prejudice,—tho magical word which veils much in oblivion,—and which I almost seem to catch in music."

"The dance waits for us," said Thora.

CHAPTER XX.

WHEN Jacob awoke the morning after the ball, his first consciousness was an undefined mortification; as if, some way or other, he had the night before made himself ridiculous. With anxious uneasiness, he brought all in review before his mind—every word that he had said, every situation in which he had been placed; and although each separately passed through the examination without his being able to take exception against it, yet still did the whole collectively produce that painful consciousness.

He said to himself, "It was all so novel to me. I was out of my senses! What can that girl think of me! O, perhaps she will not recognise me when we meet again—perhaps I should not even know her—no, perhaps not; she was in a ball-dress then."

Nevertheless, he fancied he could not avoid going to call, about something very important which he had to say to Wilhelm Fangel. Accordingly, somewhat later in the day, he presented himself at his father's house. When Thora saw him, an expression of glad recognition passed over her countenance, and in the same moment all his uneasiness vanished, and an infinite happiness filled his whole being. Her mother was in very good humour, because her daughters had danced so much. She said to Jacob, "You must excuse all the bustle we are in to-day;

you know how it is in a family when the daughters come home from a ball in the morning. But do us the pleasure of coming here to-morrow evening."

Jacob returned home as gay and light as a bird. The next evening he made his visit; and went again and again as often as he could. All his reflections during this time were nothing else but the declaration of that feeble warfare which reason and honourable principle wage against love. Reason has a presentiment that love will be the death of it; it sets itself, therefore, in opposition to it; but all its efforts only tend to make the victory easier for the crafty, smiling Eros.

Without giving the detail of the whole struggle, it is enough that this one sentiment only sunk deeper and deeper in his soul. Every word of hers, every word that concerned her became important; the slightest change in her countenance awoke in him the most torturing anxiety; trifles, which had hitherto been of the utmost insignificance to him, awoke the most painful reflections.

A time now began from which all his former life seemed to him dead; nothing for which he had hitherto cared and striven after appeared to have any value in his eyes; it seemed as if he had began a new life which had reference only to this young girl.

It is, perhaps, a more striking than beautiful image, to say that a lover resembles a drunkard. As this one, dejected and languid after the last night's carouse, invigorates himself by a fresh glass, so does the lover also seek alleviation for his disquiet and his anxieties by hastening again to the beloved. If this method of cure did not exist, there would be neither so many drunkards nor yet so many innamoratoes.

Other young men, also, besides himself visited in the family, and sometimes Jacob felt himself in that state of mind when he seemed to hate this girl with his whole heart. The feeling which governed him, and which irresistibly impelled him towards her, seemed to him a dark and evil power. He was as uneasy in the chain that bound him, as if some other person had laid the fetters upon him.

However painful his state of mind was, he nevertheless separated himself from his intimate friends, that he might in solitude give himself up to it. His thoughts resembled those plans which people lay out in sleepless winter nights, and with which they are almost always dissatisfied when it is day and they are once more engaged in the business of life.

His common place book was filled with entries, having reference to his own state of mind:—

"—— A travelling merchant has caught and sold the tiger of the desert. They have given it milk and fine bread instead of warm blood; they have patted its striped skin with their delicate hands, whilst sharp thorns have pierced its brethren. When the storms bring back to it the remembrance of the wood, it wishes for a moment to escape. It cannot: it has accustomed itself to milk and fine bread, and to the caressings of their delicate hands.

"—— The high-priest Phinehas, son of Eleazar, son of Aaron, the brother of Moses, took a sword and ran it through a Jew who loved a heathen woman; both he and she perished by the same weapon.

"—— It is written that the enemy shall inherit the possessions of those who ally themselves to the heathen. It is a dreadful curse! But yet, to see her belonging to another!

"—— How can it be, that upon a woman's lips should dwell a smile which drives one mad? Looking at it simply, the lips are only flesh and blood, and the smile, perhaps, only a mechanical movement. Yes, it is very easy to say so to myself here, at home: but the moment I see the smile, my reason is gone; I am dizzy; I am as if drunken with happiness.

"―― He walks about in a scarlet coat with epaulettes; wears a feather in his hat, and a sword by his side: and I—am a Jew!

"―― Gemoro says that a man must learn to ride, to fight, and to swim. I am possessed of all these qualifications. I am a knight disguised in a Jewish gaberdine. The misfortune is, however, that I cannot put off this garment. It burns my vitals, like the shirt of Dejanira sprinkled with the blood of Nessus.

"―― As a child, I nearly murdered him. It was an anticipated, a prophetic hatred; and now he would do me the injury for which I would strive to take his life.

"―― Was it a mere accident that she left the room by my side, and that she took my arm before I ventured to offer it to her? Did she know that he was with us also? . . I might have asked her. But if I had discovered that this uncertain hope was a cheat―― O this state is terrible! I could almost doubt whether there was a God, when he permits that a human being should suffer thus intensely.

"What if she is a coquette, and merely amuses herself with me! if I am tortured merely to gratify her vanity! Do not sport with my feelings, thou girl, who believest in Christ! The poison fang is not extracted.

"―― Would God that she had died in Holstein! Ah no; for then I had never seen her."

After Jacob had passed some time in this manner, he was one day surprised by a visit from Martin. Yet it was not the visit itself which was so surprising, for Martin had already been many times with him, although he had been driven away by Jacob's distracted or taciturn manner. It was rather the determination of Martin to stay, spite of everything, which surprised him. He took a pipe, seated himself, and puffed out long volumes of smoke, which were only interrupted by occasional short observations and replies.

At length Martin said: "I am come at an inconvenient time I see very plainly; but the intention of my visit must be my excuse. I have got an interesting disease under treatment, and I don't like quite to trust to my own skill. I would now, therefore, do you the honour of consulting with you."

"What sort of a disease is it?" asked Jacob.

"The thing is soon told," replied Martin. "I have a patient who suffers from general debility. I have prescribed the usual means in the usual doses—wine and good living among the rest,—and now he has swallowed a whole bottle of brandy at once, and so he has brought on a most violent brain fever."

"And so you ask my opinion," exclaimed Jacob, and burst into a loud peal of laughter. "And must I give you my learned counsel?"

"Yes, 'because thou art the man, O king!' as the prophet Nathan said to David," replied Martin, "you are the patient."

"I!" exclaimed Bendixen; "are you mad?"

"Yes, you! I prescribed you a teaspoonful of the Christians every other day, and you have gone and swallowed a whole bottleful!"

"How dare you," exclaimed Jacob, almost beside himself, "apply such a vile comparison to——" The word died upon his lips; he could not bring himself to pronounce the name of his beloved whilst an unpleasant idea was present to his mind. "What could induce you——"

"Be quiet, Bendixen," said Martin, in a calm voice. "I came prepared to find you violent. I told you that my patient was in a high fever. Folks in love are always violent. But remember it is a friend who speaks with you; that he is not talking for his own interest, but solely for yours. If you are so unreasonable as no longer to endure my sympathy, because it does not exactly chime in with your inclinations, just say the word, and I am gone."

Jacob had not the wish to utter such a word, and Martin continued:

"I made use of an ordinary simile; but it does no harm. On the contrary, perhaps there may be some advantage in presenting the raw material reality in opposition to ideal pictures and day-dreams. Be a sensible fellow, and don't any longer go dreaming about a fair face. All the world knows that you go almost every day to the Fangels, and that you make a fool of yourself with your love-lorn look!"

Jacob felt humiliated and tortured by a sense of shame; it was with difficulty he could bring out the words, "Has *she* said that I made myself ridiculous?"

But Martin had not the heart to pursue his advantage or to win his aim at the cost of truth; therefore he replied good-humouredly, "I have not said so; I have merely said what I imagine to be the case."

By these words Martin lost all the ground that he had gained. He had not considered that the lover recognises no other judge than the beloved, and that all the rest of the world is to him indifferent; nay, in fact, does not at all exist. Jacob again breathed, and now for the first time set himself really to combat with Martin.

"What have you to say against this girl?" demanded he.

"Against the girl!" replied his friend; "nothing at all. She is a very nice girl—for a Christian."

"But what if she now loves me, spite of my being a Jew?"

"That she does not," said Martin; "at all events she will not marry you."

"I beseech of you, Martin," said Jacob, with dignity, "not to injure the lady of whom we are speaking, by insinuating that she would love me without wishing to marry me."

"She cannot," returned Martin, "no more than a Brahmin maiden could marry a Pariah! Or, yes—she might, but he could not; for what sort of a marriage would that be in which the wife believed herself to belong to a better caste than her husband?"

"Love does away with all differences," remarked Jacob.

"Yes, if you lived in a wilderness where there were no kindred and friends and acquaintances of the Brahmin maiden, who would fancy that they defiled their honour by offering their hand to the Pariah. Recollect, my friend, that a man does not alone marry the girl, but all her connections; at all events, her family. And the girl herself—even supposing that she in your courting days forgets that you are a Jew, still, perhaps, as the wife, when the ardour of love has a little cooled, she may now and then remember it. Only think, suppose that when she was angry she should some day taunt you with being a Jew!"

Jacob trembled, and was silent for some moments; at length he said, "But a girl of education and refinement would never do so—no, she never would!"

"And then," continued Martin, "there is the law of the land. Who can marry you?—a Christian priest? And in what religion are your children to be educated?—in the Christian? As children, they will suck in antipathies against the Jews with their mother's milk, and learn to despise their father. Only think, if your own child, sitting upon your knee, and to whom you were teaching its school-lessons, should suddenly interrupt you with the question, "Father, were they not the Jews who crucified Christ? The hateful Jews! If I had one, how I would beat him!"

"Martin, what a horrible picture you draw!" exclaimed Jacob, as if speaking to himself.

"And just consider," continued Martin; "marriage is something higher than the mere connection of two people to bring children into the world. There is a religious element in marriage—its own peculiar spirit, in which the man and wife are bound together for a much higher union. But there is something inimical between Christendom and Judaism; like the flames of Atreus and Thyestes, they may burn side by side, but they cannot become one. I do not know whence this dark, indescribable enmity proceeds. Can it be the curse which was pronounced by Him who died at Golgotha? Is it His blood which is between us? I do not know. I do not know its origin; but I ask you, have you never in your life observed the curse which rests upon us, or have you now suddenly forgotten it?"

Jacob approached Martin, pale as death: "Blood between us! Martin, do you really, then, believe there is such a dark power in shed human blood?"

"What is amiss with you?" asked Martin; "you look as if the very hair on your head were about to rise! Don't frighten yourself; I did not mean anything in particular."

"But you, Martin—you yourself? Have you never thought about getting married?" asked Jacob, whose thoughts had evidently taken a turn.

"Bah!—I!" replied Martin; "when I get a good practice, I shall look out for a good connection in some Jewish family or another. I shall make a good income—lead an active life; and therewith I shall content myself."

"Yes; you, Martin—you are a lucky fellow," said Jacob.

He sat silent, gazing as if into vacancy; and then, as if in a prophetic ecstasy, exclaimed, "I know it—it is a misfortune! A mysterious curse has been uttered; but I defy it! Let the cup be filled with the deadliest poison, yet will I drink it!"

"Shall we go and have a game at billiards?" asked Martin.

This sudden change in the current of his thoughts acted so

violently upon Jacob, that he turned round, and stared at his friend.

"Yes, you may look at me," said Martin; "I only mean, that if you have made up your mind to be mad, you need only be so in one way. There is no need for you to shun the world —that only makes you more completely crazed with love. As far as I am concerned, I wash my hands of it."

"Well," continued he, as Jacob silently turned towards the window, and looked out; "have you determined?"

"Yes," said Jacob, and heaved a deep sigh; and as he went out with his friend, he clasped his hands together, as if to hold fast by a resolution which was ready to slip from him.

CHAPTER XXI.

FRAGMENTS OF THORA'S LETTERS TO HOLSTEIN.

... "Thou mayst imagine, dear Wilhelmine, that I received great attention at this ball. There was a Lieutenant Hvidhorn and a Lieutenant Engborg, who paid me such zealous attention, that they very soon ran in each other's way, and then looked like two chanticleers who will fight about a barleycorn. It is the most amusing thing I know, to see two gentlemen in this position, and to hear how they overwhelm one another with compliments.

"There was also at this ball a very remarkable young man. I do not exactly mean that he was so remarkable because he was very handsome or elegant—no; the remarkable thing was, that though he looked like any other well-bred, well-dressed young man, yet that I was told afterwards that he was a Jew. Thou canst imagine my surprise, when I recalled your old Jew —that nasal-toned, wretched, miserly being, with all the qualities of a thief, excepting that he will steal in a roundabout way and always give some trifle to boot for that which he steals And, after all, this young man is a Jew! It seems to me almost impossible. The very thought of him talking through his nose, seems to me like some great sin! No; the name Jew, as far as he is concerned, has no other signification than as it indicates a race, just as a surname is given to soldiers, to show from what country they come.

.. "This man, perhaps, may seem to me to have a much higher moral and intellectual stature than he really has, because I, unconsciously to myself, regard him from so low a point of view. Only think!—he is not only one of the distinguished students at the university, but he also sings, and his voice is so tender and delicious! I always think about your old Jew. Ah! only let him sit down to the piano, and sing a ballad!

. "Jew!—there is something dark—something of hatred and contempt about that word; yet, every time I contemplate it near, all that is repulsive vanishes like a shadow. There is, in reality, no imaginable ground for hating and despising a human being, because he holds a faith different to our own. And yet, every time this word presents itself afresh to my thoughts, it conveys afresh these strange ideas. It may be because there is something foreign, wonderful about this people, which is descended from the East, and which, though living among us, are so strangely foreign to ourselves—or, I don't know what it is. This is all I know—that I don't understand it. It may be quite wrong, also, to judge them all according to those specimens which I have seen in Holstein; it is, perhaps, as if any one should judge the Danish ladies by the old fishwomen on the shore. I prefer, rather, imagining this people as living proudly shut up in their dwellings, like Rebecca in Ivanhoe—concealing themselves under a miserable exterior when they venture forth, and only sending an occasional true representative out into the world, to receive its homage and glory, and then to return back, and receive his reward. It may be that this is all wrong; but every other idea is unpleasant to me.

.. "Saladin was, of a truth, a great king, and a brave, magnanimous warrior; the Saracens were as chivalrous as the Christian crusaders. I have read so in history, and in Sir Walter Scott. The Jews are, in reality, their countrymen, for they, too, are Orientals. And they also have had great warriors in the time of the Maccabees. And, in fact, even Christ and the apostles were Jews.

"There is something remarkably expressive in his physiognomy. He is the only one, of all the young men who come here, in whose countenance one seems to see the soul. When Lieutenant Engborg comes, the first thing that catches my eye is his uniform; in Kammerjunker Hvidhorn I notice, in the first place, his waistcoat and gloves. On the contrary, I never remember once to have noticed how he was dressed. I don't even know whether he has large or small feet—although he must have had small ones, or they would have struck me. His countenance is his whole person. Lately he was in a very bad humour, but it so happened that he suddenly smiled, and the effect was as if the sun had suddenly burst through the clouds; I turned to the window involuntarily, to look if it were not so. It is, however, very extraordinary to find such qualities in a Jew.

. . . "It is now very evident to me that when other people talk it is only to say words. When he speaks it is to utter thoughts. He is almost too intellectual. And then his way of thinking is so extraordinary—takes me so by surprise. He looks at almost every subject from the opposite point of view to which I have been accustomed, and yet we often come to the same result. I fancy that we think differently, but that we feel alike.

. . . "My sister laughed at me the other day, and said that Bendixen was in love with me. She did not mean it, of course, but still it made me very angry; I was ready to cry. I can assure thee that it has never occurred to me, that *he* could fall in love with me, although in my vanity I have believed it of all the rest. I have really never thought about it; it seems to me as if I fancied he was already engaged; as if he already had chosen for himself a beautiful girl of his own nation, the most excellent of its daughters, with whom he will sometime retire and be happy, hidden from all the world. For this reason my sister's words took me by surprise, and also, because I felt I don't know how to write it—I need not however send the letter after all—that I myself would have been very glad to be this daughter of his people. But if he loves me can he overlook this difference?

"He loves me! he loves me! Now it is morning, and I have sat the whole night before the candle, with my arms on my knees, thinking of nothing else than the words which he said—'Thora, I have always loved thee; my dead mother sang about thee!' And every time I repeated these words to myself, I almost laughed aloud for joy. What extraordinary words—'I have always loved thee; my dead mother has sang of thee!' There was a mysterious power in the sound and in the voice: never before had such a rapturous, bewildering sensation rushed through my ear to my heart; I was dizzy; I first awoke to consciousness when I felt myself clasped to his breast. How happy he looked! His lips moved, his cheeks were quite pale, but in his eyes there was a pride as if he had conquered the whole world—I became quite proud of myself."

"February 17th, 1830.

"Dear Wilhelmine,

"I will now write a connected letter. I have began several, but I will send none of them.

"I am betrothed! Yes, my child; I have not kept my promise about what we talked—that I would never marry. That is the way of the world! He is a student of the name of Bendixen; and he is handsome and amiable, that thou mayst believe. What a happy life we have had of late! One of our relatives, a distant relative of my mother's, died lately; therefore, for appearance' sake, we have been obliged to live very quietly, and to ourselves. But what happy charming days with him and my family! And then, thou hast no idea what honour and respect is shown to a girl by her family when she is betrothed; it is as if every day were one's birthday. Make haste, my dear girl, and be betrothed! This is the best advice thy friend can give thee. For the rest it is quite as well that this death has occurred just now, for my beloved has the queer fancy that he cannot endure to be congratulated. When any of the few people who come here have offered him their gratulations, he looked quite frightened, and we have heartily laughed at him. He laughs himself, and says that it comes from the Latin proverb, which says that the gods are envious, and therefore he is afraid of being wished too much happiness; and then he looks at me, as if he feared lest the envious gods should take me from him. But it is a whim, a mere fancy, about which I will not dispute with him. All men are fanciful, and since he also will have his fancies like the rest, it is best that he should have them as quietly as possible. But he is so kind, and so good! My father and mother like him, and my brother is an old friend of his, so that I am the happiest girl on the face of the earth. Thou canst fancy how anxious I was lest my father should have any objection to the match. Thou knowest my father very well: he is good and kind to us children, but he has his own opinions; and when there is some one with us, he sits sometimes quite still, and listens to what we are talking of, and then gets up suddenly, with a little smile, and goes into the counting-house. I was afraid he might have something against Bendixen; but that day when Bendixen went into my father's room—Oh, I shall never forget that day!—I stood in the parlour that was next to the counting-house, and was all in a tremble; it was just as if sentence was going to be passed upon me. Then the door suddenly opened, and I heard my father say, 'You are an excellent young man—that is enough. Nay, there she stands; take her in God's name;' and then, putting his arm round my neck, he kissed me, and said, 'Now I will merely go in and fetch thy mother; excuse my absence.' Oh, how dear he is, my good old father!

"Yes, my dear Wilhelmine, I am happy! Mayst thou soon be as happy, thou poor little thing, is the wish of

"Thy friend,

"THORA FANGEL."

CHAPTER XXII.

Rich wonderful spring-time of love! Thou hast a bliss which none can sympathise with, excepting those who are inspired by thee, and that is of itself a proof that in thee abides true happiness. Thou art as still and noiseless as the glance which is exchanged between the lovers; thy speech is a speech of freemasonry—the word which to the uninitiated conveys no intelligence, and appears disconnected, or from which he turns away angrily, has a fulness and an intoxicating odour for those whom it is intended. Thou art in reality the spring; the soul without wishes or desires, cradles itself in happiness, and untroubled by a single care, allows itself to be borne along by the glad waters which flow through it. There are those who rejoice because they have never come under thy influence; but secretly there is in them a consciousness, as it were, of a germ within their souls which has withered ere it came into blossom.

It is but short this time of Paradise. Sometimes it endures no longer than the eyes of the husband perceive that the form of his beloved is fair and pleasant to look on; then come the senses with their longings and hopes, desires and conflicts, and the bloom is rubbed from the wings of Psyche. Or the angel of life drives him forth, like our first father, to eat his bread in the sweat of his brow, and when Cupid must bear burdens he becomes pale and loses his wings. There may, it is true, come quiet evenings when he rests after the labour of the day, and disporting himself in the beams of the descending sun, raises himself once more upon his wings; but a melancholy smile plays around his lips, he thinks upon the morrow, and softly drops again to the earth. Or, be it in what form it may that the cherubim comes, he yet comes surely, and shuts up the gate of paradise. Yet, for all that, man has been there; his heart has thereby become enriched, and he preserves his treasure in memory.

It was a bitter winter evening. According to the Almanack, the season was advancing towards spring, and the winter, as if in anticipation of its approaching close, seemed to be making a violent effort to retain its dominion. The snow fell in large flakes, which were driven about by a keen east wind; the lamps threatened to go out, and here and there shutters, which had broke loose from their fastenings, clapped backwards and forwards before the feebly-lighted windows. Jacob was almost alone in the streets; buried in his own thoughts, he was unregardful of the weather, and strode hastily forwards towards the dwelling of his new friends, at whose house, for the first time since their period of mourning, an evening party was to be given.

He was just approaching the street where they lived, when two gentlemen passed him. As they came onward, with rapid strides and their heads bowed down, a fragment of their conversation reached his ear, in an interval of the storm. "It is a sin, though!" exclaimed the one, in a tone of surprise, "that lovely girl"—the remainder was lost in the distance which was quickly left between himself and the speakers.

A burning stab seemed to pass through Jacob. These words need not of necessity refer to him; but at this moment they came to him like the voice of a supernatural power, and as if accompanying his own thoughts. So long as he had had only one thought, one subject, the love of Thora, his path had been the ascent of a mountain where the view was concealed from him; but now, when the goal was neared, when he stood on the desired summit, with the prospect extending round him to entirely new objects; now, when he stood with Thora in his arms, he began to consider how it would be regarded by others.

Here now was the reply which he had shuddered at giving himself; here was it now fully expressed. People would call it a sin that this lovely girl should be betrothed to a Jew.

When he entered the brilliantly-lighted drawing-room where the family were assembled, the ladies, for the first time since their mourning, in their splendid attire, the house appeared to him almost strange, and he felt, as it were, a terror in being there. Thora, in her silk dress, looked remarkably elegant, and her reception of her lover, which was more constrained than usual, because she was afraid of her splendid new dress being crumpled, seemed to him to be the condescension of the brilliant lady to him.

The merchant, contrary to his usual custom, spent the evening with his family, and the behaviour of his wife and children towards him showed an increase of affection and regard, as if in acknowledgment of his kindness. He was an elderly little man, with an intelligent friendly countenance, and polite and refined manners. He had passed his earliest youth in a family where the remembrance of the chivalrous period of Caroline Matilda was still vividly retained; and he himself had lived through the excitement which the first French revolution extended over Europe. He was a knightly democrat, a citizen without fear and without blame. It was his pride that he was independent of every great man, and that he could set his hat as high as the king himself, as he used to say, and no less to exhibit a certain chivalric courtesy to the fair sex. Thus he would open the first dance in his own house, and it was really a pleasure to see the elderly man conducting his partner with the gaiety of a youth, and the politeness of a courtier. There was only one thing which caused regret to his family, and that was that he was so fond of spending his evenings at the club, where he talked politics with his friends of the year '90, and played at l'ombre; they regretted this, because it deprived them of his company. His wife could not conceive why he could not have his political talk and his game at l'ombre as well at home, neither why the wretched wine which he paid for out of the house tasted better than the good wine from his own cellar; "but that is the way with men-folk," said she.

Although Jacob cherished an almost filial respect for this man, yet he was so unaccustomed to his society, that he always felt a certain constraint in his presence; while the delight of the others, in which he could not participate, made him, at that moment, still more estranged from them.

Shortly after his arrival, a carriage drove to the door, and the company was increased by two young ladies, friends of Thora, or, as we should say, the younger was Thora's friend, while the elder was the friend of her sister.

From the very first moment when Thora received this young lady in the most affectionate manner, Jacob felt a repugnance towards her. She was very fair; her countenance round, and rosy-lipped; the nose short and somewhat turned-up; the upper lip curled, as if in derision; the eyes lively and defiant. In short, there was in this countenance such a want of respect for others, so much liveliness, archness, and sarcasm, that the whole produced that indescribable effect which would cause a Jew immediately to say, "She is a *nischainto*" (foe to the Jew), a feeling which is, perhaps, nothing more than the consciousness that to such a fair person, the dark physiognomy of the Jew is very repulsive, and at the same time suggestive of ridicule. Jacob was so strongly impressed by this feeling, that he dreaded the consequence of this young lady's intercourse with Thora.

When a girl is betrothed, her attention to her female friends is, in the first instance, greatly increased. She will, as it were, prove to them that so far from being wholly occupied by love, she does not in the least forget them. At the moment when they actually have lost their interest for her, in the most natural way possible she affects to have a much greater regard for them than she really has. Thora, therefore, and her young friend Sophie, had a vast deal to say to one another before they took their seats. Sophie surveyed Jacob with a searching glance, and then whispered: "Thy beloved is handsome though! What beautiful dark eyes he has!"

Thora blushed, glanced at him at the same time, and cast down her eyes.

He narrowly watched these glances; he saw Thora's blush, and imagined with torturing apprehension that this very probably had been called forth by some allusion, more or less delicate, to his being a Jew.

At length the ladies seated themselves; still, amid the almost general conversation which now took place, Thora and Sophie occupied themselves many times by whispering together. Jacob would gladly have given a year of his lifetime to have been able to join in with this discourse and prevent their secret communications; but all his thoughts perpetually revolved round the same point, and he was scarcely in a condition to reply to the questions which from time to time were addressed to him.

The family observed the change which had taken place in Bendixen this evening. He, who in the family circle was accustomed to be so cheerful, so cordial, so amiable, now sat gloomy and apart, his glance wandering restlessly around; and even if he were not altogether unpolite to the ladies of the party, yet there was in his whole demeanour a want of attention and cheerfulness which operated painfully upon the whole company.

Lieutenant Engborg came. He immediately fell into deep

discourse with the ladies. He might have brought with him some extraordinary tidings, so great was the interest with which people questioned and listened to him; by the same rule, his conversation must have been very witty, judging by the bursts of loud laughter which it repeatedly called forth. Jacob sat alone, as if he did not belong to the company; at various times, it is true, he made attempts to join in with the conversation, but every unsuccessful attempt made the next endeavour only the more difficult.

Thora saw that something was amiss, but could not comprehend what it could be. She said to herself, "He cannot possibly be angry because I do not show any preference towards him in the presence of all these people? What if he should be jealous? Yes, let me only see that; I'll soon make an end of it!" And then again she began a conversation with some one, apparently with great interest.

Many guests arrived one after another, but the number of guests only increased Jacob's strange uneasiness. It was evident that he endeavoured many times to gain the mastery over himself, but on every occasion something immediately afterwards occurred which, as it were, threw him back upon himself, and he again became absent and gloomy.

Late at night, when the guests were all gone, the merchant walked with long strides up and down his bed-room. At length he stopped before his wife, and said:

"Mother, didst thou notice Bendixen's behaviour this evening?"

"Yes, I fancied that he was rather cross," replied the lady, hanging up her dress.

"I have been vexing myself about him all the evening," continued her husband. "What strange behaviour for a young man to ladies. I am myself very fond of him; he is an excellent, good fellow, and I would certainly be the very last to upbraid him with being a Jew; but still I fancy that his behaviour this evening is the consequence of his being a Jew. A Jew is not chivalric; he has not been brought up in a chivalric manner. But when he is betrothed to a Christian girl, he ought to study these things a little."

"I fancy," replied the wife, "that he was only vexed because he could not be alone with us. But thou art right; it is all very well that we should like him, but he must yet see people, and he must not imagine that he is to rule the house."

"It is a delicate matter to meddle with," said the merchant, after some reflection. "I cannot undertake to be his educator, and one must only speak to Thora about it with the greatest circumspection."

The married couple talked still farther on this affair, and were agreed on one point; namely, that it was a subject that must be treated with the greatest possible delicacy, and that therefore it should not be hurried, but still that they would avail themselves of the first suitable opportunity which offered itself.

CHAPTER XXIII.

The opportunity did not soon present itself; and now so many days had passd that they hardly looked for it. Either by accident or by management on the part of Jacob, of which the family knew nothing, he had for some time only been to the house when no visitors were there; thus he was once more amiable and most agreeable in his manners, although his countenance bore traces of suffering.

On Saturday evening, Thora said to him—"Thou wilt come here to-morrow morning?" He became pale, and there was an expression in his face as if it was with difficulty that he suppressed some painful emotion.

"Art thou ill?" exclaimed Thora.

"Oh, no!" said he, and passed his hand over his forehead; "it is nothing of any consequence; I shall soon be better."

"Oh, no, thou art ill!" continued Thora, with tender anxiety; "thou hast looked so poorly for several days. Stop at home to-morrow morning; I will see if my mother will not go with me to pay thee a little visit."

Thora did not observe that the appearance of indisposition vanished from Jacob's countenance at these words; she regarded his silence as confirmatory of her fears, and would not rest until he had promised her that he would take a carriage home.

Jacob, however, on the following day was perfectly well, and when on the next Saturday she asked him to come on Sunday morning, he promised to do so.

Contrary to probability, he found her alone.

She was almost astonished by the expression of childlike joy with which he looked around him; now contemplating her, now the room, as if they had met after a long separation. There was something in his manner which affected her, without her being able to explain to herself what it was.

She sat by his side and stroked the hair from his forehead, and looked into those eyes which gazed at her with unspeakable tenderness. Although she felt that she loved him, it seemed to her, when she met this expression in his eyes, and heard the tender tones of his voice, that she did not love him sufficiently, was not sufficiently grateful for this deep love. On her side the conversation was only by a few words. He, on the contrary, said much, but in that suppressed tone in which the profoundest passion often speaks, as if it feared to give the reins to itself; but the words were so clear, so explicit, so forcible, and now and then developed themselves in imagery which betrayed the southern home of his soul.

She bent over him with a still deeper and warmer affection, and as she thus sat, Jacob suddenly fancied that he again perceived in her eyes that penetrating two-fold, deep glance, which he had once before observed, but now stronger than ever. And again the blood rushed back to his heart with resistless impulse.

He was silent, and she drew him still closer to her bosom.

The mother and sister came home, and interrupted this *tête-à-tête*.

Jacob rose to meet his future mother-in-law with the greatest politeness, assisted her and her daughter to take off their things, and asked, "Where have you been so early, dear ladies, and in all this grandeur?"

"We have just come from church, where we heard Mynster preach," replied the mother. "Thora, hast thou not a cup of coffee for me?—it is so horribly cold."

Soon after Jacob took his leave, but not before he had promised to come again early in the evening.

When he was gone, the mother said, as she set her coffee-cup somewhat hastily down upon the tray, "There is something dreadful in this man! I fancy that he cannot endure our going to church; what, would he have the whole family re-baptized? Such a face as he made when I said that we were just come from church! Good heavens! can he not be as tolerant as we are!"

Thora was wounded by these remarks, and began to weep.

"Nay, don't cry, my child," said the mother; " there is nothing so very bad after all! Thy father and I have talked together about him, and we are agreed that thou canst alter him in many ways for the better. A girl, when she is betrothed, has great power over her lover. If thou managest well thou canst accustom him to be a little more chivalric, as thy father says, and to get rid of his ill-humours. He is very fond of thee, heaven knows, and thou canst wind him round thy finger."

Thora's tears ceased to flow, because her thoughts were rivetted by her mother's words.

The evening came. They had visitors with them, and again that unaccountable cloud was diffused over Jacob's countenance. It was not that he was either unpolite or silent; there was, in fact, nothing to complain of in him; any one who had not seen him in his brighter moments, might not perhaps have found anything remarkable in his behaviour; he was only quiet; it was only a certain uneasiness, a something akin to anxiety, which showed itself in his features; and this it was which annoyed the family. They wished that the future son-in-law should be cheerful and make the house cheerful, and cause people to say, "That is really an amiable young fellow that Thora is betrothed to."

He excited among the guests now present similar feelings as

regarded himself, as on the preceding occasion; and yet something still must be mentioned. When Thora met him on his arrival in the passage, she patted him on the cheek, and said, "Now let me see that thou art very cheerful this evening."

What was the origin of this injunction? was the instantaneous suggestion of his mind. Had there been remarks made about him in the family?—perhaps a quarrel and reproaches.

When Jacob, in the course of the evening, conversed with the lady of the house, he thought he perceived an acerbity and an unfriendliness in her tone which he had never observed before; and when he turned to the merchant, the latter replied to him with a politeness which was almost too polite. Jacob turned aside; his lips quivered, and tears filled his eyes. From this moment he became more silent and introverted, so that again the attention of the visitors was turned upon him.

Thora herself felt that the behaviour of her betrothed was singular; and when he was gone she seriously began to think by what means she could produce a change in him.

CHAPTER XXIV.

THE following morning Jacob sat and prepared his coffee, with that profound attention which people often seem to bestow upon mechanical occupations, whilst, in fact, they are thinking nothing about them.

"It is a good thing, however," said he to himself, as he turned the tap of the urn, "that Martin is away. I am almost frightened lest he should soon come back; although he is, after all, the only one with whom I can speak freely."

Jacob again sank in deep thought, which was only interrupted by some one knocking at the door, and immediately after the door slowly opened, as if the person about to enter had not expected to gain admittance.

It was Martin.

"Martin!" exclaimed Jacob surprised, and rose to meet him, "welcome, good friend! It is wonderful though, for I was just then sitting and thinking of you."

Hush!" said Martin, and continued to stand at the door, with a solemn countenance, "hush! disturb not my emotions, I approach a betrothed man! I enter—it is most extraordinary! You are at home, lucky fellow! you despise neither food, lodgings, nor cleanliness, and yet you exist on love!—I congratulate you!"

"Thanks, thanks, Martin! But come away from that door, come and sit down."

"So be it!" said Martin, and entered. "But, seriously speaking, how are you, my good fellow? Though it is not much use inquiring—of course, you are in a fever—in a fever of rapture——"

Jacob constrained the muscles of his face, and the expression of his eye, so that happiness should beam from his whole countenance, and that he might emphatically reply to the inquiry. With the same forced gaiety did he compel Martin to sit down on the sofa, gave him a pipe, and said—

"Let me give you a cup of coffee. Something you must have for your congratulations, especially as you offer them so beautifully!"

Martin cast a hasty glance at Jacob, while he poured out the coffee, lighted quietly and in the most scientific manner his pipe, and seated himself most comfortably on the sofa. When he had tasted the aromatic liquid, and convinced himself that it was excellent, he said—

"I will drink your coffee, Bendixen, but you may very well imagine that it is not exactly the beverage which should be drank on an occasion of this kind. I expected to have seen an array of seven and twenty champagne bottles, to which the appropriate seven and twenty shots should have been fired. Or, perhaps, you have already had the firing?"

"No," replied Jacob, and smiled.

"Good heavens!" continued Martin, "What sort of fellow are you! When a man luxuriates in the seventh heaven of love —when he is so brimful of happiness that he dances, floats over the earth,—how can such an one, I say, sit in his room and quite prosaically pour out his coffee from a tin coffee-pot? Why, at all events, does he not let the water run over, whilst he is lost in those beautiful eyes, which are for ever beaming before him? Why does he not forget his bread?—why, in his abstraction of mind, does he not eat his bread without butter, whilst in thought, he is grasping the hand of first one and then another in the family of his beloved, petted and caressed by aunts and cousins, and passed about among the friends and acquaintances of the family, proud and admired as the very best of all good fellows? Love!—Is this thy so much exalted power that .   but Bendixen! You don't really look enraptured; your eyes no longer are bright; your smile has vanished, like the bubbling fountain in the desert!"

During the foregoing brilliant description, Jacob had actually forgotten to assume a correspondent countenance, and sat listening to it with a sad and melancholy air.

"You yourself understand it," said Martin; another time will do just as well for feigning; for are you not aware that I know too well not to see that you are not gay, in the way which you wish to make me believe? What is in the wind, my dear fellow?" asked he, in a grave and sympathizing tone; "do not the family behave well to you? do they persecute you?"

"No!" replied Jacob; it would be in the highest degree ungrateful of me were I to utter the least complaint, or express the slightest cause of displeasure. Ah!" continued he, "if the truth must be spoken, it is not they, it is I who cause myself annoyance and sorrow."

"Did I not think so?" said Martin to himself.

"It is I who vex myself; I cannot help doing so. Oh, I cannot describe to you the painful circumstances in which I often find myself! It goes so far, that I am annoyed if I have to go there when they have visitors. It seems to me almost as if it were a want of due respect to the family, to let it be seen by their guests that they are going to have a Jew for their son-in-law. And even when I am there I am miserable, if I see two people talking in an under tone, or glancing at one another, or exchanging a smile, unless I know what they are talking about, or smiling at. I have not eyes and ears enough to serve my purpose; I am rent to pieces as it were;—and yet, perhaps, their glances and their smiles are the most innocent in the world. It may be so very likely, but I have filled my mind with apprehension. When I keep away I am always longing to be there; for it seems to me that my presence may prevent remarks which have reference to me. And then, besides that, when I am not there that conceited puppy, Lieutenant Engborg, comes dangling about my beloved!"

"What then, in order to make the unhappiness complete, are you become jealous?" remarked Martin.

"No;" returned Jacob, "but he already paid his court to the same girl, and now, when she has decided in my favour, it seems to me that honour requires him quietly to withdraw himself There is a certain degree of impudence in going to the house, just as if no change had taken place. It seems to me as if he expected that his time would yet come."

"But is he not somewhat liked by the family?" asked Martin.

"Yes, a little," replied Jacob; "but that has nothing to do with existing circumstances."

"No, but all this is, in fact, of quite subordinate importance, if you only get on well with the family, and you yourself say that they treat you with all possible delicacy."

"But have you never remarked," said Jacob, "that there is a delicacy which wounds? The misfortune is that there is any occasion for delicacy at all. Their delicate silence has in it something painful to me, for I have become so much accustomed to certain words that I always expect them. If they would only for once talk about Jews in my presence, and even joke about them!—That would be a kindness to me, for it would prove to me that that they had for once quite forgotten that I was a Jew. But not the slightest sound about Jews is heard, although innumerable occasions occur when the word must have been on their tongues. Not long ago, they were talking about a man whose name was Jacobson. I read on every countenance the wish to inquire whether he was a Jew, but I was present; they were vexed and were silent. It is never out of their thoughts that I am a Jew; my presence is a constraint upon them; they cannot talk so confidentially, so unrestrainedly, with me, as if I were a Christian. My greatest happiness would be to become merged into their sphere; to vanish as an individual and live as a portion of their family life; but every moment plucks me out from among them; I am but as a stranger in their domestic circle. Our blood will not unite in foster-brotherhood; there is a mysterious mischief-bringing power standing between us which divides us one from the other."

Martin sat with bowed head, and was silent long after Jacob had ceased speaking. At length he said—

"I could have told you at the beginning precisely what you have told me now. The thing is that we are Jews, and the worst of it is, that we know it so well ourselves. Therefore, I did my best; but it is now all one. I am your physician, and I will continue to be so, although you have gone beyond my prescription; but if you had a patient who had taken cold by his want of care, and by his disregard of your advice, and thus had brought himself into a consumption, you would not let him lie in a helpless state because the consumption was owing to himself. Will you have my advice?"

Jacob had thrown himself upon the sofa, and now lay with his hands over his eyes, and made no reply.

Martin for some time walked up and down the room; at length he said—

"You may ask me why I come here and thrust myself into your confidence? I may ask myself the same question, for I really do not know why. It lies here within the ribs, and will out; and if I were not a sworn foe to the materialists, who say that feeling has its seat in the heart, I should believe that I was very fond of you. But that I am not; for if I were, I should naturally walk up and down the room, and wring my hands, and say, 'What the devil would you go and betroth yourself for? If you had only let that folly alone! If you had only kept away!' But I do not do so. I am not your friend; I am nothing else but your family physician, and you are ill. There you are lying now on the sofa; I draw out a diagnosis of your disease, and take a review in my learned brain of all similar cases. Let me have a cigar—nay, here they are—when the cigar is smoked out, I think we shall be ready. Now listen, and be filled with admiration! After due examination, various circumstances present themselves under which a union between a Jew and a Christian woman might be happy. In the first, there might be a happy marriage if a Jew from the corner of Leather-lane or Little King-street was betrothed to a Christian lady of the rank of a servant wench. By a happy marriage, I understand one in which all the promises of the betrothal are fulfilled. When such a couple are courting, there generally occurs a pretty little quarrel, at least once a week, on a Sunday, up in her garret, the end of which generally is that the lover is marched down stairs, while the lady exclaims, 'Go to Jericho with you, you cursed Jew!' after which they celebrate a cordial reconciliation on the Monday; the lover's ears being no more wounded by such an address than the lady's by the blow with which the fist of the lover regaled them. When this pair are married, the same life is continued, only that the passionate scenes may occur any day in the week, work-day or saint's day, whilst, as a matter of course, the happy moments of reconciliation become all the more frequent. Occasions of disunion being shortness of money, jealousy, and such like. That is a happy married couple with strong nerves and heavy fists. Another

15

case is when a rich Jewish good-for-nothing becomes acquainted with a poor Christian girl and her coquettish mother. He makes them presents, takes them to the shops, buys them shawls and gown-pieces; in short, becomes so indispensable, that, in order to be always together, they are betrothed. During the time of betrothal, the lover adorns his beloved for himself, after the wedding for others; nor will I be understood not to have said that also during the betrothal he may not have done the same. Finally, I have bethought myself of a case in which a Jew may marry a Christian lady for the sake of wealth, or for some other worldly reason. That is an arrangement—a bargain, as if for oranges; they find that one-half of the wares are damaged, and, therefore, they set a higher price upon those that remain. At the time when you took the infection of that strange, sublime rapture called love—I beg your pardon, when you fell in love—I was frightened. I had no rubric ready by which you might be suitably treated; I was afraid that you might get into a dilemma, by which the soul would be pressed out of your very life. Now, however, I am ready for the case in which a Jew like yourself, a handsome, well-meaning young fellow—nay, hold your head up!—has stumbled upon a Christian family which, as far as it is possible so to be, are tolerant, and endeavour to make amends for a deficiency by constant attention; who are possessed of this almost incredible peculiarity, that under all circumstances there is no one so solicitous for the family as the family itself. In this case a perfect, nay, a romantic happiness is possible, if only the Jew will be wise enough; not, like the porcupine, to set up his quills at the approach either of friend or enemy, and thus become intolerant. Bendixen! Compare your engagement with those other betrothals; thank your God and Creator, and be reasonable and happy! Do not sin against God's gifts. If the others have forgotten that you are a Jew, or even seem to have forgotten it, forget it yourself, or, at all events, seem to forget it. The girl loves you; there is not a doubt about that. Why do you not speak to her of these things?—why do you not compel yourself to touch with her upon these delicate feelings of yours? Give her your full confidence. There! now we have the true remedy! Talk to the girl, man! By so doing, you will have a confederate in the family itself—the most powerful confederate— the only one which, in truth, you need! Now I have done; *dixi*, I have spoken, and both my coffee and myself are become cold!"

Long before Martin had ended had Jacob sprung from his seat, once more gay and full of life.

"You are right, Martin!" exclaimed he; "you are perfectly right. I have been blind, deaf—I have been a—why have you not regularly abused me? I have deserved it! Oh! I am now alive, I am as if new-born——"

"Yes," interrupted Martin, "I also lay great stress upon the science of obstetrics."

"Don't laugh at me," said Jacob; "you have freed me from all my pusillanimity and childishness! You are my benefactor; yes, in truth, my benefactor! When shall I be able to do so much for you?"

"I hope never!" exclaimed Martin. "Heaven preserve me from being so mad! But, since we are talking about making returns—why, I advise you to get married; employ me as your doctor, that will be a little practice to begin with. But, on second thoughts, you are a doctor yourself, and, therefore, I must give you my services gratis. However, this you *can* do— when you have the wedding, and I come to congratulate you, give me champagne instead of coffee."

As soon as Martin was gone, Jacob hastened to his betrothed.

On his way thither, he said to himself, "Yes, I will make a full confession to her of all my childishness; she shall see into every crevice of my heart. She will stand by me, and like my good angel, chase away the evil thoughts."

His heart was light, and his eye beamed with happiness as he ascended the steps to the house.

CHAPTER XXV.

As usual, they had visitors. The moment was evidently not propitious for his errand. But his powers of mind were in such active movement, his determination gave him such energy, that he thought not of impediments.

The company was engaged in lively, and tolerably loud, conversation when Jacob entered the room. A French lady was there, together with the family, with whom she was staying, Lieutenant Engborg, and a few other young men.

Jacob's arrival for the moment filled Thora with anxiety; but his countenance was so unusually cheerful and cordial, that she immediately lost all fear and received him with her most affectionate smile, and, with a certain degree of pride, introduced him to the French lady as her betrothed. This lady probably thought that his position in the family required that she should pay him particular attention; she immediately, therefore, drew him into the conversation, which was again continued, and which was gay and amusing, and had reference to what she had seen during her short residence in Copenhagen.

Of course, all spoke in French, and Jacob soon perceived that Lieutenant Engborg had much more fluency in the language than himself. He said to himself that this young man should not long have the advantage of him in this respect; but, for the moment, there was no help. He was not accustomed to feel himself overcome in any contest where man meets with man. The arrogance of the lieutenant, however, was painful to him, and there were moments in which he was conscious of jealous bitterness; as now, for instance, when Thora, who also spoke beautiful French, was able to keep up a much livelier conversation with Engborg than with himself.

Jacob bethought himself with uneasiness and vexation of the object for which he had come, and the company who stood in the way of his precious purpose became irksome to him. He had not, however, much time for reflection: he was borne along by the stream of conversation. Almost against his will, he talked a great deal, as if to punish himself for not talking well. He joined in the laughter of others, although he himself felt no cause for laughter.

Coffee and cake were handed round. "Try this," said Thora, in the midst of a lively conversation, presenting to the French lady the heaped-up plate; "this is true Danish wheaten-cake; you will not find its equal in France; it is sent us by my aunt from the country. It is true, Bendixen!" said she, addressing Jacob; "and perhaps my aunt also will soon come herself. Oh, I am so glad that you then can make the acquaintance of my sweet aunt Matilde!"

Without paying much attention to this information, Jacob replied:

"It will delight me, if your aunt is only as good as her wheaten-cake; I will now eat a piece to her happy arrival."

Jacob said *pièce* instead of *morceau, pièce* signifying a whole loaf; on which the French lady exclaimed, laughing, "Indeed! you must either be very fond of her then, or very hungry!" on which Thora and the lieutenant burst into hearty laughter. It seemed to Jacob as if the lieutenant compelled himself to laugh, whilst Thora laughed with all her heart. It ought to have been just the contrary. He was all the less inclined to excuse this involuntary outburst, as he had not cordially sympathised with the merriment of the others. He fancied that he was an object of ridicule to this company; that he had been humiliated and rendered absurd, though respect for the family ought to have preserved him from this. Nothing more was needed to chase the superficial cheerfulness from his countenance, and to exhibit instead displeasure and mortified feeling.

So sudden was the change of his countenance that the two ladies, perceiving it, involuntarily became silent, on which the lieutenant burst afresh into peals of laughter.

"Lieutenant!" exclaimed Jacob, in a voice tremulous with passion, turning round to him.

The lieutenant seemed to quail before him, and was silent.

The silence which had thus suddenly fallen around him, and in which Jacob seemed to hear the echo of his own exclamation, made him instantly feel the folly of which he had been guilty. In vain he now endeavoured to give a renewed impulse to the conversation; all the powers of his mind seemed arrested by the required effort, and in the course of a few seconds he endured a real martyrdom; he felt himself fearfully lonely, and yet it was, as if the eye of the Almighty was riveted upon him. He suffered under the curse which is imposed by an isolated youth, and by the mind not having acquired the polish of social life.

The sound of the stage-coach suddenly pulling up before the house, released both himself and the company generally from the petrifying influence which had fallen upon them. All hastened to the window to see who had arrived. Jacob blessed in his heart the stranger who had come so opportunely.

"Mother!" exclaimed Thora, "there is my aunt!"

"Yes, good heavens! my aunt," chimed in her sister; and, clapping their hands, they ran out of the room to receive her.

The visitors took their leave, and Jacob, who was abashed and dejected, would have followed their example, if it could have been done with propriety.

When the aunt had embraced and kissed her sister and her nieces, and inquired after the health of the absent merchant, Jacob was introduced to her as Thora's betrothed.

"I congratulate you!" said the aunt, very coldly but politely. Jacob bowed most respectfully.

"But how happens it that you are come so unexpectedly, dear Matilde?" asked Mrs. Fangel.

"Good heavens! the occasion is a happy one!" replied aunt Matilde. "You know that ever since the death of his sister, my husband has lost all desire to continue at the parsonage, although it is so good a living; therefore he made inquiries after a living in the city. In the spring we got a letter to say that the living he wished for was at his service; and as soon as I heard that, I had no longer any wish to remain a country parson's wife. I set off, and now you have me, and here I shall stay till my husband comes. Good heavens! How I have longed after Copenhagen!"

"Oh, that is delightful!" exclaimed Thora's sister; "so then my uncle will be our parish minister! And he can marry you, Thora!"

"Thora!" interrupted the aunt, with a keen glance; "can she be married by a Christian minister?"

So unexpected and so startling was this exclamation, that Jacob at first could hardly believe his ears; the next moment it seemed to him impossible that it could be said in any other spirit than that of sheer stupidity.

Question and answer in the meantime were uninterruptedly interchanged. Whilst the aunt replied, Mrs. Fangel had already a fresh question on her lips.

"When does your husband come? Does he enter on the living immediately?"

"Yes; he only stops till he has sold our rubbish by auction. We shall get everything new here from top to bottom."

"But will not aunt go and change her dress?" asked Thora's sister.

Thora had walked silently to one of the windows; Jacob stood with a sorely perplexed mind in another window, and drew figures on the pane of glass.

"Yes, thank you, my child! But let me first have a cup of warm coffee. Ah, see there, Mr. Lieutenant!—" exclaimed she, casting her eye on Engborg, who had not left with the others, and who had approached her—"Ay, and you really," added she, in an under tone, "have let my niece be carried off from just under your nose!"

Jacob heard these words. It was not possible for him to doubt their meaning, yet he could not take offence at them. The aunt seemed to him like a demon who had broken loose to persecute him.

At length she went to change her dress. He longed to approach Thora; to excuse his behaviour to her, and to have thus early such an understanding with her as might secure him against this horrible woman; but Thora, with a look of displeasure, also left the room and followed the others into the chamber.

He stood in torturing anxiety; so much did he dread any word which might possibly be exchanged among them. Of a certainty his countenance must have expressed the musing of his soul; for, some time afterwards, when Thora approached him, she pressed his hand tenderly, whilst she gazed into his face with eyes full of tears. In a moment Jacob's suffering was at an end; but it was only for a moment; for, in the next, he asked himself, how long will she retain affection and regard for the Jew, whom she allows to be persecuted under her own roof?

Jacob was seated at table by the aunt, as if it were intended to bring them amicably together; but the first words she addressed to him were, "Nay, I'm pleased. Then you do eat with us!"

Shortly after, she turned towards him, in a friendly manner, and asked about his birth-place, his rank of life, and so forth. When he had given her some information on these subjects, she asked,

"But what do your family say to your having betrothed yourself to a Christian girl?"

Jacob had self-possession enough to give an evasive reply, but he sat as on the rack. He would have given a year of his life if he could have silenced that tongue—if he could have prevented it from uttering those poisonous words, to which the whole company sat listening with profound attention. He felt as if madness were raging within him—as if a burning hatred arose within him of all those who heard these words, and more especially of her who uttered them.

She, however, in the meantime, had passed on, with the same ease and the same indifference, to other conversation with some one else at table; and seemed not to have the slightest idea, either of the pain she had occasioned, or of the aversion which she had called forth.

Wilhelm Fangel now joined the party. At sight of the aunt, with whom he had spent so many happy summer holidays, he rushed to her, and flung his arms round her neck. After this he offered, as was his custom, his hand most kindly to Jacob; but, unluckily, Jacob was in no humour to receive a hand which had so lovingly pressed that of the aunt, and he received Wilhelm's greeting with a cold "Good-day to you."

He felt that all eyes rested upon him—that they regarded him as the destroyer of the family joy; and his heart was filled with a sort of evil satisfaction in the thought that he could recompense them with some of the unhappiness which they, so calmly, had caused him to endure.

When he went home, he seemed to himself to be in the conition of a somnambulist. There were moments when he rearded the whole as a dream; the next moment, however, the eality stood clear and torturingly before him. As he opened is door a bitter smile curled his lip, at the thought of the tener, loving emotions with which he had last closed it.

CHAPTER XXVI.

A FEW days afterwards the post brought Jacob a letter; and a fervent joy, not unmingled with melancholy, filled his heart, as he recognized the handwriting of his father.

He read:

"Long life to thee, my only son!

"I have received thy letter, whereby I learn that thou, because of our great sin, hast betrothed thyself to the daughter of one who is not a Jew. Hast thou rightly considered what it is that thou hast done? Listen to the serious words of thy father. Thou art descended from pure and spotless Jews; our fathers' fathers have united themselves only to Jews; they have never forsaken the God of their fathers. But what is in thy mind to do? What would thy mother—may peace rest upon her!—she who now reposes in the garden of Eden, and who is the intercessor for our sins—what would she have said, if she had lived, at thy wishing to unite thyself with the child of the Christian? Thou art not a fool; thou mightest have chosen for thyself a bride from among the richest of thy people. Dost thou believe that thou canst be happy with the daughter of a stranger? Dost thou believe that she can ever forget that thou art a son of Israel? And thy descendants,—wilt thou tell me what is to become of them? Wilt thou be able to bring them up according to the law? My son—my only son! Thou art blind; thou art going to destruction; thou wilt cause thy father to rend his hair, and curse his birth! Must I, like the poet, say of my house, 'Its honour is gone from it?' Yet, why do I speak of myself? My heart is become grey, and bows towards the grave, after which I long; for since the death of thy mother I am lonely, and now thou goest far from me, never more to return. But the blame is mine, and mine only; I myself sent thee into the midst of temptation; and yet I, by the side of thy cradle, prayed God to remove all blessing from my head, and lay it upon thine! I give thee now only my best advice. Thy uncle and aunt, and all our relations here, are angry, and will not speak to thee; they believe that thou wilt allow thyself to be baptized. But I still am thy father. The Lord God will forgive me because I cannot curse thee. I extend my hand towards thee. My son, bow thy head, and receive my blessing.

"'The Lord bless and preserve thee! May the light of his countenance shine upon thee; may he be merciful to thee, and incline his countenance towards thee, and give thee peace!'

"Thus says thy affectionate father to thee."

Scarcely had he gone through this letter, when some one knocked at the door, and an elderly Jew entered and begged an alms. He could not have chosen a more favourable moment than this, when the letter of his father had made the Jews, and all that belonged to the Jews, precious to Jacob. It pained him as much to see this Jew begging as if he had been one of his nearest of kin; and he gave him bountifully. The old Jew believed that there was some mistake in this liberal gift, and hastened away, with the words, "May God bless you!"

These words, and the accent in which they were spoken, sounded to Jacob as the church-bells on a Christmas morning may sound to the Christian. An indescribable, vehement, painful longing seized him; he envied the poor Jew who now went among the Jews. The veins of his forehead were swollen with impatience. Home!—home! into the paternal arms! And Thora?

Like the bird tethered by a string, which flies boldly aloft, but is suddenly checked in its flight, and moves in circles around that one steadfast point,—so were the emotions of Jacob by this name, and then took another direction.

Thora! All those beloved emotions which the heart had forgotten awoke with redoubled force. The image of the beloved stood clear and graceful, and filled the heart with the blessedness of affection, until a movement of the mind suddenly recalled the late circumstances, and thus flung their dark, threatening shadow over the picture.

"What ought I to do?" said he, at length.

"Let it be as God in heaven will!"

At this very time the Fangel family sat talking familiarly together at the supper-table. The merchant was at his club.

Wilhelm walked up and down the room, and approached the door several times, as if about to leave it, but, fascinated by the subject of conversation, resolved to remain.

"That is, in fact, a very gentlemanly young man," said Aunt Matilde, when Mrs. Fangel had expressed her surprise that no one had seen Bendixen for the whole day. "I had imagined him to myself with a low-bred Jewish countenance; and I had determined quietly, in my own mind, that I would get him out of the family before long. And he has not been in it much of late; but now that vexes me. You have not bad taste, after all, dear Thora,—if one could only get accustomed to his being a Jew."

Thora was silent. She had it, however, on her tongue to say, "Mind your own business, dear aunt."

"I have always liked him," said Mrs. Fangel; "he is a respectable, quiet, and upright young man. The only thing I do not like in him is the temper which he has shown latterly. Before he was betrothed, he was always so cheerful and kind; when he used to look at me with his large dark eyes, it was with such extraordinary tenderness, as if he would beseech of me not to deny him Thora. He looked as if he could have gone through the fire for me;—but as soon as he was betrothed, it was all over."

"Perhaps his family are opposed to the match," suggested the aunt.

"I don't fancy so; he never speaks of them," said the mother.

"I believe it, nevertheless," exclaimed the aunt, who prided herself on her knowledge of human nature.

"No, I don't think so," said Mrs. Fangel; "he has his own independent fortune,—and why need he trouble himself about his family, if he only loves Thora, and that I am convinced he does."

"You might easily find out what is amiss with him," said Thora's sister to Wilhelm; "you have always been such good friends."

"I don't intermeddle with my sister's love-affairs," replied Wilhelm. "My sister has chosen her own lover; I have nothing more to do with it. Besides, did you not all see how short-tempered he was also to me the other day? Nevertheless, this I will say for him: he is a noble fellow in reality,—nor have I a friend whom I esteem more than he; but he has his faults like all of us."

"If I must speak my honest opinion," said Mrs. Fangel, "I fancy,—nay it is almost ridiculous; but don't you remember, Mille, the day we came from church? I almost fancy that he cannot bear our being Christians."

The aunt burst into a loud laugh, and exclaimed,—

"Do you then think that he wishes us all to become Jews?"

"No, certainly not; but I fancy—nay, I don't exactly know myself—but I cannot explain that extraordinary countenance!"

"That is called demonstration in a circle," remarked Wilhelm, as he made a pause, and looked at his mother with a sarcastic air.

"It will all come right, never fear," said the aunt, after a moment's silence. "In the first place, I shall set about making him sick of being a Jew. If he really loves Thora, he will also love her religion; and the day when he is baptized I will, with my whole heart, give my blessing to her marriage with her handsome lover," added she, as she went up to Thora and kissed her.

However much indignation Thora might feel at her aunt's pertinacious interference in her affairs, she was nevertheless touched by this proof of affection from so adored a relative of the family. She did not herself make any opposition, or even risk any opposition on the subject. She thought that it was best to let the affair take its own course.

CHAPTER XXVII.

The more Aunt Matilde thought about the affair, the more interest had it for her. She anticipated, in idea, the triumph she should enjoy when she had enriched the community with a new member much in the same way as she, in her country parsonage, interested herself about a chicken hatched late in the season, or which she had reared when every one else had given it up. She determined to manage the matter calmly and with circumspection, so that she might arrive safely, though slowly, at the goal; she would hold the reins in her hand; she would adjust every word which should be spoken to Jacob; and everything should be so arranged as to conduct him towards the desired object. Amid all these arrangements, he became cordially dear to her—dear as her own triumph, because he was necessary for it.

She selected Wilhelm as her adjutant—as her confidant. She unfolded to him her whole plan of procedure; first, how she, in all friendliness, would represent to Bendixen that he was a Jew; point out to him the excellencies of Christianity; and, if he made any opposition, then combat with him most fervently, and lastly win the most glorious victory. She asked Wilhelm if he had not some theological books, in which they might find some forcible arguments for their purpose in this approaching disputation.

"I and my husband have no children of our own," said she,

finally; "and if I am so fortunate as to get this young Jew baptized, we will adopt him as our own son."

"Aunt," said Wilhelm, "you are unquestionably descended from the priest Tangbrand."

"I cannot bear that you should say so," replied she, somewhat nettled by this observation; "I am not intolerant. It does not annoy me at all that the man is a Jew; it is not so much for the sake of his own eternal happines that I would have him baptized; but since he has betrothed himself to a Christian girl, he ought to become a Christian."

"Yes, aunt," replied Wilhelm, "but I doubt, nevertheless, whether your method will be successful. According to what I know of Bendixen, he will not believe that you talk to him about Christianity and Judaism merely out of friendship. If you would make a Christian of him, you should treat him as if you knew no other than he was a Christian; be gentle and kind to him, and he may, perhaps, become a Christian before he himself knows that he is one."

"Yes! that's the right way, truly!" exclaimed the aunt; "let him go on, and remain a Jew until he becomes a Christian of his own accord! Yes, that's beautiful!"

"That was what the wind said when it would compel the traveller to throw off his cloak," said Wilhelm; but, as far as I myself am concerned, I will have nothing to do in the business. Bendixen is a little affronted with me at this moment. But he will get right again; and as for ladies' affairs, I shall not trouble myself about them."

It was just as Wilhelm had said. The aunt did not succeed with her gentle measures. Bendixen sought merely to avoid her. He only came to take a walk with Thora, or to accompany her to the theatre, or for some other purpose of pleasure, and left the house as soon as possible. In a few days Aunt Matilde was out of humour.

"I tell you what, Thora," said she; "your lover had a great deal better fix your trysting-place in the street; then he need not come here at all."

"Yes," said Mrs. Fangel; "it really begins to look as if he hated us altogether."

Jacob received a hint of this from Thora, and the next day he made a particular point of paying attention to her mother, invited her to go with them to the theatre, and in the evening conducted her and her daughter thither; and when he was alone with these two ladies he was most agreeable and kind, and the former good understanding was, for the time, established between them.

Often now, when the aunt expressed herself bitterly towards Jacob, the mother took his part.

"Such a betrothal as this I have never seen before!" said Aunt Matilde; "it is exactly as if it were some mysterious affair, and nothing but the mother must know about it. He never comes to the house when there are visitors; and as to us, he never speaks a word to us."

"He has not a great deal of time," said the mother, deprecatingly; "he is reading for his examination; it would be a good thing if all young men were as industrious as he is."

One day, however, there came an invitation for Wilhelm and Mille from the family of the Privy-councillor, with whose daughter Mille had gone to school. It was the custom at the Privy-councillor's to give a party every spring; and before Thora had gone to Holstein she had been regularly invited there with her sister. This time, however, she was not mentioned in the invitation.

"It was very extraordinary though, that they have not invited Thora," said Mrs. Fangel, as she sat looking thoughtfully at the invitation.

"And if they had done so, they would have been obliged to

have invited her lover also," said Aunt Matilde—"and that you may very well know they will not do."

"I did not know that!" said the mother.

"I know very well that I should never have thought of inviting a Jew, if I gave a great party!" exclaimed the aunt.

"But, perhaps, they do not know at the Privy-councillor's that Thora is come back," said the mother, after some consideration.

"How should they not know that?" exclaimed the aunt; she will soon have been at home half a year."

"That's quite true," said the mother in a low voice.

A deal was now said on the affair. The mother declared that Mille should not go; and Wilhelm declared that he would rather stay at home.

"There is no help for it," said the mother; "Mille must not go to a place where her sister is not reckoned good enough to be invited."

Silence fell over the domestic circle. Wilhelm drummed with his fingers on the window-pane; and the ladies, out of humour, sat down to their sewing.

Jacob came. He accosted the mother most kindly as usual, but she recceived his salutation very coolly. Wilhelm took up his hat and went out; Mille put her pocket-handkerchief to her eyes, and left the room likewise.

When Jacob was alone with Thora, he asked her what was amiss.

"Oh!" said she, "it is nothing but childishness. Wilhelm and Mille are invited to the Privy-councillor's, and because I am not invited they must now remain at home. That is what she is crying for."

The moment Jacob heard these words he understood the whole thing. The pain and vexation which it caused him was, however, counterbalanced by the heart-felt gratitude which he felt to Thora for the delicacy with which she had mentioned it. He took her in his arms, and deliberated with himself whether he should not at this very moment acknowledge his weakness to her; ask her whether she could bear with it, and whether she believed herself strong enough never to see the Jew in him. But while he was thus combatting with himself, Thora said—

"Thou must not let it trouble thee so! I do not care about going to the Privy-councillor's! If I have only thee!"

After those words, it seemed to him almost a sin to express any doubt.

As he went away, he said to himself, full of confidence, "Let them all be against me, if they will: she is attached to me with a faithful and loving heart!"

CHAPTER XXVIII.

They told the merchant about this affair at the Privy-councillor's; he smiled, and was silent.

From this time, however, Mrs. Fangel often fell into deep thought; and on one occasion Thora surprised her in tears. She approached her with anxious foreboding, and inquired tenderly why she wept; her mother, however, embraced and kissed her as she replied, "Thou canst not do anything for it, my dear child!"

When Jacob came, she received him as a guest who deserved courtesy; but it was plain to see that even this cost her an effort. Mille did not stand on ceremony; she left the room as soon as she saw him, and banged the door after her. The aunt received him with a sarcastic and significant manner; and when Jacob looked beseechingly towards Mrs. Fangel, as to remind her of the good-will which she had lately shown him, she at first cast down her eyes, and then pretending business elsewhere, left the room.

He was thus left alone with that dangerous foe; and he was weaponless also, for he dared not enter into controversy with her, lest it should lead to a quarrel, which, in the present state of the family feeling, might break off his engagement with Thora.

That family, hitherto so cheerful, had now become silent and gloomy, and to none was this change so terrible as to him. If on a spring-day the mild sunshine and the blue sky awoke as it were a new life in his breast, and he hastened cheerfully and with a yearning heart to his betrothed, it was only necessary for him to see the house from a distance, and at once it seemed as if the sunshine were clouded, and he entered with an uncertain and anxious gaze.

But it was not so much their want of cordiality to himself which distressed him, for to that he was beginning to be accustomed. It was much more on account of Thora that he suffered. He had a presentiment that love is a flower of the sunshine; it may endure through a violent tempest, and afterwards raise itself with twofold beauty; but when it must remain in the shade, without sunshine and without dew, it bows its head, and withers away.

Under these circumstances it was a relief to all parties when the merchant one day declared that the family should remove to their country-house. The wife, it is true, suggested that it was yet very early in the season, and that no other families had left the city; but the merchant adhered to his resolve, and they went.

This change was at all events good in one respect; they saw each other much less frequently. Jacob, however, often reflected with bitter uneasiness that Thora was in consequence much more under the influence of her aunt. This painful consciousness often took possession of his mind as he sat among his books, and he would then rush forth, as full of terror as if some threatened misfortune hung over him; but when he reached the place, its unfriendly atmosphere soon drove him back again to the city.

CHAPTER XXIX.

MARTIN and Jacob continued to meet; but both avoided any conversation on this subject. Martin could see plainly from his friend's countenance how things were going on; but as he no longer knew how to advise him, he thought it better not to interfere at all; while Jacob, on his side, shrunk from even the mention of this unlucky engagement, which he dreaded to think was so insecure.

One beautiful day, at the close of July, Martin accompanied him as far as the gate of the city on the way to the Fangels' country residence. Martin went on, looking at all that surrounded him—at those who walked, or drove, or rode, as well as those who disputed with the drivers about the fare, so much per person. At length, turning to Jacob, he said :

"You are very dull to-day; although, as to that, you have always been so of late. What a glorious fellow you used to be formerly!—then one had the hope that one should make a regular physician out of you. Look there!"

A Jewish family had drawn up in a four-seated Holstein-carriage, and as they only occupied two of the seats, they sat there patiently waiting for more passengers, and sped on the time by conversation about family affairs, which the father every now and then interrupted by a kind warning to one or another of the children not to tumble out of the carriage, or by a timid "So, so" to the horses, if they lifted up their heads.

Martin pointed to them, and said, with a smile, "I have half a mind to remain here; when the driver mounts his seat, the father of the family will perhaps put up a prayer for a happy journey."

Jacob, whose thoughts at the sight of this Jewish family had taken quite another direction, said, with a sigh, "This day week my uncle's eldest daughter will be married."

"Nay, there is no need for you to sigh about it," said Martin; "you are really quite mournful."

"But I should like to go to the wedding," said Jacob, after a little thought.

"Well, then, go."

"Yes, but they have not invited Thora," returned Jacob.

"You surely do not expect that your betrothal with a Christian girl is publicly acknowledged by the Jews!" exclaimed Martin; "will you have both the bag and the purse?"

"No," replied he, "I should be very well satisfied if I had merely my share in one of them."

"It really is quite terrible to see how you are perpetually hanging down your head!" exclaimed Martin. "Good heavens! man—make an end of it! Pluck up spirit and talk with your beloved; she is, after all, nothing more than a woman."

"Nothing more than a woman!" repeated Jacob—"yes, you should only know how much mischief a single woman can do."

"What!" said Martin, "does your beloved cause you mischief? Is it already gone so far with love? Ah, thou great god, Cupid!"

"On, no—the aunt," said Jacob.

"The aunt? What sort of an aunt is she? When did she drop down from the clouds? I thought that heaven had permitted a perfectly amiable, auntless family to fall into your hands."

"She is the wife of a country parson," replied Jacob; "I cannot give you an idea what a Jew's foe she is."

"A parson's wife! I can very well understand," returned Martin. "They are the most intolerant people in the world—far worse than Turks, or even than parsons themselves. Such a parson's wife manages her household, receives tithes and offerings in kind, and never sees a Jew bring a goose, nor even a chicken. What thoughts can such a poor woman have about Jews!

"Well, and your parson's wife?" continued he, as Jacob remained silent.

"She has caused me to repent what I once said to you, that I wished they would let me bear in the family that I was a Jew. It was a defiance of Heaven, and I have been punished for it. She hardly ever talks of anything else; she treats me as if it was her firm determination to drive me out of the house."

"It is a pity she did not come before the betrothal," remarked Martin.

"Why so?"

"Then, perhaps, you never would have been betrothed," said Martin.

"Oh, don't talk so," said Jacob.

"But surely she will be going away again," remarked Martin "or is she a widow who will now spend her annuity here in the city for your benefit?"

"The husband has had a living given to him in the city," returned Jacob; "and he is to come as soon as he has sold their things in the country. The poor man must be under petticoat government, for she sets off and leaves him to manage everything as he can. But what good will it do if he comes and they go to their own house?—they will naturally all hang together like pea-straw."

"Well, then, come to open warfare, and drive *her* from the house," said Martin.

"That I cannot do," replied Jacob; "she governs the whole house; if I drove her away, I should drive the whole house with her. It has become impossible for me to live in the family since she came."

"Now, I'll tell you what, Bendixen," said Martin, after a pause, "get married—take the girl away from them; the sooner the better."

"But I must have the consent of the family," replied Jacob; "and before I have passed my examination and got some practice, they will, of course, not give it—especially with such an understanding as now exists amongst us."

"But you have a fortune of your own; you do not need to wait for practice," remonstrated Martin.

"I have not more fortune than I require for myself," said Jacob. "And what sort of marriage would that be in which I could not insure to my wife something like a pleasant, easy life? And Thora has been brought up in affluence."

"But her father is rich," again suggested Martin.

"But would I allow my wife to be maintained by her father?" exclaimed Jacob; "in that case we should hear them exclaim against the Jews. Besides, he is a merchant, and a merchant has always need of his money. A good dowry paid down at once I could not object to, but a yearly allowance—that would only make me still more dependent on them than I am at present. You may very well believe that I have thought over all these things; in fact, I think about nothing else."

"But I know certainly that your own father is wealthy."

"Martin!" exclaimed Jacob, "you cannot mean that I should make demands upon my father for the maintenance of a Christian wife?"

"Well, then, on my soul and happiness!" exclaimed Martin,

"I know no other way than that you should be baptized. And, in fact, that is the most natural thing: if you are attached to your beloved with your whole heart, it is a small matter for you to be baptized for her sake."

"Such reasonining as this would drive me mad," returned Jacob. "The reasoning sounds cogent enough, but I can reply to it by reasoning equally cogent. A sincere man cannot abandon his faith for mere worldly prosperity. But you know very well that I could not allow myself to be baptized,—I who every morning and night use the Jewish prayer. I don't know how it is, but I am much more of a Jew now than I used to be. I have frequently livingly pictured to myself that I was baptized, have regarded myself as a Christian; and I cannot describe to you what a pang it is to me when I meet a Jew, nor what an unspeakable relief when I can say to myself, 'but thou art not yet baptized!' In this way I think of the baptized Jews of Copenhagen, who, on Friday evening, when the Jews go to synagogue, follow them to the entrance, and remain standing outside until they hear the words, 'Arise, my friends, and go forth to meet the bride!' and then go home weeping."

"In that case, I pronounce your malady to be incurable; I bid you farewell," said Martin; "I will return to the city."

"Oh, go a little further with me, Martin; I am so shockingly out of spirits," said Jacob. "I do not wish you in my place, although you would then so much better feel what my sufferings are."

"Poor fellow!" said Martin; "would to Heaven I could discover some new Pitcairn's Island whither you might conduct your beloved, and live in paradisaical peace, separated from all the rest of the world!"

"Yes, would that such a decided course of action were possible!" returned Jacob. "Would that I could, at once, assemble all these miseries, to combat against them and dare everything, even life itself, so that I might overcome them. Anything would be better than to be thus cowardly tortured. There is reason in the saying, 'It is a slow death to have the life trodden out of one by a goose.' And I am trodden on like a worm,—and yet I dare not even once show my sting! How I do hate that woman! If the thought of my beloved did not always remain uppermost in my mind—I believe that I should have murdered her long ago."

"Your condition is really a painful one, Bendixen," said Martin. "You go about with a hollow tooth of which you would be glad to get rid, and yet you have not the courage to have it taken out. And there are, in fact, only two alternatives to choose from—you may as well hear them once more—either to be baptized, or to break with them."

"Precisely in this consists my misfortune, that whilst I am placed between these two alternatives, I can choose neither of them!" exclaimed Jacob, impatiently. "When a man stands between fire and water, and cries out for help, it is not the thing to say to him, 'Leap either into the fire or the water.'"

"Nay, then take your own course, my good fellow; run away both from the fire and the water."

"And you have not any other resource to suggest to-day?" asked Jacob.

"Lord God!" exclaimed Martin, "under your circumstances there is no other resource. I would gladly leap into either fire or water for you, of that you may be sure; but I don't see that it would be of any benefit to you. If I can be of any use to you, say so; here I am for you to command. If you don't see what I can do at this moment, but think of it afterwards, you have my address, you know. Good-bye. My compliments to the parson's wife."

As Martin walked back, he said to himself, "Now I think that I have brought the poor fellow into such a state of mind that he will go there and do some stupid thing. And the most stupid thing that he could do would be better than going on in the way that he now does."

But Jacob did nothing outrageous this evening. The nearer he approached to the village where they lived, the more his violence of temper abated, and that gloomy, dull, and yet irritable state of mind again came over him.

When Thora saw him arrive, pale and wearied by his long walk, by the heat and agitation of his mind, she fancied that he was ill, and rushed out for some reviving drops. His appearance excited uneasiness in the other members of the family, and they came round him anxiously inquiring after his health. When Thora returned with the drops, Aunt Matilde snatched the bottle from her, in order that she herself might count them out. Jacob in a few moments found himself astonishingly better. He was so unaccustomed to kindness, that he forgot all ill-will in these proofs of tender regard; he felt how much he could love these people, if they would only allow it.

As he came with Thora from a short walk in the garden, he was like one new-born, and for the first time he noticed the shoots of the vine which had wound themselves up the wall of the house. The tea-table spread in the garden parlour seemed to him more pleasant and inviting than he had ever seen it before.

Aunt Matilde met him at the door.

"Nay," said she, "you are now looking as lively as a fish. Thank Heaven! I was beginning to be so afraid lest you should die; for we poor creatures should not have known how you must be buried."

Mille laughed aloud.

The truce was thus already at an end.

Jacob felt almost ashamed of the tender feelings which he had cherished, though only for the moment; he accused himself of cowardice. "It was, however," said he to himself, "only a yearning after peace which caused my greatest joy in the kindness that was shown to me. I made myself weaker than I really was, merely to enjoy their kindness! Oh how profoundly have they humiliated me! Now I understand how my whole people may become so wrong-headed as, with the disgusting spirit of the slave, to kiss the hand which smites them!"

CHAPTER XXX.

"I am weary of it," said the merchant, one day at dinner; "I will have quiet in the family. Poor thing!" said he, turning to Thora, and patting her cheek, "thou hast not at all a happy courtship."

Thora began to weep.

"It shall not go on in this way," continued he, speaking with the warmth of passion; "there shall be an alteration. I thought it would be a good thing for us to come out here; but nothing can be worse. If the fault lies with Bendixen, I will seriously take him to task; if wrong has been done him, I will from this time forth take his part. There shall be peace in the house."

The aunt took up the word. "That there must be a change is plain enough; either Bendixen must be baptized, or else we must every one of us turn Jews."

The merchant's face flushed crimson, even to his hair; but he constrained himself, and said, "I hope, my good sister-in-law, you may not have cause to repent of the zeal with which you interfere in this matter. If you have no objection, I will myself regulate the affairs of my family."

And so saying, he rose from the table and left the room.

Aunt Matilde remained sitting for a moment in profound silence. She then turned round to her sister, and said, "That is as good as to say that I had better leave the house. That Jew has now gone so far as to make a breach in the family. But this I tell you," said she, starting up from her chair with such violence that it fell over, "this I tell you, Thora, I will not let myself be thus trampled on by your lover. I will stop here! I will stop till your father and your lover take and thrust me from the door! For what I care, you may marry a Jew. I have done my duty."

A pause succeeded this outbreak. Aunt Matilde put her pocket-handkerchief to her eyes and sobbed; the others sat with downcast eyes, each occupied with their own thoughts.

"Here he comes!" exclaimed Mille after awhile, and pointed to the window.

"Thora, do thou go out and meet him; it is not worth while for him to come in here," said Mrs. Fangel, going up to her sister.

It was now several days since Jacob had been there, and his longing after Thora had become stronger than his fear-mingled aversion to her family. Besides this, another feeling impelled him; this was a dread, a dissatisfaction in his own mind, as if he was about to do an injustice to Thora by going to the Jewish marriage, which was to take place that evening. From the moment when the clerk of the synagogue had been, and invited him according to the old formula, "You are invited to the marriage and the dinner; knife and fork and spoon you must yourself bring with you," an irresistible longing, a homesickness as it were, had taken possession of his heart. In order to excuse himself, he said, "I do not prevent Thora from going to the Christian church, and she has her family with her—what have I?"

But notwithstanding this, his conscience was not pacified.

He was now anxious to find an occasion, a suitable opportunity, of saying this to her; but as she continued to walk silently by his side, and as he, in his embarrassment, did not know what else to talk about, he called up his courage, and said,—

"This evening there is a wedding at my uncle's; his daughter is to be married."

"Indeed!" said she; "and art thou invited?"

"Yes," replied he; but it gave him pain for a moment that she should so decidedly infer that she was not included in the invitation; the thought continually thrust itself forward in his mind that there was a barrier between them.

"Yes, I am invited," said he.

"And shall you go?" asked she.

"Yes, I was thinking of doing so, though—"

"Go, my friend," said she, "and I hope you may be amused."

The tone of resignation in which she spoke touched him deeply. He felt so grateful for the readiness with which she had wished him pleasure, that he began to think what return he could make so as to gratify and cheer her.

They had now passed through the wood, and reached that point which opened to the Sound; here they seated themselves upon a grassy bank.

The afternoon sun, which was yet high in the heavens, shone hotly upon the sea, which lay like a faithful hound at the feet of the land; ships with white sails moved slowly, almost imperceptibly, in the offing, while the distant coast of Hveen shone out like a blue mist, which, softly tremulous, seemed to rest upon the horizon. Beneath the cool shade of the trees no sound was heard, excepting the occasional twitter of a bird, as if the birds themselves were too well satisfied to keep up long conversations.

"How unnatural," exclaimed Jacob, after a long silence, "appears human action, when one contemplates nature! We human beings keep up a warfare about mere trifles, and make our lives disagreeable, when we might be so happy. How compassionately mighty nature smiles upon us! It seems to me as if at this very moment scales had fallen from my eyes. Oh, my Thora, my soul is filled with repentance! I also am to blame for much of the unfriendly feeling which exists between thy family and myself. Thora, I will go at once to thy aunt, and offer her my hand; if she will give me only one kind word, I will remain from the wedding. I will belong to you."

"Wilt thou actually do this for my sake?" exclaimed Thora.

"Yes, dear Thora, and for my own sake also," returned he. "At this moment I am so happy; I see so clearly how the riddle of my life may be solved. It has been unmanly in me to have been so long afraid of showing my weakness to thee, of being willing to yield."

"Oh, thank God!" exclaimed Thora, "then all will be right. They have always said that there is nothing in the way, nothing against thee, if thou only—"

"Only what?" asked Jacob, seeing Thora hesitate.

"Would'st embrace our faith," returned she.

It is said that a man, when he receives a mortal shot, preserves for a moment his calm exterior, and then drops, as if the thought of death was too great to be comprehended in a moment. Jacob turned towards Thora as if astonished; the happy smile rested still upon his countenance, but the next moment a deadly paleness overspread his features

"My aunt—everybody thinks that thou shouldst be baptized," continued Thora.

He rose up without a word, and walked back with her through the wood towards the garden.

"Art thou angry?" asked she, with quivering lips.

"Oh, no," replied he, scarcely knowing what he said, and continued to walk on, "not angry, but very sad!"

He was so wholly absorbed that he was scarcely aware of anything, until he found himself once more in the garden-par-

17—2

lour, where there were several visitors, among the rest Lieutenant Engborg, and then the sound of their voices awoke him, as it were. He was in no humour to remain, and therefore bade them a hasty adieu.

At parting Thora said, with a tremulous voice, "To-morrow morning I shall go to town, at twelve o'clock, to do some errands; wilt thou go with me?"

"Yes," replied he, and with a hasty adieu to all, he left the house.

When he had gone some distance, he stood still, and leaned his head against a tree.

"Thus, then," sighed he, "has the serpent destroyed the flower which was so dear to me, and under which I hoped to find rest. But it is no fault of hers; they have poisoned her mind. Oh, how is she to be snatched from amongst them? I love her so fervently—"

"And yet how uncourteously I left her," continued he, as he again pursued his way towards the city; "and how can I meet her again? Oh God, thou hast laid thy hand heavily but righteously upon me!"

Thora had accompanied him a few paces from the house. When he had left her, she stood looking after him for a moment, with a bitter smile, and then burst into tears. Shortly afterwards, however, she dried her eyes, breathed upon her pocket-handkerchief, to conceal that she had been weeping, and then returned to the house and Lieutenant Engborg.

In the festively-decorated sitting-room of Marcus Bendixen, the men were assembled for minbro (the afternoon prayer), which is customary before the celebration of a marriage; the women were in another room, occupied with the bride.

Divine worship was about to begin and only waited for Marcus, who was engaged in yet once more impressing upon his wife the regulations of the occasion.

"Is her hair combed; is the silver chain bound round her; the veil put round her head, so that no one can recognize her?" asked he, as he drew his wife into a corner.

"All is ready" replied she, impatiently, "if you will only begin the prayers."

"Dear wife," returned Marcus, "thy heedlessness terrifies me! If there should be any mistake? Remember that one does not have a daughter married every day."

Instead of replying, his wife gave him a little push with her hand, and indicated with her eye that he should look towards the door.

"Jacob, my brother's son!" exclaimed he, as if surprised, when, in accordance with his wife's hint, he turned round. "There, thou canst see," said he, turning again to his wife with an animated manner, "I was right. He is still a Jew at heart!"

"How poorly he looks," said she.

"Oh, the poor fellow!" returned he. "It's plain enough that he does dance upon roses among those Christians! I'll tell thee what, it would have been much wiser of him to have fallen in love with our Mariane."

"Marcus," said the wife, "the sun is going down; is there anything more thou would'st say to me?"

"Now, in God's name!—and if there is any mistake let it lie on thy head;" said the husband, and then added as to himself, "not for a deal of money would I that he had not been here!" He went up and welcomed Jacob kindly, and then gave the sign that the prayers should commence.

All covered their heads and turned towards the east, with a low bow towards the invisible Deity. A deep silence prevailed in the room, whilst the men softly whispered the prayers and the benedictions. The crimson light of the setting sun shone upon the window-panes, and gave them the warm colouring as of painted church windows, and flung a strange glory over the little assembly.

When the prayers were ended, the steward of the bridegroom, a friend of the family, and who slept with him the night before the marriage, that he might keep watch over him, so that the evil spirit did not carry him away, according to the book of Tobit—conveyed to the woman's apartment, the present of the bridegroom to the bride: a pair of stockings, two pair of shoes, a silk pocket-handkerchief, and a prayer-book. Shortly after, the presents of the bride were presented to the bridegroom,—a bag for tephilim, in which he could place the holy chapters and the necessary leathern straps; the thalis, in which he could enwrap himself during prayers, and the shirt to be worn at the great feast of reconciliation, and in which he would finally be interred.

After this a trumpet was blown, and the doors of the drawing-room opened; and two and two the men accompanied the bridegroom, and placed him beneath the canopy under which the ceremony was to be performed; the women then led forward the bride in procession, whilst the trumpets blew a solemn march, and having conducted her three times round the bridegroom, she was then placed by his side.

The priest stepped beneath the canopy, and read aloud the marriage contract, and the bridegroom placed the ring on the hand of the bride, who immediately afterwards was enveloped in a silk garment, nor ought again to be visible before the morning after the marriage. A glass of wine was brought in; the priest consecrated it with a short prayer, and the bridegroom having drank it off, the glass was laid under his foot, and he crushed it to shivers, as a sign that as this glass could no more become intact, so should their fidelity never be sundered.

The deep, devotional silence was broken by the loud voices of congratulation, and the shrill, triumphant blast of the trumpets; the now united families embraced each other and the young couple; there was a cheerful sound of rejoicing, happy, human beings.

During the lively meal which followed, and at which the old people lived their youth over again, and in unrestrained merriment joked with the blushing bride and the happy bridegroom, while the younger portion of the company sought as it were, by their loud gaiety, to silence their own longings, Jacob found himself seated opposite to his uncle's youngest daughter, she whom he had instructed as a child. There sat she, with her pale, fine countenance, and with her large, dark eyes fixed upon him with a sort of inquisitive sympathy, as if she were endeavouring to read in his face traces of that happiness which the Christian maiden had bestowed upon him. His mind was strangely affected. The fatiguing walk which he had just had in the warm weather, and the painful agitation to which he had been subjected, had exhausted his physical powers, and given a morbid dominion to the soul. His body seemed to be in that state when the senses only slowly and reluctantly perform their offices, when the eye sees as through a mist, and sound comes to the ear as through empty space. The scene before him—all this gaiety and happiness, that young girl, with the wise, sympathetic eyes—all began to shape itself into a something of fearful unreality, as it were into a magic picture, which his guardian angel mournfully unrolled before him, as if to show him what had been intended for him. Every time his own peculiar circumstances presented themselves to his mind, a burning stab seemed to pass through his breast; he felt like the woman in the fairy tale, who, as a young girl, had eaten enchanted corn, and then beheld in church the unborn generations in long procession, advancing towards her with threatening glances, and laying their lifeless hands upon her breast, one after the other, until, with pain and terror of soul, she dropped down dead upon the church floor.

The sounds of merriment seemed to be passing away into the distance. Even the young girl appeared at length to him only as a shadowy form; whilst those dark eyes still fixed upon him seemed to bid him an eternal farewell. He reeled as he sat; he caught hold of the table to prevent his falling from his chair.

When he recovered consciousness, he saw himself surrounded by the whole company. Every one exhibited the most affectionate solicitude about him. Scarcely able to refrain from weeping, he thanked the Jews for their kindness, and hastened from the house, that he might not interrupt their mirth.

As he stood in the street, in the quiet evening air, amid the buzz of the passing crowd, he felt dejected and bewildered. He seemed to himself as if homeless; wherever he turned his thoughts, horror and fear seemed to meet him. At length he bethought himself of Martin, and a ray of comfort passed through his soul; he turned his steps therefore towards the hospital, where Martin lived.

As he approached his room, he heard voices as if in loud conversation; but it was not until he recognized Martin's voice amongst them that he entered.

In the middle of the large green-walled room stood a table, upon which were placed an ale bottle and the necessary glasses; at one corner of the table sat the host, with his long pipe; two of the guests sat in their loose house-coats on the window-sill, with their backs to the street; others lay smoking on the bed, or seated on the bed's foot; two only had chairs, because chairs were by no means plentiful in Martin's room.

Spite of the free and easy condition of the room, the countenances of the young men present bore an impression of energetic action, as if something had occurred which interested them in an unusual degree.

"Here is Bendixen!" exclaimed one; "here is something which will please him."

"Bendixen," cried König, raising himself from the bed, "have you heard the news? There is a revolution in France! Charles X. has been driven away! *Vive la République!* Look how he stands there, like an image of pure amazement!"

"Gröndal has proposed," cried another, "that the whole medical school should emigrate into France, and enrol itself in the Republican army!"

"Yes," said Gröndal, "I am sick of the poor botching work there is here. If it were not for a gallows-bird now and then gashing an overseer with one of those broad, heavy knives that they have in the house of correction, we should never see a regular wound. But there! Yes, if one went there, one could cut, and slash, and make as many wounds as one would. I fancy, now, that the Russians will march down against the French; and there are no patients that I like better than the Russians. One can trepan one of these fellows, and take away half his head, and he keeps alive for all that. I shall never forget a Russian sailor that we had last year; he had been smashed by a ship's boat, which had fallen on him. When I went to see him first, he was like mince-meat; three months afterwards I saw him, in the market, thrash a peasant of Amage, from whom he had stolen a cucumber."

"If we were but in Paris now," said one, "what a life it would be! The Jacobins mount their red caps, and declare war against the kings of the earth—perhaps against the King of Heaven also—and hurl a million of men against the foe. By Jemini! I can fancy how, throughout the whole day, the drums beat for a general muster, the alarm bells are rung from the towers of innumerable churches, and how, amid the universal commotion, the old regicides creep forth again from their hiding-places, and bask in the sunshine like gnats in the spring."

"Respect for regicides!" exclaimed König. "I should not mind myself being a regicide,—in an honest way, of course, according to the regular process—judgment and execution! If we had any other king than the white-headed Frederick! It is a cursed shame that we have not a king for practice."

"Folks must be contented with what they've got," said Gröndal. "I propose that we immediately march to Amalienborg. *Aux armes, citoyens!*"

"I must beg the doctor to step down; a new patient is just come," said the hospital servant, opening the door.

"I'll come immediately," said Gröndal, putting on his slippers.

"I'll go down and see the new comer," said another, and went out.

Several others followed the example, and before long Martin and Jacob were left alone.

"It will be better to light a candle," said Martin. "How the days shorten. A month ago, and it was light till ten o'clock. There! now we can see what we are talking about. What the deuce is come to you?" exclaimed he, the moment the candle-light fell upon Jacob. "You look as proud and resolute as—a king, I was going to say, only that class of folks is going down. The deuce! but it is very becoming to you. It is a long time since I have seen such a face as that on your shoulders."

"That may very well be," returned Jacob; "because at last I *will* do something. Martin, I shall go to France!"

"To France?" exclaimed Martin.

"Yes. I cannot stop here; I must get away from all this wretchedness. I must be off. It has come like a revelation, as

I stood here among all these healthful spirits, and felt to the very bottom of my soul my own unmanliness and weakness."

"But what has happened?" asked Martin.

"Nothing more than that she to-day let me know that I was a Jew, and wished that I would be baptized," replied Jacob.

"And will you then break with her for that?" asked Martin.

"Oh no!" said he. I know very well that it does not proceed from herself. But they have made me suffer beyond my power of endurance. I will go to France, and fight out a position for myself; then I will take her there,—I can live quietly with her there,—there they have all dark hair and dark eyes."

"And your beloved?" what do you think she will say to it?" asked Martin.

"If she loves me truly, she will wait for me."

"And if she will not wait for you?" asked Martin.

"Then she does not love me; then it will go madly enough; but it will be all the same if I stay," said Jacob.

"Bendixen," said Martin, "let us go out into the country on Sunday, then we can talk more about this scheme."

"I am seriously in earnest," returned Jacob; "if it is possible, I shall set off to-morrow."

"To-morrow evening I shall go and hear whither you have set off."

"Martin," said Jacob, "can you really, as my friend, advise me to remain here, and become utterly miserable?"

"I don't advise anything," returned he. "If I were in your place, I should perhaps do the same, and perhaps not; I cannot at all tell. But this is my true opinion: to-morrow, when you talk with your beloved, there will be many tears, and a grand reconciliation scene, and on Sunday you will go into the country,—but perhaps not with me."

"And I give you my word of honour that I shall set off," persisted Jacob.

"Hist! it is a good thing that no Christian heard you talk about your word of honour. You know very well that it sounds strange for a Jew to talk of his word of honour. But so be it, man! If you really will set off, then—yes, at all events, one faithful friend will accompany you on board. And I will, this last evening, drink brotherhood with you, dear Bendixen."

CHAPTER XXXI.

When he woke, the resolution of the foregoing evening lay heavily and oppressively upon his heart; as soon as he thought of giving it up he breathed more easily. When, however, he took a review of the circumstances, he soon became again convinced that there remained nothing for him but to go.

For a long time he walked up and down, and examined it at all points; he then set out to get his passport before he went to meet Thora. It is thus that people often, when they feel themselves to be weak, strengthen themselves by energetic action.

Lieutenant Engborg on the preceding evening paid close attention to Jacob and Thora; he was struck by their appearance as they entered the garden parlour, and by the manner in which they parted. He thought the time was now come for him to make a diversion in his own favour. What he really wished for was, perhaps, not exactly clear to himself, but something, he flattered himself, would occur to his advantage.

People are, in a general way, not nearly so bad as their actions, else there would be no going unarmed along the street. When any one, for example, will take another's beloved from him, he does not think of committing a robbery, but merely says to himself, "That poor girl is unhappy with that churl, who does not know her value; she would be a good deal happier with me;" and he consoles himself by thinking that in any case the other only gets the reward he deserves.

Lieutenant Engborg watched very attentively for Thora, as she drove into town with her father, and then followed to the counting-house whither they were going.

She sate in a little room alone, waiting for Jacob; she was out of spirits, and had some anxiety about their meeting, after the occurrence of the foregoing day.

A knock was heard at the door, and the lieutenant, bowing most respectfully, entered. She felt a sort of relief that it was not Jacob—that she had a respite; and there was, perhaps, some trace of this in the tone with which she exclaimed, "Is it you, Lieutenant Engborg?"

The lieutenant put down this shade of tone to his own advantage, and replied, "I knew that you would come into town this morning, and therefore I could not deny myself the pleasure of inquiring after your health; you seemed so unwell last evening, when I left you."

Was it possible, that amid sorrows and disagreeables, Thora's affection had decreased, or, at all events, was not at all times equally steadfast? Or is it true, as is said, that the most constant of women, with a true housewifely instinct, always wishes to have a lover in store? Or was there, merely in the tender tones of the lieutenant's voice, something which was consolatory to Thora in her present state of mind? Or—but enough: instead of calling her father in, she contented herself with saying, "I expect my betrothed every moment; it will be unpleasant to him to find you here."

"Oh! it is only out of dread of him that she is afraid of a tête-à-tête," thought the lieutenant.

"I heard you last night," replied he, "appoint twelve o'clock for his meeting with you here, and it is now only half-past eleven. In any case, the cause of my coming here is of a nature which might easily satisfy Mr. Bendixen. I only wished to tell you the sorrow I felt in seeing you so unwell, and to express a hope that it was but a temporary indisposition, which the affectionate care of your betrothed will soon chase away."

At these words, Thora's eyes involuntarily filled with tears; she sat with her pocket-handkerchief to her eyes, and with her other hand motioned for the lieutenant to leave her; but instead of going, he siezed her hand passionately, and kissed it.

At that moment Jacob Bendixen entered the room.

All three stood for some seconds unmoveable. The lieutenant regained his self-possession the first; he took his hat, and with a little bow to Jacob, was about to pass through the door. Jacob took a step or two backwards, and the door closed between them and Thora.

"Wait a moment, lieutenant," said Jacob, and followed him; "what business brought you here?"

"If the master of the house demands an account of my conduct, I will give it," replied Engborg, and continued to move on.

Jacob, however, laid his hand upon his shoulder, and said, "But perhaps you can give me an account of your visit to my betrothed? Do not be in such a hurry, lieutenant."

"Well," retorted the lieutenant, with a malicious smile, and turning round to Jacob, "I was seeking for the best means of consoling a poor young girl who has the misfortune to be engaged to a bear."

Jacob trembled with rage; but he still preserved sufficient command over himself to say, in a tolerably calm voice, "Allow me to tell you, lieutenant, that you are a dishonourable fellow! I am ready any moment to give you satisfaction."

The lieutenant made a step backward, bowed profoundly, and said, "Many thanks for the intended honour; but, as an officer, you see plainly—a duel with a Jew"——

Scarcely was this word pronounced, when the lieutenant felt the gripe of a firm hand upon him, and himself swung through the large room in which they stood, against the door they had left. There the lieutenant collected himself, and made a movement as if to order him away; but there was in Jacob's countenance, as he turned towards him, an expression of such mortal hatred, such almost frenzied passion, that he rushed from the room, and was out of sight in a moment.

Jacob stood waiting for some moments, as if to recover himself. He listened. He imagined that Thora would come out to him, if she were innocent of this meeting with Engborg, as he wished to believe her, although appearances were so much against her; and that she ought to explain all, and ought also to make the first advances. She, meanwhile, sate within, almost senseless from shame and terror, expecting every moment that he would open the door.

He waited still some moments longer, but she came not.

He opened the door of the lobby which led from the room where he stood, closed it heavily behind him, and went slowly down the stairs; at every step he took, expecting to hear her call.

Outside the gate, he waited yet again. Not a sound was to be heard; the great building stood as if there were no life within it. He repented already; he might yet have gone back, but pride withheld him.

For many hours he walked backwards and forwards in his room, listening to every sound—standing still at the least noise in the passage, in the hope that it might be a message from Thora. At length some one approached his door—some one tapped on it, and in walked Martin.

"No signs of the journey!" exclaimed Martin, as he stood in the doorway.

"You will soon see that there are," said Jacob.

"Oh, I hoped that it was all over. She will write; the family will consent, and everything will be as it was," said Martin.

"Yes, she may write," said Jacob to himself; "let her write and excuse herself, when she hears that I am gone! All will be right with my journey." And then, speaking in a more decided voice, he replied, "We shall see whether or not I set off!"

"At all events, I shall not take leave of you for longer than eight days. There is something cursed in taking leave for a long time. We will only take leave of each other for a week."

"Shall I carry out your luggage, sir? it is quite time," said the man-servant, coming into the room.

When Jacob sat in the cabin after Martin had left him, and with an almost disbelieving glance regarded the objects which surrounded him as something strangely foreign—as something wholly disconnected from himself, and which would of themselves vanish away—he was suddenly reminded, by their swinging motion, that the vessel was already under sail. Now, for the first moment, he felt that he was separated from Thora. With the anguish of despair he rushed upon deck, as if he would spring to land; but the ship was already on her way.

The perfect impossibility of return produced an almost pacifying effect upon his mind. The vast, calm surface of the ocean, ploughed only by the vessel's keel, awoke a momentary disquiet—it was as if smoothed by the Creator himself: thus it must be.

The vessel glided on its secure, rapid course, past large and small craft. A fresh sea-breeze began to blow. One of the passengers struck fire, and lighted his cigar, with a satisfaction as if nothing more important existed. The sun burst for a moment from the clouds, and shone upon the receding city and the verdant shores. The scene involuntarily animated Jacob; his blood flowed with an agreeable glow through his veins; he felt himself for a moment light and free, and in the inmost recess of his soul he exclaimed, "Now I am at liberty! I will forth into the wide, glorious world, and do battle for my whole being. How many there are who at this moment might envy me!"

CHAPTER XXXII.

THE dilgence in which Jacob was seated rolled through the barriers into Paris.

His inquisitive searching glance met in the streets, and on the boulevards, pedestrians, men of business, porters, municipal officers, but no *émeute*. The shops stood open—customers went in and out—a division of the National Guard marched along to the beat of drum, and with the tri-coloured flag displayed; but nobody paid any attention to them.

When he had placed his luggage in his hotel, he went out to inquire about the revolution; but there was nothing to learn. Here and there lay a heap of stones which had been used for barricades; but the paviors were already fixing them again in the earth with their rammers; now and then he came to a house which had been injured by the firing—but even here the masons were at work putting all again into order.

Jacob sought for the French people—the great people who had so lately in these very streets dethroned a king; but he saw only passers-by as in Copenhagen—calm, peaceful pedestrians. He sought for the republican bands—they who, at the first glance, he hoped, would see in him one of themselves, and receive him as a brother—there were none; he himself was no more than a mere pedestrian to the passers-by. Nobody noticed him; nobody troubled themselves about him—him who had risked the happiness of his life to hasten to them.

He visited the Chamber of Deputies; they were disputing violently, passionately—about a word, a single letter of the Charter. He hastened to the courts of justice; they were passing sentence on a thief who had disturbed the public safety.

His brain seemed to swim; he began to imagine that he must have sold his soul to the devil for a cheat.

He had wished so ardently to throw himself into the most violent tumult of life—into combat and danger, that he might win honour and renown. He went to the bureau of the Minister of War, that he might enrol himself as an officer in the Algerian service—but not being a Frenchman, he could not become a soldier!

He had hastened hither with his blood boiling and his muscles strung for action, and all at once he beheld himself destined to do nothing!

His disappointed tortured mind turned back with redoubled force to Denmark, and to those whom he had left. He put one thing to another, so that it seemed to him the most natural thing in the world that he must have letters. Martin would certainly tell Wilhelm Fangel where he was gone—Wilhelm would mention it to his family—they would write letters to him under cover to the Danish Ambassador.

He went to the ambassador's hotel. The secretary assured him, with the utmost politeness, that no such letters had been received. It was a painful effort to Jacob, whose heart seemed breaking, to return the politeness of the secretary, who accompanied him to the steps.

Instinct, or frenzy, drove him to the post-office. There was a sort of consolation to him in seeing letters—in being able to convince himself that letters still existed in the world. What envy he felt, one evening, of a young man who went and fetched thence a whole packet of letters!

Should he, after all, turn round and go back of his own accord to Denmark, like a schoolboy who had played truant? And perhaps then, the day after he had set off, a letter would come. No, he must remain—alone, without acquaintance, friends, or employment—alone, with himself, his disappointed hopes, his defeated wishes, his gnawing remembrances.

He threw himself, alone as he was, into the countless whirling throng. Many an evening when he, unconsciously as it were, spoke aloud to himself in his room, he was startled by the sound of his own voice, which he had not heard through the day.

It is a weary thing to be alone in the desert—but still more oppressive to be alone in a large, populous, noisy city. All the happiness of the world spread out before the eye; wealth exhibited in all its manifold temptation and attractiveness; equipages rolling past in which are seated beautiful, splendidly-attired women; friend walking arm-in-arm with friend; lovers exchanging affectionate glances; neighbours greeting one another cordially;—all this to the stranger is dead. He is excluded from it altogether; it is as if he did not belong to the human race. He seldom is placed at the board where others partake of the jovial meal—others who trouble themselves nothing about him, and with whom he would rather not eat. He wishes for nothing else than to hide himself in some desert, or at the bottom of the river which rushes through the crowded city.

Suicide!—This is the thought which perhaps suggests itself to many a heart amid such anguish; or liquor, drunken forgetfulness of all their sorrows. But Jacob was a Jew; and these people have a singular submissive patience. Perhaps they first learned this patient endurance at the time when the Egyptian, Pharaoh, compelled them to make bricks and find their own materials; and in later times the Europeans have known how to keep it in practice. They do not get drunk; but their passions are strong, like the Orientals; like the bearded Arabs, whose meal is a handful of dates washed down by a draught of water from the spring, but whose tent is full of slaves and luxury.

Accident, however—that stone which thrown into the stagnant water of human life so often awakes it into motion when nothing else will—at length befriended even Jacob.

One day as he was passing through the Rue Montorgueil, that street in which one of Charles X.'s generals had to defend himself against a shower of balls and paving-stones aimed at him by men women and children, and where the stones of the barricade were not wholly laid down to rest, as loyal paving-stones ought to be—he became observant of a disturbance, at the point where the street widens out, and branches off into two other streets. The thought that perhaps the flames of the revolution had again burst forth, awoke the spirit of life within him, and with hasty steps he approached the assembled crowd.

In the midst of the throng lay a carriage overturned, and the coachman on the ground enraged by the blows which were given him by the equally enraged men in blouses. Some of the spectators rapidly related the occasion of this scene. A carriage had driven fiercely down the street, when a crowd of men in blouses, who stood and conversed together, pointed at the driver and said something, in a tone of derision, about aristocrats who kept equipages, and compelled their coachman to drive among the remains of the barricades. In return, he muttered something about "*la canaille*,"—on which he was dragged down from his box, the alarmed horses sprang aside, and the carriage was overturned as he saw.

Jacob fancied that he heard a half-suppressed shriek from the interior of the carriage. He sprang forward; and having with some difficulty succeeded in forcing open the carriage-door, he beheld two ladies, not at all in an enviable condition, the one tumbled upon the other, and who were making vain attempts to raise themselves. Animated by ardour, which is so easily excited when the human powers have for a long time been in a state of repose, Jacob exclaimed to the men in blouses, "There are ladies here! Frenchmen, will you make women responsible for the crimes of kings?"

It is one of the most amiable features of the French character, that even the lowest among them has an inborn sentiment of chivalry and magnanimity. The carriage was raised immediately, and the coachman escaped with the beating he had already received.

The ladies could not easily regain their composure, spite of all the apologies which were respectfully offered by the men in blouses. They besought their rescuer to drive home with them.

After a little while the terror of the ladies abated; they were not at all hurt, and presently the younger of the two became eloquent in her expressions of gratitude. With all the loquacity of a Parisian she scarcely permitted Jacob to say a word.

"You have saved us from Heaven knows what misfortune! You came like an angel from Heaven! What horrible men! Did you see one of them? what eyes he had! his black beard, though, was almost handsome, but so wild! Thank God, that you came! But it is Baron Descamps: it is his fault. He is so careful about me; he will not allow me in this disturbed time either to go to or from the theatre. I am an actress, sir, the *prima donna* at the Vaudeville Theatre. But he is an old fool, the good Baron Descamps; he sends his carriage for me; I get in and—*voila tout!*"

With these words she glanced at Jacob with her large, black eyes.

"Leonie!" said the elder lady, in a reproachful tone.

"I said what I think," returned Leonie; "I have told him to his face that he is an old fool. Only think, sir, a man in his good fiftieth year—and he wears a wig! But that's all one, however—only I shall not forgive him this accident with the carriage; he shall pay for that! This is my house, sir, *Rue Faubourg Poissonniere, No. 3; Demoiselle Courtois.* I beg you will honour me with a call. I shall not play to-morrow evening —to-morrow evening at nine o'clock; it is fixed. Adieu, sir knight!"

CHAPTER XXXIII.

"Oh, how charming it is! See how the houses fly past us! Nay, see how the horses gallop along in the omnibuses; they will outgo us—à demain, thou good horse! Take care!—ah, thank Heaven, that's good! Nay, you drive very well!"

"On, on, thou French horse! There! trot away as fast as thou wilt! On, on!"

"Hyp, hyp!" cried Leonie, and laughed merrily, whilst she pinched Jacob's arm.

"Where shall we drive to?" asked she, when having got into the throng of carriages they were compelled to go more slowly.

"I don't know—to the world's end!" replied he. "If the horse had wings, we would drive up into the air towards the sun, like Phaeton. Do you know the fable of Phaeton who tumbled down?"

"Ah, have you also heard about the handsome Phaeton? Yes, how sorry I was! They broke into the coach-house, and took it out for the barricades. And a cannon-ball went through it, and shivered it to a thousand pieces. Oh!"

"What's amiss?" asked he.

"Do you see that little man in the light coat? That is M. Arthur, he who composed my Spanish Bolero; won't he challenge you because he sees you driving me?"

"Then, does he sometimes drive you out?"

"Oh, he lisps, and he smokes so many cigars! He is now courting Pauline. Oh, now I know where we will drive to. We will drive to St. Germain! Pauline is going there with her lover. Poor girl, how serious she is grown since she has become acquainted with him. They go about admiring nature and the fine arts; and I really believe they have been to church Yes, we'll meet them at St. Germain. I will introduce you to him. But pray tell what is your name?"

"Bendixen."

"Ben——! Bening——! Have you no other name? But now I think of it, ours is a very hasty acquaintance. I have only seen you once; but we are very good friends for all that. Oh it will be glorious fun! I will pretend that you are a prince! Pauline is very proud because her lover is the son of the manager of the theatre. I will overpower them; I will confound, annihilate them with a prince!"

"Is that the Palace of St. Germain?" inquired he.

"Yes, I believe so. Look, that little pavillion that we are now coming to was built upon the spot where Louis XIV. was born beneath the open sky—yes, we are all human. By our Lady of Loretto! there is Pauline with her little man! Pull up, let us alight."

Jacob extended his hand to help her from the carriage. She put out first one little foot, and then the other, as if she was afraid; he must catch her in his arms, she said, for she was so very timid.

The other couple approached. Leonie assumed an important air, and said:

"My Prince! allow me to introduce to you my friend, Mademoiselle Pauline, and her cousin Monsieur Albert. Mademoiselle, Monsieur Albert,—his Highness the Prince Ben——. I beg your pardon, Prince, but your name has escaped me."

"Bendixen."

"Prince de Ben-dix-sen. They are rather barbarous, horrible names which these Russian princes have,—but he is immensely rich," whispered she to Pauline, who, as well as M. Albert, stood in the profoundest humility.

"Prince!" again began Leonie, "allow me to ask whether you would ride upon a mule or a dragon. You know, Prince, that we young ladies always ride in the park of St. Germain."

"Whichever would be most agreeable to Mademoiselle."

They went to the man who let out horses and mules; and when Jacob and Leonie had each mounted a horse, Pauline said, "Albert, if the Prince de Bendik, or whatever his name is, condescends to ride, you must do so too."

"I will not ride," said Albert, evidently displeased.

"Will you, then, lose the opportunity of making so desirable an acquaintance?"

"I am not ambitious."

"But I am!" said Pauline, with tears in her eyes; "and if you will not ride to-day, we will part for ever."

"Pauline!" exclaimed he, "I no longer know you! my sensible, quiet Pauline——"

"I am not sensible; I am not quiet!" interrupted she. "I will have a mule. Will you have one or not?"

"Let us have two mules," said M. Albert, with a sigh, addressing the man who let them out.

Leonie and Jacob, in the meantime, had galloped down the park, as fast as their animals would go.

Leonie's was a spirited creature, and Jacob said, as he mounted his, "It shall be a steeple-chase; let go—away!"

Before long, Leonie lost her pocket-handkerchief, then her little scarf, and lastly, her bonnet; after that, she began to shriek out—"Stop him! Oh, I will never ride again! Save my life!—Ah!"

And down she fell from her horse, and rolled among the

leaves. At the first shriek, Jacob stopped his horse and leapt off. When he came to Leonie, she sprung up, and received him with peals of laughter.

"Did I not do it beautifully?" said she. "That's the way I always do when I am tired of riding."

Pauline and her cousin joined them; they also dismounted, and the animals trotting back of themselves, they all four walked leisurely together, amusing each other with laughter and merry talk.

When they came to the carriage, Leonie said, "Let us all drive back to Paris, and sup with Phillippe. He has the best *sole Normand frite* in all Paris, and red hermitage at six francs the bottle."

They did as she said.

CHAPTER XXXIV.

"I fancy that Baron Descamps cannot endure me."

These words were said in a little elegantly furnished room, something between a drawing-room and boudoir. Everything in it was small, and highly decorated, as if especially selected for a lady's use. The round table covered with exquisite copperplate engravings and lithographic prints; the sofas and armed chairs covered with crimson velvet, a work table, a luxurious *chaise-longue*, and lastly a bookcase of rich rose-wood, with glass doors, which was filled with the richly bound works of Corneille, Racine, Victor Hugo, &c.

Leonie sate by the window, and was examining a new dress; Jacob sat at the table turning over a book of prints.

At his remark about Baron Descamps, she suddenly lifted up her head and said laughingly, "He is a good old fellow, and he is very fond of me; it is quite excusable if he does not like you!"

"I am really sorry for the poor baron," said Jacob.

Leonie burst into still louder laughter. "There, you sit so gravely and make a fool of the baron!" said she, "charming, you ought to have been an actor!"

"But I am quite serious in what I say," said he, and rose from his seat.

A cloud passed suddenly over Leonie's countenance; she gazed fixedly at him for a few moments, and then said tenderly, almost beseechingly, "But you are not going to break off our acquaintance? Ah, now I think of it, you have been very gloomy and self-absorbed for several days; I have not seen one of those happy smiles which were so frequent when first I knew you? What have I done? Do you no longer love me?"

"Leonie!" replied Jacob, "I never did love you."

At these words all Leonie's cheerfulness returned; she clapped her hands and exclaimed, "Oh, this little friend of mine is a coquette! He is an original! Men in general vow that they will love a poor girl for ever!—he says he has never loved her—oh, it is delightful; just for once, by way of change."

"Leonie," continued he, "endeavour if you cannot, for once, find a chord in your soul upon which a deeper tone can be struck. I have not deceived you, and yet I have never loved you. My heart belongs to one alone; to a young girl in the North; there will never be room in it for another. Unfortunate circumstances have separated us, and I have left her, have gone alone and forsaken out into the world. Tortured in mind, miserable unto death, I met with you. I was a stranger here and without friends; accident brought us acquainted, and you have done all in your power to make my life pleasant. In your society I have endeavoured to find oblivion, to drown every recollection of her whom I love. But these recollections have only gained renewed strength in their temporary rest; they are now mightier than I am, and with them comes repentance for sins which are beyond your knowledge. Oh! I seem to myself like a miserable criminal!"

"Poor young man!" said Leonie, derisively, "have I been thy tempter?"

"I do not believe that you are capable of understanding me," said Jacob.

"You have deceived me!" returned she in an angry voice. "It is not true, I am sure, that you have been only a short time in Paris. You have made believe that you spoke bad French;

but now when you are in earnest, you forget yourself and speak like a Frenchman!"

"The passion of the soul," replied he, "can always find the right word. It makes the most unlearned man eloquent."

Leonie was silent.

"When I was quite alone," continued he, "you hospitably opened your doors to me. When no human being troubled themselves about me, you gave me your friendship, and enabled me to pass many pleasant hours in your society. You made inquiries neither about country, race, nor religion, and although I cannot love you, I shall ever remain eternally grateful to you."

Leonie approached him nearer; she gazed still more fixedly at him, as if she began to understand him, and then said, "You suffer, my poor friend; the world has been unkind to you! I only have been compassionate, and have soothed the wounded heart."

"Yes, I do suffer," said he, and laid his hand on his brow.

"Stay with me!" cried she, "forget those who have used you ill!—stay with me!—I will be faithful to you—I will receive no more presents from Baron Descamps—I will leave the theatre; I will work for you, if it is needful; I will be your nurse, your friend, your comforter; stay with me!"

"Would that you could only feel how fervently grateful I am to you," returned he, "but it is impossible; I must hence! Better by far that I wander again solitary about the streets than—"

Leonie was exhausted; she sat down and wept.

Jacob approached her, and said, "There is nothing more to say; I must now go; farewell, Leonie. Think of me as a guest whom your house received and entertained, and to whom you have given far more than board and lodging—human kindness.

I must go. Some other guest will come to whom you likewise may show pity."

He said this out of his full heart, never thinking of the satire there was in the words.

"And who should come?" said she, raising her tearful countenance; "that old Baron Descamps? I will not see him; I hate him; I detest him!"

"Oh, do not go thus!" again besought she, as he was about to leave her. She threw herself into his arms, and fainted. He called her *bonne*, tenderly unloosed her unconscious embrace, and left the house.

Sunk in deep thought and dejection, he walked mechanically along the streets. Sorrow and yearning came back into his soul like old acquaintances, and resumed their accustomed places. At every step he took he was saluted by a new recollection; and although it occasioned him pain, yet was it dear to him.

A crowd of thoughts rushed into his soul; he walked slowly and dreamingly along, and involuntarily recited some verses of a song, which until then he seemed never to have paid much attention to:—

> "This brave apparel canst thou wear,
>   Which Thora Hjörtur once possessed;
> She chose it for thy Sunday gear,
>   A maid more fair than all the rest.
>
> "And with her hands as fair as snow,
>   Each seam thus skilfully she wrought;
> Now neath the sod she lieth low,—
>   And a new love claims all thy thought."

He continued to repeat the words half-aloud to himself, until they became confused in his memory, and he could no longer recal them.

He had now, without himself being aware of it, reached the Palais Royal, and entered the garden, where children and elderly people went and enjoyed themselves in the mild sunshine.

Suddenly he struck against a man, and, as he involuntarily looked up to offer an apology, he recognized the Baron Descamps, walking with another elderly gentleman. He remained standing before the baron; Leonie seemed to him already as something in the past, and the baron like a remembrance of her.

"No offence! nothing at all to excuse!" said the baron, with some vexation, about to continue his way; but when he observed Jacob's melancholy appearance, an agreeable hope was suggested to his mind; he paused, and said,

"But what ails you? You look really as if your mistress had jilted you!"

"That is not the case, however," replied Jacob, attempting to smile; "and if I had a mistress, I should, perhaps, be more disposed to be faithless to her."

"You are not inclined to travel?" asked the baron, eagerly.

"Very much, if I only could."

"If in any way I could be of service to you," said the baron.

"That you can!" exclaimed Jacob, as an idea came into his mind. You have influence, baron; you are a deputy; obtain a post for me as officer in Algiers."

"When will you set off?" asked the baron, eagerly.

"In one hour after I receive the commission.

"Within four-and-twenty hours you shall have it. Here is my hand upon it. But now, on my honour, you shall first dine with me and my friend—Count Planhol—Monsieur Bendigsen; come, let us go to *Befaur's*."

So saying, he took Jacob's arm, and, with a beaming countenance, entered with him into a restaurant, and ordered a magnificent dinner.

CHAPTER XXXV

THERE was a storm in the Mediterranean. The frigate was tossed about as if the sea made of it a plaything for its billows. Who would have believed that it could have been so stormy and cold in the Mediterranean Sea—upon the sea which is garlanded with dates, palms, and orange groves?

On the morning of the twelfth day after they had set sail, the frigate cast anchor in the Bay of Algiers. Such of the passengers as were awoke by the regular tramp of the sailors around the capstan, betook themselves to the deck.

In the dawning light of day, the land appeared like a huge white spectre which was ascending out of the dark blue sea. To the right of the ship a steep headland ran out into the ocean, and on its summit, at some distance from each other, burned two fiery cressets on tall poles; between these two ascended the moon, red as blood, above the mountain top, so that at the moment it looked as if, in Africa, that land of enchantment, the moon also stood upon a pole. Abrupt gusts of wind came from the land, now strong and cold, now soft and mild, bearing with them the odour of unknown trees and flowers.

When the day had fully dawned, the sea became animated as it wore, and the frigate entered the harbour. The sun flung down his red beams upon the white city, which wound up the mountain in long terraces; upon the ruins of the fortress, and the distant mountain top. An animated crowd thronged the shore: men in white turbans, or red caps; Jews in long robes and with long ill-kept beards; and talkative, inquisitive Frenchmen; whilst a solitary Turk sat on a step by the water's edge smoking his long pipe, and watching the newly-arrived vessel with a grave, immovable aspect.

"Thus, then, I am now in Africa," said Jacob, as he set foot on shore; "now it is my fatherland!"

He had imagined that immediately on his arrival in Africa he should be sent against the enemy, and thus at once should be brought into the absorbing business of life,—and instead, he found himself appointed to garrison duty.

An insignificant conversation,—a scratch of the pen of the War Minister's Secretary,—had placed him in a regiment which lay in Algiers itself. At this new stroke of misfortune, it seemed to Jacob as if at a certain point his whole existence must have had a shock, so that its mechanism had become wholly out of order, and thus that it could no longer keep time with good luck.

The French officers regarded him with a certain feeling of dislike as a foreigner, who had been thrust in among them through the influence of his high connections, and waited, therefore, for proofs of his bravery and general ability, before they made any friendly advances towards him. The only officer in the regiment who approached him with consideration and good-will, was a Pole, of the name of Josinski. He was a young man, of a pale, melancholy countenance, but of tall and powerful make, and the best rider in the regiment. He spent much time with Jacob, and his conversation was principally about Poland.

"We Poles," said he, on one occasion, "serve France in all her wars indiscriminately; we are like the little Savoyards who go to Paris and work like slaves that they may support their poor parents. But we, alas! cannot send to our fatherland the fruits of our bondage. If death meets us in the field of battle all we can do is to cast a beseeching glance towards France, and pray of her not to forget Poland."

"You will seldom," said he, on another occasion, "see a Pole smile. Our awful national miseries have reached us in our mother's womb, and given a depression to the soul, from which it cannot raise itself. Oh, you do not know what it is to have no country! For a hundred years we Poles have been in the condition of the Jews, who, scattered over the whole world, still preserve legends of their holy land, to which a Saviour is one day to reconduct them!"

Jacob made no reply; and Josinski shortly afterwards began to speak of the life in Algiers, and the murderous, wearisome garrison duty.

"Neither do I find it very entertaining here," said Jacob. "I hastened hither with a burning desire for activity,—for the most exciting scenes of human life; and now I must pass my days in the most barren inactivity which I ever knew. If I am not on duty, I go to sleep to prevent my thinking, and the more I sleep, the sleepier I become."

"If one could only ride out hunting in the mountains," said Josinski, "for hunting there is! But then, instead of bringing anything home in one's own bag, one runs the risk of having one's own head carried home in the pocket of a Bedouin! And the French say that they have conquered this country!"

One night the drums were heard to beat in the city; the garrison hastened to the scene of action; men and cattle in confused throngs were entering at the city gates. The Arabs had made an attack in the plain, plundered and murdered many, and had spread terror even to the walls of the city.

A small troop marched out to chastise the foe, whose light bands vanished as rapidly as they had come, leaving behind them smoking ruins and headless trunks to bear witness to their course, whilst the French troop endeavoured by a forced march to overtake them.

The wild Kabyles rushed down from the mountains in aid of their Mussulmen brethren; and the desert sent forth its Bedouins in their white, fluttering burnuses. Strengthened by these allies, the enemy formed again for attack, and skirmishing took place through the whole day between the French advance guard and single troops of the foe. In the meantime, a general battle was to be fought on the morrow.

In the French camp all was in the most lively movement; for the nearness of the enemy and the consciousness of the approaching fight excited every one alike. The soldiers sat or lay stretched out round a large fire, which had been kindled as a defence against the keen night wind which blew from Atlas. Some were drinking and making merry; others talked in an under voice with their companions about the beautiful France, and their beloved at home; while others again—and they were mostly the youngest soldiers—talked loudly and uninterruptedly about all imaginable things; they were in a state of feverish excitement, like lottery gamblers the night before the drawing of the prizes; the elder soldiers, who had been more frequently in battle, talked about the enemy and his mode of warfare, and gave good advice to their younger companions. One old soldier, of the time of Napoleon, had assembled a group of listeners around a separate fire, and entertained them by stories of the glorious old times, when the man with the little hat informed his soldiers the night before the battle that they would be victorious.

The officers walked about in the camp, in lively and loud conversation about the Boulevards of Paris, as if the war did not concern them, but only the common soldiers; and yet the soldiers knew very well that on the following day their officers would advance before them against the enemy.

After awhile the animation subsided; the soldiers wrapped themselves in their gray cloaks, and stretched themselves on the ground before the fires to sleep. The watchword of the sentinel at the extreme post was alone heard through the camp, or the bark of the jackall from the surrounding desert; while now and then a wild, dull cry in the distance showed that the foe was awake.

"Have you already been in battle?" asked Josinski from Jacob, as they sat together in the tent.

"No; I sit here and think what a strange thing it is that I have never yet even heard a regular cannonade; and yet it seems to me as if I was quite familiar with it. I cannot perfectly understand my own feelings, nor yet convince myself but that, some way or other, I must have some remembrance of it."

"It is probably some remembrance of your military exercises, which you imagined as an actual battle. I could almost envy you. You have still before you to experience that proud, wild excitement which seizes upon one at the first salvo, when the cannons thunder, the balls whistle through the air, and blood spouts forth,—that bacchanalian, bloodthirsty horror, when every second may bring death, and one hurls oneself against the foe! The first battle resembles one's first love. One is almost lost in one's own feelings. Afterwards, with use, one becomes much cooler, and more indifferent, and thinks rather about how one behaves in the eyes of those who are observing us."

"I will not say anything about myself," said Jacob; "but I hope that I shall not show myself to be a coward. I have longed for this moment."

An ordnance officer entered the tent. The general had

received despatches, which were accompanied by a letter-bag; here was a letter for Lieutenant Bennigsen.

"Perhaps a letter from some true, fair lady in Paris," said the Pole, with an arch smile; "I will leave you alone."

The letter was sealed with black, and bore outward signs of having travelled far and wide before it had found traces of him to whom it was addressed. It was from Benjamin, the old clerk of his father, and announced, after long circumlocution, the death of the old man. After this came a long statement of money matters, and how the trustworthy Benjamin had so placed the capital as to secure its producing a good return.

Death is a fearful reminder; and now every grief which he had occasioned to his father stood at once clearly before him. All the memories of his childhood returned with extraordinary distinctness, and the picture of his still youthful, though lost life, was spread out before him. On this his thoughts, wrung by repentance, turned to his father's death-bed, and to his long-deceased mother. He saw her again, so gentle, so pale! He saw his father in his loneliness as his last hour approached! What was his having been alone in a foreign city in comparison with his father being alone on his death-bed? His anxious eyes had sought with infinite longings for his only son, and his last thoughts had been tortured, perhaps, by the agonizing certainty that that son would never pray a kadisch over him when he lay in the grave.

"But I will pray for him," cried Jacob, whilst tears streamed down his cheeks; "let them hear on the outside that I am a Jew. What care I? Yes, I am a Jew!"

And he began to repeat, aloud and fervently, the prayer for the soul of the dead:—

"Thou shalt, oh, my father, have a kadisch yet again!" said he, when he had ended; and once more he repeated, out of his full heart, the Jewish formula of blessing for the dead, and blessing of the God by whom death is sent.

But the prayers had as little power as the tears to relieve Jacob's heart. Much more was necessary than prayers once, or even twice repeated, before the burden could be removed from his soul;—there was a whole life for which he had to weep. Nor was there a single point in future on which to sustain hope; because his love, even if the Christian maiden continued faithful to him, seemed hopeless, and, at his moment, in the highest degree sinful.

The drums and trumpets summoned the troops into motion; they were formed into long line, according to the general's plan of attack. Jacob mounted the horse which his orderly brought to his tent, mechanically, and as if in a state of stupor. He saw, with a feeling of perfect indifference, the blue tops of the distant mountains shining in the morning sun; and without any feeling either of fear or warlike joy, he heard the wild signal-cries of the enemy, while the earth thundered beneath the hoofs of the cavalry.

The orders of the colonel were, that the regiment, after making a circuit, should post itself on a level plain. Arrived here, a troop of Bedouins suddenly presented itself, which, covered by a ditch and wild fence, seemed ready to oppose the French cavalry, pointing against them with their long muskets. Head after head, in innumerable multitudes, presented itself, their white bernuses fluttering in the morning wind,—their white caps making a strange contrast with their brown countenances and black beards. At the near approach of the enemy, the foremost row rose up to their full height, in their long white attire. Jacob involuntarily checked his horse. Thus stood the Jews clothed in the synagogue, on the great day of the Feast of Reconciliation; thus also were they laid in their coffins. It was as if his father stood there, arisen from his burial-ground, multiplied a hundred fold; or as if all the holy Jews, newly risen from their graves, were thus assembled against him.

The signal was given for the attack; but if it had cost him his soul's eternal happiness, he could not at that moment have fired upon those beings. The trumpets sounded; the fire-arms poured forth their murderous contents; and the troop which Jacob commanded flew past him to right and left into the smoke-cloud of battle, and he alone remained immovable.

It was but for a few moments. He regained his consciousness, and with this became aware of his position, and began to think what his companions—what the army would say to his conduct. He put spurs to his horse, and compelled it, without looking before him, over dead and dying, friend and foe, in wild career after the regiment. But the regiment had already chased away the light foe, and were now recalled by the general from the fruitless pursuit.

It did not escape Jacob that he had sunk in the opinion of his companions. Hitherto he had not enjoyed more of their regard than it was necessary for them to pay him as an officer; now, however, he was despised by them. This was not shown by words, it is true; but he was too much accustomed to the silent insult for it to escape him for a moment. They have, in Danish, a simple but significant expression for him who is an object of contempt or ridicule; they say, "He is crushed." It is really so; even the body seems to feel the humiliation; it contracts, as if it would make itself as small as it could, that it might hide itself.

In the afternoon, when the army had again betaken itself to the camp, Jacob walked backwards and forwards in the most solitary of its outskirts. He felt dejected; he knew himself to be dishonoured in the eye of the world, without being so to his own conscience. In vain, however, sought he for the means of explaining his conduct, or excusing himself to the world. He was driven almost to despair by that fruitless agitation of mind—embittered both against himself and the whole world.

"But it is a good thing, after all, that they do not know that I am a Jew," said he to himself, "else they would say the Jew Bendixen is a coward; now, at least, I have the satisfaction of knowing that they merely say, the man, the officer, Bendixen, is a coward."

A French officer came up to him, but passed him without appearing to see him. The blood boiled in Jacob's veins; all his hatred concentrated itself in hatred of this man.

"It cannot be that you did not see me, De Terry," exclaimed he.

The officer stopped, turned towards him, and replied, with an air of the most perfect surprise, "Ah, in truth, Mr. Bennigsen, you are right; I did not see you. I really believe that you have at times the power of making yourself invisible."

"How am I to understand that?" demanded Jacob, with quivering lips.

"Just as you please," replied the officer, with the most polite smile.

"Then permit me to send one of my friends to you," said Jacob.

"Mr. Bennigsen, I am at your service, with the greatest pleasure."

Jacob went in search of the Polish officer, who, in the first instance, seemed to wish to avoid a conversation with him; but when he heard that it was to speak with him about a duel, his countenance brightened, and with a warm pressure of the hand, he undertook to become his second.

At the appointed time the two adversaries stood, with their seconds, before each other. The time was short; very little was said about apologies or concession; the seconds placed the pistols in their hands, and at a sign given by the Pole, both were to fire.

The sign was given. De Terry's ball whistled over Jacob's head. Jacob's ball entered the heart of his adversary.

He spun round like a top, and then dropped to the earth.

In the evening Jacob awaited in his tent the unavoidable consequences of this event. He was indifferent as to what those consequences might be; he seemed to himself like some one carried away by a strong stream, against which it was in vain to attempt to strive.

Josinski entered hastily.

"Good news," cried he. "A patrol has found poor De Terry, but without his head. One of the devil's Kabyles, who are swarming around us, has earned his piastre at your expense. It is said in the camp that De Terry, having ventured out too far, has fallen into the hands of the enemy, and we have escaped a court-martial."

A faint expression of satisfaction passed over Jacob's countenance. Fortune is an enchantress; even when she has given up everything, she will befool with a smile.

CHAPTER XXXVI.

"You lead a very pleasant hermit's life here," said Josinski, on one occssion, when he paid a visit to Jacob, at the little outpost of which he had now the command.

Jacob replied, with a melancholy smile.

"I can very well believe that the behaviour of the officers must be disagreeable to you," continued Josinski. "I was so afraid that you would be challenging them for it; and in that case you must have fought with one half, and the other half must have been your seconds. Don't be vexed that I bring this history back to your mind. I, for my part, am convinced that you are not afraid of danger. When you stood before the ball of De Terry, one might have believed that you had been accustomed all your life to stand before pistol balls; and, of a truth, it requires some courage, also, to maintain such a post as you have here."

"You are now judging too favourably of me, dear Josinski. It is not courage which I show, if by courage I am to understand that strong feeling which is called forth by an interest in in the thing, and which, for its sake, causes us to defy danger. I am indifferent, careless, about life. It is said that they who suffer the extreme of sea-sickness, lie stretched out under the influence of the malady, and would hear, with the greatest indifference, that the ship was about to sink. That is my state of mind."

"It would be just the same with me," replied Josinski, "if it were not for a secret hope which at times passes like a stab through the breast, and drives the blood more rapidly through my veins. For the rest it would be a sin to say that you live among too many defences," said Josinski, interrupting himself, and glancing round the barrack-room; "but what books are these that you have here?"

"They are some which got by chance among my things when I left my own country, and which have been a great comfort to me here. I wish that you could understand them. They are stories about Icelandic heroes, and are written in an extraordinary manner. They treat merely of actions, while the feelings and impulses which gave birth to them must be added by the reader; nor can one ever be tired of thinking them over."

"Tell me a little about them?" besought Josinski. "Thus we shall study northern literature in the African desert, and pass the hot hours of mid-day in an agreeable manner. I am no Frenchman; you need not be afraid that I shall immediately make use of the information you give me for a treatise on the old Icelandic character."

Jacob smiled, and said, "I will gratify you with pleasure, though I am afraid that the best part of them, the spirit of the north, will evaporate in a translation. Perhaps it would be the best if I were to shut the book, and relate something from memory. At this moment I recollect two different stories. I will begin with one about a child:—A man, named Trorsten, lived at enmity with his neighbour, who was called Steinar, a wicked but very brave man. One day, as Thorsten, with a small number of attendants, and in company with his little son, Grim, then ten years old, were travelling in a country place, they came to the edge of a great wood, and here they were met by Steinar, with a superior body of followers. Thorsten said to his son, 'Run into the wood, and wait there till the fight is over,' after which he went against Steinar. 'After the fight,' says the story, 'they sought in the wood for Grim; they found him sorely wounded, and by his side lay the son of Steinar, and he was dead.'"

"Do you not feel this as I do?" asked Jacob. "One is seized with a secret terror—one is almost afraid of casting an eye into the wood, and becoming witness to the mortally-embittered conflict of the two boys."

"Yes, that is really true. Go on. This little specimen excites a wish in me to hear more."

"One of the best heroes in Iceland was Gunnar, who dwelt at Hlidarende Grange—no—whilst I am telling about him, so many things come into my memory I know not how to make any choice. I will teach you Danish. Then you may yourself read about the affecting friendship between Gunnar and the wise Njal, and of the enmity between their wives, Bergthora and Halgerda; of the quiet irony with which the husbands alternately paid a fine to each other for the deaths which their violent wives caused in their households; of Gunnar's glorious deeds, and of his last fight, when his wife refused to cut off a lock of her hair for a bowstring, so that his life might be saved, because he had, two years before, given her a box on the ear."

"Are these stories, then, the reading of the common people in Denmark?" asked the Pole.

"No, not as far as I know," replied Jacob; "but now I will tell you how Njal died. His warlike sons, all of whom lived with him, had killed a chieftain, and for revenge his people set fire to the house where they lived. It was towards evening when the flames burst forth from all quarters of the building. Flose, the leader of the marauders, came to the door, and besought Njal to come forth. Njal replied, that he would not forsake his sons, since he could not revenge them. 'Do thou go out, wife,' said Flose to Bergthora, 'for on no account will I be the death of thee.' 'I was married young,' replied she, 'and I promised Njal when I married him, that we would share weal and woe with each other.' On this the husband and wife passed from the door into the house. Bergthora was now desirous that her little grandson, the son of her daughter, should be carried forth from the burning house, but the boy besought for himself: 'It seems better,' said he, 'that I should die with thee and Njal, than that I should leave you.'

"On this, Njal ascended the marriage-bed with his wife and the little grandson, and bade the house-servant to fasten a fresh ox-hide over the bed, so that their bodies should remain uninjured; and thus the three laid themselves down to die."

"This lofty contempt of death," said Josinski, after a little pause, "is one of the qualities which distinguish the uncivilized people amongst whom we are. In this respect the Arabs resemble your Icelanders. I saw an instance of this as I rode hither. I had ridden somewhat in advance of my company, when by chance looking behind me to examine still more carefully a ruined wall, probably the remains of a mosque, I perceived a Bedouin who was taking aim at me with the utmost coolness. But this coolness was my salvation; I threw myself down by the side of my horse, so that I could hang with one leg in the stirrup, and scarcely had I done so, when the ball whistled over the head of my horse. The Arab was now my man. I drew forth my pistol, turned my horse, and rode up to him; but as I approached he crossed his arms over his breast in the most cold-blooded way possible, and stared at me with his coal-black eyes. I could not kill him; I left that to the soldiers who hastened to the spot."

"Did they kill him?" asked Jacob.

"Yes, that I believe they did."

"Ah!" said Jacob, "I cannot deny but that I feel a sort of sympathy for these people. The right is on their side, and they defend it with wild bravery. And then there is something strange and poetical about them; they seem to belong less to the earth than we do. They speed lightly over it; they have not bound themselves down to it by walls and defences. And yet when one sees their proud powerful forms, they seem as if they were more fervently loved by mother earth than we. To see an Arab in that white garment with its ample folds by the side of a French soldier, in his clumsy scarlet breeches, and his absurd-looking chacot! To see Colonel Yussuf by the side of a French officer! He seems formed by God as a model for a warrior; courage beams from his whole being, so that one fancies that the bullet must turn aside from him. I can never contemplate him without feeling a kind of pain that he has forsaken his own people; how one's heart would bleed to see him in a Christian army!

"Therefore is it," continued he, "that I am sluggish and indifferent. I would gladly, more than gladly, distinguish myself and become honoured. But I cannot fight against this people. I seem to myself like a mercenary; I murder, if not exactly for pay, yet for reward; for it is murder, even in open fight, if one does not kill for a righteous cause—or, at least, in the belief that it is so."

"Better go over to the Bedouins," said Josinski, in jest.

"Oh, no! we Europeans are bound together by civilization. I love the French—at a distance; I love them for the thought's sake, which God must have had when he created them."

"Yes, it is strange," exclaimed Josinski; "these people, who individually are so egotistical, frivolous, and vain, as a nation feel a sympathy with all other nations, and are ready to sacrifice life for them. I hate every individual soldier; but when I see a regiment marching forth, my heart throbs with pride."

"Masses always make that impression. One loves not each individual citizen, yet one loves a whole people."

"Much might be said against that," said Josinski. "I for my part love every Pole that I meet,—he is a little bit of my fatherland. I picked up the other day a button in the streets of Algiers: it was a button from a Polish uniform, and it seemed to me a sin that it should lie in the dirt."

"That is because your fatherland suffers. A son of rich, proud England cannot endure to see an Englishman abroad."

"Yes, my fatherland suffers; hear, will you?——" The Pole stopped in the middle of the sentence and fell into thought.

A corporal came with a message, and Josinski left the place.

A few hours later, when he was alone, Jacob stood in an opening of the palisadoes which surrounded the buildings. In the distance he observed a cloud of dust which was rapidly approaching, and presently perceived that it was a man on horseback riding at a furious gallop. As he could not tell whether it might not possibly be a Bedouin, who had vowed the head of a Christian to Allah in his morning prayer, and as in that case he might, by mistake, have a design upon *his* head, he prepared himself for fight. As the rider approached, however, he recognised him, to his great astonishment, to be Josinski. He rode as if directly against him, pulled up his horse with such violence as almost threw him upon his haunches, and then leaping from his saddle, flung his arms round Jacob's neck. Jacob was as little able to understand the broken exclamations of the Pole, as to conceive the cause of the rapture which beamed in his countenance.

At length burst forth the words, "Revolution! The Russians are massacred in Warsaw. The Poles have risen!"

"Hurrah!" said Jacob, "Yes, it is in Danish I exclaim, God be thanked!"

They again embraced each other.

Josinski dried his eyes, and said,—

"We two rejoice together alone in the desert; but I am certain that at this moment there is rejoicing over half Europe. You have said that you wished to fight for a righteous cause; now, I ask you, do you consider the cause of Poland to be a righteous one?"

"Oh, Josinski! it is almost blasphemy to ask such a question! I will go with you to Poland——."

"Why do you hesitate?" asked the Pole. "Does any objection arise in your mind?"

"No; it was only the thought that perhaps there might come a letter to me from my home."

"Write to them, and tell them that for the future they must address their letters to you at Warsaw instead of Algiers. Or, is there something else?——"

"No; it was only a passing thought. At this moment the colours of heaven fade; my private affairs are small and insignificant in comparison with those of Poland."

"Then let us be off!" exclaimed Josinski; "there is no time to lose. We must away if we would thus desert. If only no Arabs may be lurking in the way! My friend, do not think ill of me if you see that from this time I am careful of my life here in Algiers!"

CHAPTER XXXVII.

THE ATTACK.

"I am as hungry as a Kalmuck!" said a young officer, who in the darkness of night was accompanying Jacob through the village. "According to good Captain Dalgetty's example, I have buckled my belt tighter on the march; but the tighter buckle it, the more my stomach cries out for provender. Perhaps you have been so lucky as to get good quarters, and, if so, will invite me to be your guest—nay, these are they!—no, thank you! I prefer going farther, and foraging on my own account."

Jacob entered the hut, which resembled less a human dwelling than one of those mounds of earth beneath which the farmer buries his potatoes for the winter. Within its naked clay walls nothing was to be seen besides three half-naked children, who were lying upon a little damp straw, and stared with looks of terror upon the intruder.

The corporal now came in. "This is a poor lodging for you, lieutenant," said he, "and the provision is not much better. Here, however, is some bread and brandy, if you'll tackle to. The Russians must give us breakfast to-morrow morning; and it will be a warm one I think!"

"Thanks, my good Soltau. But are there no inhabitants? Is there no mother for these children?"

"God knows! I see none."

"Where is the man to whom this hut belongs?"

"He may be looked for in the dog-kennel. I drove him out to make room for the lieutenant."

Jacob thought to himself,—"Perhaps he may be such a Pole as my father used to entertain at his table."

"Soltau," said he, "I would rather go out into the fresh air; let the man come into his own house."

"He'll creep into it soon enough, if he sees the lieutenant and me go out; the lieutenant may be very easy on that score."

"Tell me, Soltau," said Jacob, when they were again in the open air, "how can you be so unmerciful as to drive a man out into the cold from those little children? I have on other occasions seen you gentle and full of human kindness towards your comrades on the march."

"Unmerciful, lieutenant, towards such a creature as that!" exclaimed Soltau. "If he could get a guilder for cutting all our heads off, he would do it. If our position was not as good as it is, there would be half a score of Jews on the way to betray us to the Russians."

"But there are Jews," said Jacob, "who serve in the army like good Poles."

"Under arms—that is another matter," returned the corporal; "he who will slay the Russians is my comrade, even though he were a Turk. An old soldier like me does not require to see the certificate of baptism. But if we had not these rascally Jews in Poland, there would be so many traitors the less."

"But why do they not hang up these cursed spies as an example and warning to others?"

"We hang a couple every day," replied the corporal; "but they swarm like rats."

"Are there actually none but Jews who are traitors?"

"No, heaven defend us, lieutenant! Every one of these swinish peasants is a traitor; he hardly knows that there is a country which is called Poland; but we call every traitor a Jew."

"That is another thing," said Jacob, laughing. "Lend me your bottle."

At that moment a shot was fired beyond the village; they could see the flash through the darkness.

When they came to the place where the bullet had fallen, they found some horse-soldiers gathered round a man who lay upon the ground and moaned. They were talking loud, and threateningly.

"What is amiss here?" asked Jacob.

"Wait a moment, lieutenant," said the corporal, and bent over the man. "Did not I think so? It is our host! On the way to Stoczek, no doubt! Thou miserable son of a dog," said he, addressing him; "thou cursed Jew-traitor!"

"The man who lay on the ground cried in a voice of piteous bewailing, "I am no Jew! I am no Jew! I am a Christian like yourselves! I am your brother—all my misfortune be on you!" exclaimed he, in Polish Hebrew, and in an under tone, so that it seemed like lamentation. "Oh, oh! I am Michael Wucziewicz; the holy archangel Michael is my patron saint, blessed be his name! Mamzer ben hanido—oh, oh!"

"Ah, you wretch! what were you going to do at Stoczek? Confess, you dog!"

"I only wanted to fetch some eggs for the great gentleman who was quartered with me—oh, oh!"

"What! You would fetch eggs would you! Is there nobody here who has a bit of rope?"

"I will confess!" cried the Pole. "I will tell you how many Russians there are at Stoczek. I know where General Geismar is—only let me live—oi shema Yisroel!—oh! oh! oh!"

"Give me a rope!" said one of the soldiers.

Jacob, who was half-inclined to smile, partly at the soldiers, who did not understand the Jewish curses that were uttered, and partly at the wretched man himself, who had no idea that he was understood, now interfered between them.

"Conduct him to the colonel," said he; "perhaps he can give important information. No!—take the rope from his neck; you have already fired at him—that will do."

"The shot has not done him any great harm, lieutenant. It has only grazed the skin; he fell down out of sheer fright. But as you command it, we will take him to the colonel."

Shortly after, the officers were summoned to the colonel, and received orders to lead the troops silently and cautiously against Stoczek.

"By two o'clock the general will be here, on his way to Filipowko," said he, at parting; "if we could only conduct him as a guest into a conquered town!"

The officers hastened to their posts.

Through that severely cold winter night the army advanced silently towards the town, then in the possession of the enemy.

Outside the first house lay a Russian sentinel frozen to death, with his brandy-bottle by his side. His comrades were rioting within the house, along the walls of which were ranged their arms. The Polish soldiers entered with fixed bayonets, and overpowered all without noise or resistance. Taken by surprise and surrounded, the Russians everywhere surrendered, all except a few hundred men, who succeeded in assembling near a large shop, which they obstinately defended until the Poles set fire to the town.

The colonel rode into the town, his countenance expressive of trouble. "You have not done well," said he; "this fire may conduct hither the whole of Geismar's forces upon us this very night. Let all our outposts be secured as well as possible, so that the Russians may not surprise us as we have surprised them."

At day-break great noise and exultation was heard in the direction of Filipowko; they were the cavalry of General Dwernicki which were arriving. At the same time there was seen from the opposite side of the town the advance-guard of the Russian army, which was hastening on to recapture the town.

This was on that 18th of February when the first battle was fought in open field for the independence of Poland.

Like an enormous snake, wound onward the columns of the Russian army against the Poles, and annihilated under their advance the little troop which had possession of the wooded heights on the other side of Stoczek. The artillery drew up upon the heights, and commenced their fire. Both infantry and cavalry advanced from either side.

General Dwernicki, at the head of a squadron of lancers, made a halt and watched the Russian movement. After a short deliberation, he turned to his officers and gave them their orders.

The squadrons formed into line behind Dwernicki. He rode to their front; paused for a moment and contemplated their determined, warlike aspect; then, stretching forth his hand, he cried, with a loud voice, turning at the same time his snorting charger to the foe :

"Poles! Lancers—forward!"

The trumpets brayed forth their martial defiance; the earth shook as they dashed onward.

Yes, you were astonished, ye Russians. It was wholly against the rule, to fight as Dwernicki did. But it was not two kings who were come to battle to decide whose cannon could sweep down the greatest numbers; it was not a battle which was fought according to mathematical science. Our own sinewy arms must fight it out; you yourselves have made them strong by your oppressions!

Ha! that was a combat. No firearms—man against man; one Pole against three Russians! Hark! how the swords clink! how the helmets are cloven asunder! how the lances are shivered! The eagle of Poland slays with her wings and drinks the Russian blood!

They yield—they give way—a piece of the fatherland is won! Forward!—the whole land shall yet be won! The field-pieces are taken; the artillery forces cut down; the infantry are overpowered;—they fly!

Forward! forward! you reserve forces, and complete the work which the hero has begun.

The wild pursuit extends as far as Seroczyn; a Polish town is taken—it is set on fire. We will rebuild it in independence. Forward! Down with the Russians! He prays for pardon! Let him live—the imperial slave! Hurrah! The battle is won—Poland is not lost!

CHAPTER XXXVIII.

THE MARCH.

Jacob came riding slowly back to the field of battle. He was almost stupified; it was as if he had been absorbed by some strong passion, and that his blood could not again become calm.

"The lieutenant now sees that I was right yesterday; the Russians have given us a breakfast!" said the corporal, as he held Jacob's stirrup, and pointed over the field where groups of Poles were encamped among the Russian baggage wagons.

Jacob was silent. He said to himself, "That man can remember what he said yesterday! If God were to descend in thunder and lightning, would he remember to take off his chacot to Him?"

"What! must we turn back?" exclaimed a lancer, who was leading a splendid Russian charger by the bridle; "turn back, already? Why do we not go directly against St. Petersburgh?"

"And so leave them to burn Warsaw!" said Soltau. "Yes, it has always been a prey."

The name of the holy Warsaw touched the heart of the Pole. "No!" said he; "let us go back, then."

"Creutz may run away just as well as Geismar," cried another lancer.

"He can run better," cried a third, "because he has more cavalry."

"Let them all come together," cried several; "we'll make them all give way! The girls of Warsaw shall sing about the cavalry of Dwernicki!"

"Hurrah! Lieutenant Bendixen!" cried a captain of horse, who sat on the ground among several officers; "come and take a glass—a bottle, I should say, because we have no glasses." The captain knocked off the neck of a bottle with the hilt of his sword, and added: "The Russians are, and remain to be, stupid fellows—see whether they cared about corkscrews! Nay, lieutenant,—no ceremony. To-day rank goes for nothing; we have all fought equally well for old Poland. Yes, sit down—here, by my side. What the devil! I am sitting upon a Russian—a colonel! That was very amusing, if it was his wine that we were drinking! Nay, at all events, he was present at the feast, poor fellow!"

The Polish artillery force came past with the Russian field-pieces which they had taken. The cavalry drew together and formed themselves into a long double line, between which the artillery was drawn forward amid songs and exultation.

"I should like to know," said the captain of horse, "why the old fellow gives folks all the trouble of this cannon."

"What's that, captain?" asked an officer, in surprise.

"Why, don't you see that he can only take cannon with him for pomp? It is a sin to use so many horses for mere luxury. As long as the Russians have arms, he can be in no want! Hark! ho has ordered the signal for mounting. He never thinks that it is not wholesome to ride so soon after dinner."

The army advanced in long lines across the frozen fields. Everywhere was heard song and hilarity; regiment exultingly saluted regiment when they encountered each other; stories of the late battle alternated with prophetic assurances of future success, and the Polish national song echoed from the dark wood which skirted the plain.

The march proceeded uninterruptedly; the sun set; and by slow degrees silence fell over the advancing army. Comrade conversed softly, almost in a whisper, with comrade; songs were heard only here and there, and that to low, pensive airs; the soldiers wrapped themselves in their cloaks, and gave themselves up to that strange spirit of melancholy which breathes through the winter evenings of the north.

Jacob's feelings were in a state of excitement; wine and conversation had roused him; his mind struggled against that silent sorrow which seemed to influence all things around him.

"Soltau!" cried he, checking his rein; "when one looks at you, one would not imagine that you rode from victory."

The corporal rode up to Jacob's side, and lifted his chacot respectfully, as he replied, "I beg pardon, lieutenant, but I have been very happy to-day."

"But yet not happy enough? We have not, perhaps, killed Russians enough to please you?" said Jacob, with a vivacity unusual to him.

"Why, yes, lieutenant, that is exactly it. The pleasure over those that we have killed is not so great as one's vexation for those who have escaped."

"What barbarity!" exclaimed Jacob. "One might almost believe that you were a Russian. Kill flying foes!"

"It may very well be barbarity, lieutenant," said the corporal, gloomily; "but ever since the time when I first tasted their blood has the longing for it been awakened in my soul. Now that I have seen the cursed Russians again, all the old recollections rise up and demand their blood!"

"That is true, Soltau; you are a Pole!" said Jacob, more gravely.

"Yes," continued the corporal, "and that I have been this half-century. I have lived through all the misfortunes of Peland from the time of Kosciusco. I was in Prague when the Russians besieged it."

"In Prague?"

"Yes, I was there. I was at home with my mother; my father fought that day among the Poles, and fell. But we knew nothing of his death; we sat in uninterrupted expectation and listened. We heard the horrible thunder of the cannon, and in the intervals the clash of arms. It ceased; and the most dreadful yell resounded through the streets, as if of wild beasts. I was frightened—I was only eleven years old—and as the yells approached I crept behind my mother. The door was burst open by the butt-ends of guns; soldiers in green uniform, all stained with blood, and with blackened countenances, rushed in. My mother was run through with a bayonet, she fell upon me, and I became suffocated, as it were, with my mother's blood. But I had a sister——don't let us talk of that," said the corporal, interrupting himself, and passing his hand over his eyes. "When I see a Russian, it seems to me, that he it was who murdered my mother. And when I have cut him down, it seems to me again that I have been mistaken, and that it is some other: I give no quarter."

Shortly after, he continued in a calmer tone—" I was drawn as a soldier; I was to serve in the Russian army. But I deserted. I knew that death by the knout would be my punishment if I was retaken; but I deserted nevertheless. Thus I was at Austerlitz—at Austerlitz with the great Emperor! The Russians retreated over a frozen lake, and I heard the command given that the artillery should fire upon the ice, and thus cause it to break. It was done; the Russians threw away their weapons—they sank—they stretched forth their arms and cried for help—as the Polish women had done at Prague.

" In Friedland I was severely wounded; and then soon after, when the power of the Grand Duke was again established, I settled myself down at Warsaw, and married. I lived in Zaeroczym-street, and kept a provision-shop, where I did well, although the Emperor fell. If I had given up the whole of my provision dealing, I could not have saved the Emperor. But you can credit me, lieutenant, that was a hard day when the Russian guard again marched into Warsaw with their fluttering banners and ringing music, and the Polish soldiers were obliged to leave the arsenal. That day I repented me that I had not gone in 1812—and, at all events, had the pleasure of seeing Moscow burning. But when I looked at my countrymen, I could very well see that the Russians would be driven out again—yes, I could very well see that, lieutenant. It has been somewhat long in doing, but it will be done only all the better.

"When I think about it, I cannot understand how we can have held out so long. You know that they violated the constitution which they had given to us by oath; not that it mattered much to me; for we could not see that it was of any benefit to us; and, besides, I thought, if it is not stronger than that they can break it, there cannot be any very great strength in it. But then they will root out our old Polish language, and our children must learn Russian! And our lawful rights are withheld from us—yes, and more than that, they trample right and justice and human equality under foot. The best men amongst us are arrested and sentenced to the knout and sent to Siberia. Judges are paid, so that they will do just what is required of them. A man dare scarcely speak his opinion in his own family; a single word is sufficient to cause the house to be surrounded during the night, and a father of a family to be taken from his wife and children; and they never more behold him! All their property become confiscated; and people who one day have been rich, have gone begging on the next. Senators and high-bred ladies may be seen wheeling barrows;

and one may not even weep at such things, lest one gets into trouble oneself for so doing. Yes, lieutenant, we have been treated as if we were a people rejected of God, and only created to be tortured by the Russians. But you certainly have heard enough about these things before you came hither?"

"Yes, at home I read various accounts of the misery of Poland; but when people themselves are well off, they do not enter with a living interest into the sufferings of foreigners. But this I must tell you, once for all, Soltau, my countrymen, the Danes, are a peaceful people, but if they were to be persecuted thus, I do not believe that they would bear it for fifteen long years."

"Ah! lieutenant, remember that the Polish youth were almost destroyed in 1815; we must indeed wait till our children are grown up before we could have a revolution. Besides, we expected a change in 1825, and wished first to try what Nicholas would do. But he was soon tried. And God knows how long it might have been if Nicholas had not got the idea of making war on France, and of using for that purpose the Polish national treasury and the Polish army. Thus would all the Polish fortresses be placed in the hands of Russian soldiers. After this we knew that we must either break or bear."

"But what *we?*" asked Jacob.

"We conspirators—we old and young Polish soldiers, students, citizens, noblemen—*we* altogether."

"But how did it happen that you were not betrayed, arrested, and sent to Siberia?"

"Could they arrest a whole nation, lieutenant? The emperor knew that there was something on foot, but he did not know when it would break out. Many a time we determined that our rising should take place on a certain day, and every time he came to know, and had his Russians in readiness. At length, however, he grew weary of the blind alarm, and when the head of the police mentioned to him on the 29th of November that

that evening was the appointed time, he called him an infamous deceiver, and knocked him down-stairs. But the 29th was the right day, and it was arranged that the scholars of the military school at Lazienki, just outside Warsaw, should begin by making an attack on the cavalry-barracks, and give us in the city a sign by setting fire to a certain house. That evening the Polish sappers, to the number of many hundreds, assembled at my house, because they were to begin at this point, and get possession of the Alexander church. In order to mislead the police, I had a ball that night at my house. There were, of course, not many women there, but the men folk made no ado about that, but danced with one another, whilst they were thinking about quite another dance. I had posted my eldest son, who was only eight years old, outside, and desired him to keep a good look-out in the direction of Lazienki. At six o'clock, the lad came running in, and whispered to me, 'Father, there is a fire at Lazienki.' On that I went into my bed-room and drew out from the bed-clothes my old carbine, and put on my old woollen jacket, and as I thus went, I stood at the door of the dancing-room. You should, lieutenant, have seen the joke! The musicians leaped up and seized upon axes and sabres. The dancers threw aside their frocks, and forth gleamed their weapons. The police, taken by surprise, cried out 'In the emperor's name!' But we said, 'To the devil with you and your emperor!' and cut them down, and hastened out to the Alexander church. What further happened that night I am not the man to tell. I noticed that we had become very numerous; the Russian cavalry rushed in amongst us—in every window lights were burning, bells were ringing, houses in flames, Russians yelling, cannon thundering—that *was* a night! I know, however, this, that the next morning there was not a living Russian in Warsaw, but perhaps all the more dead on that account, and forty thousand armed Poles standing in the streets. Lord

Jesus! what a sight it was when the flag of Poland fluttered from the tower of the Alexander church, and the masses of people below waved their hats and fell on one another's necks, and amid loud acclamations, wept for joy.

"There was only one thing which happened," continued the corporal in an altered voice, "which I wish had not happened. I'll tell it to you, Lieutenant; I ought not to be exactly ashamed about it. The Russian officers and traitors endeavoured to sneak out of the city; but wherever they were discovered they were struck down. There came riding up General Trembicki, and desired to go out to the Russians. He was our most able, best-beloved General; he always treated his soldiers like a father. We crowded round him, and prayed him to remain amongst us; but he replied sternly, that he was faithful to his emperor, and that we were rebels. I threw myself on the ground before his horse; but he cried, 'Stand aside, Soltau! or I will ride over you!' I placed my carbine against his breast, a score of my comrades did the same—I closed my eyes—and—fired."

"Soltau!" exclaimed Jacob, in horror.

"Yes, Lieutenant, I did it! God is my witness that it grieves me still! But Russia did not get General Trembicki!"

They rode on for some time in silence; at length the corporal again began; at first in a lower voice:

"In the afternoon we had a great delight; the first Polish provincial regiment marched into the city and joined the Revolutionists. That was a fellow, General Szembek, who commanded it! He rode quite alone into the camp of the Grand Duke, and said to him, that he wished to go to Warsaw with his regiment; but that, in the first place, he desired to be released from his oath of fidelity. The Grand Duke was so confounded that he absolved him from his oath, and away he rode. And he was as good as his word, the good Grand Duke!

He was driven away from his comfortable, quiet possession, and stood with his guards up to his knees in water. On the following day the Polish provincial regiments gathered round his camp, and cut him off from all resources, so that he was reduced to a state of great suffering, both from hunger and thirst, and the last was the worst.

"We were forty thousand strong in Warsaw, all men capable of war; we wished to go against the Russian guard; the ten thousand men who were perishing of thirst, would have laid down their arms at the sight of a Polish cap. A deputation was then sent to the Grand Duke, and on the 3rd of December an amnesty was declared, under which it was permitted that the troops of his Imperial Highness, the Grand Duke of Constantine, should be allowed to depart, and should receive supplies at the expense of Poland as far as the frontiers of Russia."

"How could they be guilty of this terrible imprudence!" exclaimed Jacob, with an earnestness as if the misfortune might still be prevented.

"Yes, why?" replied the corporal, and shrugged his shoulders.

Jacob remembered that he was conversing with an inferior, and made no reply.

"There was no remedy for it," replied the corporal. "Ten thousand Russians, more or less, would not ruin us. We got volunteer troops from the whole of Europe; such fellows as that French colonel who swam over the Vistula to reach us, are as good as many thousands of thin-legged Russian guards. Nor can anybody complain of us Poles ourselves. Then when the manifesto was published which called the whole nation to arms, you should have seen! They came in from the country with flails and scythes, and desired nothing more than to be led against the Russians. Many a father and mother came travelling from a far distance, bringing with them their half-grown sons, whom they gave up to the Minister of War. It was, perhaps, no very great thing that the rich people sent their plate into the mint; but when, on the Sunday afternoon, the servant girls came thronging up to the ramparts to work at the defences instead of going to the dance—yes, Lieutenant, we may well sing—

'Still, still is Poland not forsaken.'"

Here the corporal ceased. They now approached a town where the General had made a halt. The army at large obtained a night's rest for themselves, as well as they could.

Early in the morning, before the sun had risen, the outposts announced that a strong body of infantry and cavalry were advancing against the camp to the right; and immediately the Polish forces drew up in order of battle on the outside the town.

A light winter fog covered the plain, so that it was not possible to see to any distance; the soldiers stood therefore in anxious expectation, awaiting every moment to see the enemy advancing through it. Suddenly, however, a breeze arose and dispersed the cloud of fog, and the rays of the ascending sun fell upon long lines of armed men bearing the Polish flag and banners. They were the volunteer corps—miners and peasants from the surrounding district of Woiwod, who had risen in a mass. The Polish forces broke their line as by an electric shock, and the two parties rushed into each other's arms.

The thunder of cannon was heard in the distance.

"What does that mean?" asked they of their new-found brothers.

"They are other volunteer Poles, who have thrown themselves upon Creutz and Wirtemberg; we are on our way to help them."

"We will go altogether against Creutz and Wirtemberg!"

CHAPTER XXXIX.

LETTER FROM JACOB TO MARTIN.

"IMAGINE a camp. In the middle lie some tumble-down peasant huts; they represent the palace where dwell the General and his staff. Around these, dark grey tents (because we have no other washerwomen than the clouds of heaven), and tents built of boughs and earth. On every hand swarm soldiers and horses; and smoke ascends from innumerable holes in the earth, because we cook our victuals like the gipsies in the park; the Russian prisoners are being led through the narrow alleys of tents, and a spy has been hung upon a dead tree, and so on.

"Imagine to yourself various small troops being sent out to forage, and that at the head of these is Lieutenant von Bendixen! They meet a troop of the enemy; the corporal asks Lieutenant von Bendixen whether they shall make an attack—yes; here the people ask advice from me just as I at Copenhagen used to ask it of thee! Such a foraging as this is the reason of your getting this letter. We had come into the neighbourhood of a tolerably large farm-house, in Polish Molestock, and greatly delighted, were riding up to it, when we discovered that it was already in possession of the Russians. My corporal rode up to me and asked, "Do you command, Mr. Lieutenant, that we go away, or that we fall upon the place?" That was mere etiquette; I could see that the old fellow did not conceive anything but an attack possible; besides, the Russians were already aware of us, and were about to ride out against us, so that it was no great heroism in me to command them to fight. Thus began one of those skirmishes which are the most interesting —that is to say to the spectator. The Jews are right when they say, there is no sport too great for an eye-witness. Thus we make an onslaught, and in about the course of a minute I find myself between two Russian soldiers. The blow of one, which was very well intentioned, I parried, and gave him one in return, by which means his Imperial Majesty the Autocrat has one Russian the less to rule over, but at the same moment, the other struck me so violently on the wrist that the reins fell from my hand. I could not now turn my horse, and my head prepared itself very quietly to be split in two. I believe I tried to think of you, but everything spun round in my head. Just, however, as my adversary was about to raise his arm, a pistol-ball passed through his breast. For the first moment, he looked as if taken by surprise by something or other, in the next he fell from his horse. The Russians were put to flight, and after we had killed a score of men, and had ourselves lost about half a score, we were masters of as much straw as we could buy at Vestervold for five dollars. That we carried home in triumph, and all praised the heroic deed. I calculate that my share of the booty is about as much straw as a poor Copenhagen family would buy on their flitting-day for their bed, and therefore I am advanced to the rank of first-lieutenant. In the meantime I am obliged to remain in the camp for the present, and therefore I write you a long letter.

"You can now very well perceive that I am in a different state of mind to what I was when I wrote to you from Algiers. You might then see between every line sorrow and repentance because I had left home; it was hardly possible that it could be otherwise, because my thoughts were there day and night. I felt that my mind might just as well have been a stagnant pool in Denmark as in a foreign land, even though I had been persecuted by remorse, by torturing longings and miserable uncertainty. If I, on the one hand, was tormented by the ill-will and contempt of the family of my betrothed, so, on the other, had I also to endure a similar persecution from the Jewish officers, and was not able to enjoy even the little mite of comfort which I could have at home in a good bed and a good meal.

"Here it is quite another thing. An entirely new life has begun for me. Here I am become, as it were, participant in all that concerns humanity; I have permission to do battle for a great and righteous cause, and I have respect for my own actions. It is true that I fight with a closed vizor, like Ivanhoe at the great tournament; yet, if I were to open the vizor, and they were to see the countenance of the disinherited, of the race of the fugitive, they would not deny the merit of my deeds.

"The only thing which I can object to in the life here is, that one almost ceases to exist as an individual, and becomes a portion of the whole without any self-volition. But then, again there are other moments when life seems like an ocean, and each one resembles a swimmer who sees no limits to his desires; all the powers of mind and body seem to be in a whirl of exultation, and the soul is possessed by an almost frenzy of joy in its own freedom.

"And then I have the firm belief that I shall not die here. In the first battle in which I took my part, I suddenly saw, as plain as possible, the churchyard of Norrebro. Since then, I am convinced that my grave will be dug there; and as they, of course, will hardly be at the trouble of embalming my body and sending it there, in case I should fall here, it is quite necessary that I convey myself home alive.

"When I return, I shall in truth find *her* worthy. Oh, I have not forgotten her! When it is all quiet around me, especially at night, that little drawing-room seems to stand suddenly before me. I see her sitting there, and it is to me as if my body had escaped home; I feel almost out of my senses, and I cannot conceive how I could set off. There are times when it seems to me that even if she remained unfaithful to me, I could console myself with the happiness of Poland, in having taken part in that great struggle; but at other times, when my comrades are casting fearful glances into the future, I console myself secretly with thoughts of her, although the next moment I am angry that I allow myself this egotistical comfort. Nevertheless, I am happy; I have two beautiful hopes to gladden me, and the poor Poles have only one—the hope of their unhappy fatherland.

"Dear Martin, I have often, nevertheless, a painful presentiment, principally on account of your long silence. She ought, however, to write first candidly to me. She is innocent; I believe it—I know it; but appearances were against her, and it would be unmanly of me to write first. In the meantime, I console myself with the persuasion that the letters have not yet found me. God grant that it may be so!

"The surgeon is come; he insists upon it that my arm must be amputated. He is a tall, thin German, originally a barber; but here he figures as *Doctor Medicinæ et Chirurgiæ*, and he has a spite against me, because I understand the management of wounds better than he does. He says, that as I am such a skilful surgeon, I should have stayed at home. Yes, if I had had him to cut off the parson's wife, what a sorry figure he would have made! Now, she will surely have some respect for a first-lieutenant in the Polish National Army! And let me only get a letter from Thora!—if I would not then be a captain of horse before many hours were over, you should call me—a **Russian**! If I should come home as a captain of horse, in a **splendid uniform**, should I not then cause the Jew Bendixen to **be lost in excess of light**, so that no one could see him?"

CHAPTER XL.

A DARK CLOUD.

Some months later, the army lay in a well-defended camp on the frontiers of Austria. Dwernicki had thus secured to his soldiers a few day's repose, after having been for a long time pursued by a superior force of Russians. An oppressive silence prevailed through the camp; the spirit of the general alone was in activity, calculating accurately upon his position, like the sea-captain, who conducts his vessel through breakers and tempest.

Two officers, outside the tent, paced backwards and forwards, in deep conversation; they were Jacob and Josinski.

Jacob said, "I am glad, Josinski, to see you again. How lucky it was that it was precisely you who were selected to convey the despatches! And you are now major! I congratulate you with my whole heart."

"I cannot rejoice over my own good luck, when I think of my country," said Josinski, thoughtfully.

"Your country!—Poland! What new trouble is there? Have you not, in the great battle, driven the enemy from Warsaw on the right side of the river, whilst we have swept the left side as clean as a house-floor? Is not the whole of Poland on foot, from the Russian frontiers to Austrian Gallicia and Prussian Posen? Are there not thousands of peasants here in Walhynia ready to join us? Because we are just now somewhat hampered by a superior force, are we therefore to lose courage at once? Old Dwernicki will hit upon some expedient."

"Ah! you do not know, dear Bendixen, how affairs stand. What avails it that we have conquered at Grochow, at Wavre, and at Dembe?—that we have blown up the Imperial Guard, and cut down both his 'Lions of Warna' and his invincible cuirassiers? What avails all this beautiful enthusiasm, which made me so happy—which, when we, after the battle of Dembe, pursued the retreating foe, and suddenly saw that there were Poles already in pursuit of them—the inhabitants of Dobre, who had taken the field under the command of their burgomaster? —that the regiment, which almost consisted of children, put the Russian veterans to flight?—that the Russians retired as soon as they saw the fourth regiment of the line advance with fixed bayonets? What does all this profit us?—what does it avail us? Skryvnecki sits down quietly after his victory, so that one might believe rather that he had been beaten. Instead of throwing his forces upon the dispersed, beaten, terrified Russians—cutting them to pieces, taking them prisoners, cleansing the whole of Poland from their presence—he settles down into a state of inexplicable inaction, allows them to reassemble, and gives time to the emperor to strengthen them with new masses. It almost looks as if he himself had become afraid of his own boldness, in striking at the Colossus till it reeled. Now he lets Dwernecki here be pursued and harassed to death. Poland will lose six thousand of its best men because Skryvnecki will not move his great army, which burns with desire for battle. Oh, I am sometimes ready to go mad with impatience! It is fortunate for me that I have been sent here, or I should have murdered Skryvnecki, my general."

"But is, then, the condition here so desperate?"

"With thirty thousand Russians between us and our brethren; in a position which certainly is almost invincible, but with the Austrian frontier at our back! Yet once more do the Poles put confidence in Austria, although they have twice before paid so dearly for doing so. See if the Austrians do not open their frontiers for Rüdiger, to enable him to attack us in the rear, perhaps even to help him! The persecuted Poles may expect anything!"

Josinski was called into the general's presence, and Jacob walked thoughtfully to his own tent.

The 27th of December, 1831, was the day when the Russian general, Rüdiger, entered the neutral territory, and fell upon the rear of Dwernicki's forces; and whilst Dwernicki believed in the friendly disposition of Austria, his army was disbanded, and their weapons and cannon surrendered to the Russians, from whom they had so lately been taken in victory.

It was eleven o'clock in the forenoon; the attack had commenced, and the Russian cavalry had passed the frontiers. The little Polish army was hemmed in on all sides. At that moment Dwernicki took a sudden resolve to cut his way through to the neutral territory. Some squadrons were ordered to a desperate attack, as a forlorn hope, so that the foe might be occupied, and the retreat covered.

There was a moment's stillness during the necessary preparations; the squadrons drew up in the face of the advancing hostile masses. At a moment like this, the mind is in a state of supernatural activity; recollections of the past, anticipations of the future, hurry past with mad speed, and yet all is clear and distinct.

"As a child I put faith in omens," said Jacob to himself, whilst he was conscious of the scene in all its threatening majesty; "by the wick of a candle I told the fortune of a plaything; by the garments of a passer-by I augured of my success with Thora's father. Now I will foretell the less by the greater if we succeed to-day, I shall have a letter"——

The trumpets sounded; the spurs were driven into the sides of the horses; the cavalry raised once more the Polish battle-cry, and like a hailstorm dashed they against the Russians. The first ranks were overturned, killed, ridden down; the whole living mass bowed like a field of corn beneath the tempest.

Then, from another side, was heard the Russian word of command, and rattling forward at a hard trot came a dense troop of cavalry, and fell upon the Poles. The lines were broken, and a confused, desperate, close fight commenced. The little Polish army was whirled round as if in a maelstrom.

Jacob saw a Russian lance pierce the breast of Soltau; yet once more the Pole raised himself in his saddle, and with an expression of mortal enmity, sought for the Russian; but before he could return the blow, sank himself from his horse, amid innumerable wounds.

Jacob saw nothing more. Curses, blows, sabre-cuts, pistol-shots, sounded around him. He mechanically parried and returned blows, until he found himself at the side of Josinski behind the Russians; and following their example, the two friends spurred their horses to the wildest gallop.

The horses stumbled, but there was not a Russian to be seen. They were saved—they were in Poland; whilst the remainder of their comrades might listen in an Austrian dungeon for tidings of the war in Poland.

CHAPTER XLI.

MICHAEL WUCZIEWICZ.

AMID incessant dangers they escaped from that part of the country which was now overrun by Russians. Occasionally they took refuge with the Polish peasants, who shared with them the few necessaries of life which the enemy had left them; at other times they spent whole days and nights in woods and unfrequented places, without any other means of sustenance than the roots which they dug up from the earth.

One night, as they were lying on the damp ground, and after having in vain attempted to sleep, Josinski said,—

"If it were any other conflict, and with any other foe, I would suffer myself to be captured. The bravest men are conquered by hunger. But I will never yield myself alive to the Russians. I am only sorry for you."

"You must not grieve on my account, Josinski!" replied Jacob. I endure my present sufferings and hardships with a certain kind of pleasure. I regard the whole as an appointed penance, as an ordeal fire through which I must pass to atone for some earlier passages of my life, and that I may become worthy of future happiness. Only it is not necessary that you should pass through this penance with me!"

"You are a strangely brave comrade!" said Josinski, and pressed his hand.

"It is at bottom nothing but egotism," said Jacob; "I promise us both compensation for the sufferings we endure. Sometimes, when I am profoundly thinking about my own affairs, the insane fancy comes into my mind that everything which happens here in Poland only happens on my account, in order that I may come forth from it all a better man; that all the powers of my mind—the qualities of my soul—may thus escape becoming rusty. By the aid of my medical knowledge I am able to inform you that the brain sometimes gives birth to such like conceits and fancies when the body is weakened by long fasting."

"Your jesting tone almost drives away my hunger. Hark you; it is in reality cowardly to lie here and bemoan ourselves! Let us go out of the wood and take the chance of fortune. If we meet with Russians we will fall with weapons in our hands —so that in any case it is all one."

"As you will, Josinski. Fate perhaps speaks by your mouth as it did by that of the Pythian priestess, when she sat fasting upon her tripod!"

They left the wood, and arrived at its outskirts, looked forth over the plain to a vast extent. The moon was low in the heavens, and a portion of the wood threw its shadow in the direction of a solitary house. At the distance of some hundred paces to the west lay a village, where they could distinguish the passing to and fro of soldiery a little to the right, and in the full moonlight marched a Russian sentinel.

Jacob grasped the arm of Josinski. "I recognise this spot," whispered he. "You must trust yourself to my guidance."

They crept along that portion of the plain which lay in shadow and reached the hut, the door of which they cautiously opened, and at that very moment the Russian sentinel reached the part of the wood which they had just left.

Both cast, involuntarily, a thankful glance towards heaven.

As their eyes the next moment turned from the mild brilliancy of the heavens upon the interior of the hut, Josinski laid his hand upon his sword.

The room was almost dark. In one corner, upon a low unplaned table, stood a small lamp, which cast its feeble uncertain light upon a man who sat in a half-raised, half-bowed position, as if keeping himself in readiness to spring forward. His eyes flashed through the dusk-light of the room, first upon one and then on the other of the intruders, as if he were considering with himself upon which he should first make an attack. His black cloak was torn across the breast, and at his side stood some strange victuals, two eggs, and a loaf of bread overstrewn with ashes.

Jacob withheld Josinski's arm, and advanced into the room, giving at the same time the Jewish salutation, "Peace be with you!"

The Pole drew himself together; his eyes seemed to start from their sockets, as if to pierce the gloom and see the countenance of the speaker.

"Who comes here in the dress of a Polish soldier to a faithful Russian?" exclaimed he, "you are a traitor! you shall die!"

"I am a Jew as you are," returned Jacob. "Rise up, son of the Jewish people, and help thy brother!"

"Hence, traitor, I am no Jew!" cried the man, "my name is Michael Wucziewicz! The holy archangel Michael is my patron saint!"

"Will you let these words pass your tongue while you set— schivvo*—in sorrow, perhaps, because of a beloved child; while the death lamp is burning and while Mal'rh hamoves, the angel

---

* Sorrowing for the dead—the most fearful ceremony of the Jews, and which lasts for seven days. The garments of the mourner are rent; no work is done; he sits alone; nor even says "Good day" nor "Farewell" to any who may approach him.

of death, is perhaps still hovering over your house? Why at least do you not add, 'Mamzir ben hanido?'"

The Pole had sprung up; he laid his hands upon Jacob's shoulder, while he stared into his face and cried, "Tell me what part of the law is read by the Jews on Saturday?"

"That part which begins with the word Eikef," replied Jacob, after a moment's thought, while the Pole gazed at him with most excited attention.

"Enough, you are a Jew! Baruch habo besheim Adonoi! Blessed be he who comes in the name of the Lord! Praised be the God of Israel! A son of his people passes my threshold and calls me brother! I have laid myself down at the door of the synagogue, and no one would tread upon me;* I have bared my back, and no one would smite me. God's holy book has been closed against me; my children are buried, but I could not say Kadisch (the prayer for the dead) over them! I have been as a beaten dog. Tell me, what it is that thou desirest from me, 'thou blessed son of Israel?'"

"In the first place, something to eat."

"Merciful God!" exclaimed the man, and fetched some bread. "Would God that I had something better to give thee. Is he also a Jew?" asked he, as Jacob divided the loaf with Josinski.

"No; but I pray thee to conduct both him and me to Warsaw."

The countenance of the Pole grew dark; and he replied, "A Christian has entered during my time of mourning. I will thrust him forth, that his fate may be accomplished, and that he may become a dead dog!"

"Then I go too!" exclaimed Jacob, and placed himself be-

* This has reference to his having been baptized; when, on having sent intelligence of it among the Jews, they had refused to receive his message, and had treated him with silent scorn.

tween the Pole and Josinski. "If he dies, I will die with him, —and our blood be on thy head!"

"But with what oath can I bind his tongue, that he may not betray that which he has beheld?" said the Pole, in a terrified voice.

"He will give his word of honour."

"A beautiful pledge! Will you assure me, in the name of the King of Israel, that I may trust this man?"

"That I will."

"So be it, then," said the Pole, with a sigh,—and went into a dark portion of the room, whence he dragged forth two bodies. "Help me to take off these clothes?" said he.

"Russians!" exclaimed the two friends, when by the light of the lamp they perceived the uniforms.

"Yes, Russians!" cried the Pole, with frenzied gestures. "Yes, I also carry on warfare, with my own hand! My children, my two innocent little ones, were run through by the Russians when they returned, after you had conquered at Stoczek. But they give gold, and I serve them! Ha! ha! ha! —I serve them!"

"But the Poles also give gold," said Josinski.

"Ha! ha! ha!" laughed the man; "and I serve the Poles also! The district-governor took a fancy to my wife. He compelled me to be baptized; his fellows dragged me to the church The Christian priest gave me the name of Michael Wucziewiez and the holy archangel Michael became my patron saint. And when I was baptized, the governor said I could not any longer be married to a Jewish woman,—so he took my wife. She is at the castle with the governor, and my children were murdered by the Russians! Ha! ha! ha! Blessed be this war!"

He sprang away to the low seat near the lamp of death and the bread strewn with ashes, and, placing himself in a bent position, murmured some Hebrew prayers, whilst he rocked his body backwards and forwards.

After a long interval, Jacob said to him, in a gentle voice, "Forgive me, Rabbi? It is written that in time of need ceremonies may be dispensed with; or, 'Need breaks the law!'"

The Pole stared at him, as if he did not recognise him; then collected himself, rose up, and bade them put on the Russian uniform. When this was done, he asked if either of them knew Russian; and as Josinski replied in the affirmative, he desired him to say to the Russians, who possibly might come in his absence, that he was gone to the general. "I am now going to the general," said he, "but I shall soon be back again."

"To the Russian general?" exclaimed Josinski.

"Yes; how can I go with you without a pass?" replied he, impatiently.

When he was gone, Josinski said, "Perhaps he is gone to fetch the Russians here?"

"Oh, no! be quite easy on that score," replied Jacob. "Let us rest for an hour; I am weary."

It was almost light when the Pole returned. He placed some victuals before them; and when they had eaten, he bade them accompany him. But when he stood in the doorway, and the faint light showed him the countenance of Josinski, he sprang towards him, exclaiming,—

"No, no! he shall not leave this place alive, unless he kneels before me and lets me set my foot upon his neck."

Josinski turned to Jacob with a smile.

"That he cannot do," said Jacob; "he is a Polish soldier."

"Then he shall die!" screamed the Pole.

"Rabbi," said Jacob, firmly, "you would not shed my blood! Of this, however, be assured, I shall share the fate of my friend. You must save him."

"What am I to do?" moaned the Pole. "I have laid my hands upon my murdered children, and have sworn by the life of my head, that no Christian who comes within my power shall pass my threshold before I have trampled him in the dust."

"It is written," said Jacob, "that a man is absolved from his oath if it endangers the life of his brother."

"So may God forgive me," said the Pole reluctantly, and advanced towards the door.

"Stop!" cried Jacob, catching him by the arm; "these evil thoughts may return to you on the way, and you might murder him. Go not hence before you have given him *scholaum* (peace)."

The Pole, after an evident struggle with himself, extended his hand to Josinski, and said, "*Scholaum!*" and then, with a deep sigh, passed before them from the hut.

After they had gone on for a long time in silence, Jacob said to Josinski, with some little embarrassment in his countenance, "Josinski, you are now aware of what I would so willingly have concealed—that I am a Jew."

"I have known it for a long time," replied Josinski.

"How came that?" exclaimed Jacob, in surprise.

"I had a suspicion of it when we were in Algiers, and latterly I have become certain; principally from the solicitude with which you endeavoured to conceal your interest for the Jews. But what does that matter?" added he, grasping Jacob's hand; "there is not so very much difference between us. I believe that the Messiah has already appeared; you, on the contrary, that he has yet to come. I was satisfied; for I myself believe that the Messiah of Poland will come. I long to know something on this subject; I long to know what is the present state of affairs, and yet I am afraid of what I may have to hear."

He hastened his steps, to overtake the rapidly advancing Pole.

"My friend," said he to him, "what news is there from Warsaw, and the Polish generalissimo?"

The Pole made no reply, and Josinski repeated his question; the man, however, continued to walk on without replying. On this, Josinski turned to Jacob.

"I fancy that he hates me," said he, "because he is obliged to save me. Do you speak to him?"

"Why do you not answer the question of my friend?" demanded he.

"Answer him!" said the man, contemptuously; "why does he not call me by my name? 'My friend.' *His* friend! I am not his friend. If he speaks to me, I am called Rabbi Chivo."

"Rabbi Chivo," said Josinski, speaking mildly, "tell me, if you know, where the Polish generalissimo is, at this time?"

"He is at Prague."

"At Prague!" exclaimed both Jacob and Josinski in one breath. "Has he been beaten?"

"Yes; at Ostrolenka."

"My God! my God!" cried Josinski. "Ask him if he knows anything about the revolt in Podolia, Lithuania, or Walhynia."

"All put down—driven away!" replied the Pole to Jacob's question.

Josinski folded his hands, and heaved a convulsive sigh. In Jacob's soul arose a bitterness against the Pole, for the malicious satisfaction with which he seemed to speak of the misfortunes of Poland. He pressed Josinski's arm, and let the man go on before him.

"Ask him," said Josinski, after a considerable silence, "what general that was to whom he went in the village."

"It was the generalissimo," replied he, when they had again overtaken him, and Jacob had put the question.

"The generalissimo!—what, Diebitsch himself?"

"Diebitsch?—no! He is dead of the plague! It was Pashkewitz Eriwansky! Hark!" continued he, drawing Jacob towards him, "what are you going to do at Warsaw? I tell you what,—misfortune broods over that city. Go over to the Russians! the eagle of Russia is mighty, and it has gilded talons."

Jacob turned from him, without making any reply.

"See if you can learn anything more from him," whispered Josinski.

But the Pole either knew nothing more, or would not tell it. Many times he glanced at Jacob, as if he had something upon his heart to say to him; but every time he turned away again, shaking his head.

CHAPTER XLII.

BENJAMIN.—THE FALL OF WARSAW.

A FEW days after their return to Warsaw, Jacob was sent for by the superintendent of police.

"I have sent for you," said he, "merely to know if you can give any intelligence respecting a man who has been taken up as a spy. He persists that he knows you, and that he has only come here in search of you. We believed for a time that he knew you to be dead, and therefore that this was a mere excuse. But now that you are returned, it is as well for you to go and see the fellow before he is hanged."

"What is his name?" asked Jacob.

"He is a Jew; he calls himself Benjamin."

"Oh, general! he is innocent!" cried Jacob, starting up. "For God's sake let me hasten to him, that I may not by any possibility come too late."

Jacob flew to the prison.

Benjamin, pale and exhausted, was lying upon straw in a damp chamber, his teeth chattering with fever.

"My poor, dear Benjamin!" cried Jacob, flinging himself upon him, embracing and kissing him, "thou here! in this horrible place, my poor Benjamin!"

Benjamin gazed at him, with a faint smile; seized his hand, and kissed it.

The jailor beckoned Jacob aside, and whispered to him "Do not touch him—he has the cholera!"

"Not touch him!" cried Jacob, with tears in his eyes—"he must go home with me! I will immediately go and make preparations for his removal."

In the evening, when the old man had woke out of a short sleep, and was asking in his feeble voice, innumerable questions from Jacob—interrupting himself the replies to tell about his journey and his imprisonment, Jacob said—

"Hast thou not brought either some letter or message for me, Benjamin? Didst thou save nothing when they plundered thee?"

In the midst of his sufferings, a crafty smile played on the old man's lips; he desired Jacob to take one of his shoes and cut it open,—"I have hidden there a letter from your friend, Levy Ben Martin. He said I must take great care of the letter. It was a lucky thing that I found such a good way of hiding it. They were famously cheated!"

With trembling hands Jacob cut up the shoe, took thence the letter, and read as follows:—

"The peaceful Martin sends greeting to Bendixen, the man of war!

"Thou art in reality hardly deserving that a rational man should write to thee, because one does not know whether the letter will find thee alive. In the meantime, I will for a moment suppose that thou art alive, and will inform thee of all I have done and suffered for thy sake!

"For a long time I prayed every night, 'Oh Lord God, do not this day permit that Jacob Bendixen be shot, either by an Arab, Bedouin, Kabyle, or the like.' Yes, I really did so, and I felt myself relieved thereby. But now comes a letter, telling me that thou, already, in the month of December, hast set off from Algiers to Poland; and thus, whilst I was insuring thee against Bedouins, and such like, thou hadst set out for the country of the Kossacks. Thou art, perhaps, by this time gone to Java, Abyssinia, or Guinea, and they are shooting at thee with poisoned arrows, whilst I am doing my very best to keep the life in thee among the Cossacks. If I am to pray for thee, therefore, thou must oblige me by sending thy intended line of travel, with the exact date when thou wilt arrive at each place, so that I may come at thee, or, at all events, know whereabout to look after thee, if on any occasion thou hast, as they say in the advertisements, absented thyself from thy place of abode, and not lately been heard of.

"I send this by a man who will hunt thee up, be thou wherever thou mayst! He came to me, and said that he had taken a long journey, from Funen hither, to inquire where thou wast, and that now he would travel all the rest of the way to find thee out.

"'Benjamin,' said I to him, 'are you also going mad? It is indeed the cat running after the kid.* Don't you think that the vagabond can be killed without your being by?'

"'Let me be quiet,' said he. Then when I told him that thou wast in Poland, he was delighted, for there dwelt Rabbi Nathan Fürth. He had dined one Sabbath with Rabbi Philip, and was taken with the lad.

"But when Benjamin heard that he would have to cross the sea, and when I went with him on board a Danzig skipper, he almost lost heart; he looked on the water, and asked whether he could not travel by land. But when I told him that in any case he must cross some sea, and that the land journey would be tedious, he murmured, 'In God's name, then!' went home, and packed his things. He bought an orange for thee; and I

---

* A merry Jewish song, thus:—"The cat ran after the kid, and ate it: the dog bit the cat; the stick beat the dog; the fire burnt the stick; water quenched the fire; the ox drank the water; the butcher killed the ox; death's angel killed the butcher; then came the Lord and killed death's angel."

believe he meditated taking some boiled meat with him, for he said, 'Poor lad! he was used to good living at his father's, and very likely he has much ado to eat their camp-fare.'

"What do you think,—supposing you had stopped at home, and had lived quietly and respectably with this Benjamin and me, and two or three other good friends, playing a game at *l'ombre* once in awhile, and on Saturdays eating your scholet, even though it be cooked on a sucking pig.* Do you believe that Thora Fangel would have married Lieutenant Engborg any sooner for that?

"Yes, my friend, married she is—so that you now may come quietly home. I think that you have sense enough not to disgrace me, after all that I have done in your education, by going and making yourself ridiculous—for example, by shooting yourself. Consider; it is not any such heroic action, when one has so many fire-arms to choose from. If, in the devil's name, you make away with yourself, this I do require of you—have so much regard to my good name and reputation, as your friend and counsellor, as at least to do it in a proper manner. Let a little time pass that people may see that you did not do it in a hurry, and afterwards repented of it; and if after due reflection, and with a calm mind, you decide upon the deed—fix for a moment your thoughts upon the green parlour of the hospital, where Gröndal and I sit contentedly and smoke our pipes, whilst you are going to blow your brains out; see, also, in thought, for a moment, the grave of your father and mother— and which has laid neglected for a whole year; and, after that, then in Heaven's name,—go to the devil!

"I have made mself regularly angry with thinking that you should go and behave like a child. If I were with you for a

---

* *Scholet* is a Jewish Sabbath dish, and so much liked by them, that even of those who abandon the usual religious ceremonies, it is said jestingly, that they cook scholet on a sucking-pig.

moment I'd have a good round with you! It is best that the letter now waits awhile, till I have filled a pipe and let my rage cool a little!

"Of the particulars of the wedding I know nothing. Since you left, Wilhelm Fangel has been very savage against me, because of my intimacy with you. König told me that his sister was told that a servant-girl had listened and heard the quarrel between you and Engborg. There was a deal of gossip; the old merchant got to hear something about it; you were flown away with the wild geese, and so the match was brought about.

"It is not very agreeable, that I know well enough. You have probably gone and fought before Warsaw as if it were a holy city which concealed your dulcinea; and now you see that you have fought like a Don Qui——, no, it is not worth while for me to write the name at full. But now the worst is over; the operation is performed, and the wound will soon heal if it is properly treated. In order to divert your mind, you can go and travel about in peaceful countries,—that is the best remedy against love. After what I have seen of love, I cannot compare it to any other illness than that which, in every day conversation, is called hypochondria. If one can divert the patient's mind from his disease it is gone!

"Now do you go and make a little journey of pleasure, and afterwards come home and show them that you are not any longer in fetters. Benjamin immediately said, when I told him what I have proposed, 'Very good.' Rabbi Hirsch in Middelfarl has a daughter—she has a deal of money and is not married. Come home, Jacob Bendixen! Will you give the parson's wife the pleasure of saying that she has caused you to blow your brains out, or else make a cripple of yourself? Put on a merry face the first time you meet them in the street, or go up to them in a friendly way and offer your congratulations. Do whatever you like, only be rational, and let the Poles kill the Russians, or the Russians kill the Poles—what the deuce can it signify to you? And, if the Russians do even take Warsaw, you can just as well become *Doctor medicinæ et chirurgiæ*, and in time get a capital practice!

"I know nothing more to say. If this dose does not do you good, it is not worth while to waste a recipe on you! and in that case,—

"I am, with unspeakable contempt,
"Your former friend,
"LEVI MARTIN,
"*Cand. chir. et med.*"

Jacob had risen from his seat; he pressed his forehead against the window-pane, and gazed out with an unconscious glance. It was towards the end of summer. The evening was dark, but the heavens clear; the stars looked down from heaven, like quiet serious eyes; the houses reared themselves like living beings towards heaven, as if longing to breathe a purer air.

All at once burst forth a red blaze, and coloured the roofs of the neighbouring houses; a wild shriek resounded from the ajoining street—"Down with the traitors!" which was followed by a yell of triumph. The strong sound of horses' hoofs, as if of advancing cavalry—cries of onset—the report of fire-arms—fearful cries—a sudden silence—and then again wild yelling tumult. In that last despair the deceived Poles fell on one another.

Everything passed like shadows of mist before Jacob.

At length all became still. He was awoke by hearing his own name suddenly shouted in the room. When he approached Benjamin's bed, he saw that his countenance had become livid, and that he fumbled with his hands.

"Are you there?" stammered the dying man. "I would

say something; it is Jacob, son of Rabbi Philip—don't I know him? My wife bore me a son; Jette—she was so beautiful! There is the angel of death! There comes he!—woe, woe! Where are the good Jews who receive the confession of the dying? Oschamti, bogadti, gosalti, tofalti, sheikar! (I have sinned, I have done unjustly, I have stolen, I have lied!*) There is she—there is Jette! Jacob, son of Rabbi Philip—your mother died for grief of you! Oh, schema Yisroel!"

These were the last words of Benjamin—he was dead!

Jacob sank down before the body.

He tried to weep, but his burning eyes were tearless.

"The Russians are here!" cried an officer who rushed into the room.

Jacob rose up, seized his arms, and rushed to Wola.

"There is no such need yet," said Josinski, with flashing eyes, as while hurrying along to execute some commission he met Jacob; "in a few hours it will begin. Lay your ear to the ramparts, and you'll hear the cannonade at a distance. But it will be vain to attack these fortresses with these defenders. And if they, wearied with fighting, should withdraw themselves, to-morrow will arrive the twenty thousand fresh Polish troops under Ramorino, who will annihilate them. Now are we sure of them! Now will Poland conquer!"

Josinski proceeded on his business, after giving Jacob a warm pressure of the hand. "It would be a sin to tell him that I have a presentiment of evil," said Jacob to himself. "Let him keep his hope a few hours longer."

He leaned against the ramparts, and looked towards heaven, when one star after another grew pale and disappeared; a faint crimson light began to show itself in the east, whilst the rest of

* The words of the confession.

the sky appeared to become darker; and strange, thin misty shadows seemed to move through the air.

"Thou God above!" exclaimed he, turning towards the crimson streak, and stretching forth his hands; "Thou Lord of the human race—if so thou art! I have vowed that if I come living out of this day's fight, I will shed the blood of one man! I have vowed it to thee! I have spoken it to thee, thou God of Life and Death!"

He felt a hand laid upon his arm, and when he turned round he beheld Rabbi Chivo.

"Kol Yisroel ochim! (All the children of Israel are brothers!)" said he, in a solemn voice.

"And what of that?" said Jacob.

"Go away from this place, brother," returned he; "I tell thee, he who is called Ramorino, comes not. He has been sent five days' march from hence. He comes not before Warsaw is taken."

"Rabbi Chivo!" said Jacob, "you have saved my life; now I will save yours—go!"

"To-morrow will be too late!" said the Pole, beseechingly; "I shall seek for you, and only find your corpse. I tell you this city will fall! It is as a sawn-through tree; they will give a sign and it will be thrown down. Go over to the Russians, if you have a wish for war."

"Hence, Rabbi Chivo!" exclaimed Jacob, and grasped his sword.

"Nay, nay! don't make any disturbance!" said the Pole, timidly; "This is what one gets by trying to serve a Jew!" murmured he, as he slowly turned to leave him; "a Christian would not have done so!"

A cannon shot gave the sign, and the 6th of September broke over Warsaw.

Hundreds of bomb-shells hurled into the city exploded with

destructive thunder; works which had been raised as if for eternal monuments, were blown into fragments; yet still amid the ruins stood the defenders of Poland.

The enemy pressed on yet nearer; long salvos of musketry resounded; nearer and still nearer advanced their mortal foes, and now they fought with fixed bayonets.

Once more yet the Eagle of Poland raised itself victoriously; the Russians gave way.

A ball struck Jacob's breast, as he stood in the foremost ranks of the hot *melée*, fighting by the side of Josinski; and he now lay on the bloody ground a half-unconscious witness of the frenzied fight.

There was a pause in the conflict; and the command came that a certain number of the Poles should withdraw from Wola, to other points of the ramparts. The regiment of Josinski was among these; the faithful leaders of the suffering fatherland obeyed the command, and parted from their brothers whom they would never again meet.

The thought that Josinski had left him, sent a pang through Jacob's heart, and he sank into total unconsciousness.

CHAPTER XLIII.

In one of the Prussian frontier provinces, on the river Neisse, is a country town, surrounded by low hills. At one end of the town, the hills receding form a half-circle around a fertile valley, through which flows the river. Scattered, solitary houses, lie outside the town, extending into the valley; and these houses, when seen from the hills in the direction of the town, seem with their pleasant surroundings like sportive children who have hastened onward before their parents.

In one of these houses, which belonged to a family of Polish descent, had Josinski and Jacob found an asylum. As soon as Jacob's wound permitted it, Josinski had secretly, and encompassed with danger, betaken himself with his friend across the strongly-guarded frontiers. But the fatigue of this perilous journey, and his own distress of mind, as well as his deep sympathy with the fall of Poland, had again thrown Jacob on a sick bed, and the most beautiful time of the year had been passed by the two friends in suffering and sorrow.

It was now the end of summer; and the time of their separation approached. The nearer it came, the more taciturn and almost severe became Josinski; he seemed almost to be angry with Jacob because he would leave him.

The last evening, when their baggage was packed, and lay on the floor, amid arms and other necessaries of travel, he went out several times, on the pretext of taking a walk in the country, but every time he came back without doing so, and seated himself silently by the window.

At length he said, "Thou, too sittest the whole evening without saying a word; one might think that we were a couple of lovers about to separate for ever."

"Josinski," returned Jacob, "I have been thinking of all the hours we have spent together. Who knows, whether we shall ever meet again?"

"Let us not part," said Josinski; "go with me."

"Thou knowst what it is that drags me home. Far better that thou shouldst go with me to Denmark,—do so. It is not too late for thee to alter thy plans."

"What could I do, without means or purpose, in Denmark? No I have already weighed it deeply; our ways are no longer the same,—we must part."

"Every place is suited to the occasion, began Josinski again, after a long silence. "Beyond these bright well-known hills everything lies in a sort of enigmatical gloom; it is like the future. Among the dark masses a little stream alone is moving it leaps down over the cliffs almost like a living thing; now it is lost in darkness; now it catches the spectral moonbeams, as if a sudden thought had suddenly seized it, but which, the next moment, is lost. That is the never-slumbering recollection of my fatherland."

"No one knows," again continued he, "of how much he is capable. A year ago, in Warsaw,—when Poland yet had a people, an army, and while victory smiled on our arms,—then would the mere thought of such a time as this have seemed to me as if insupportable—as one which would have broken my heart. Now that it is here, an actual living reality, I am still alive, and eat and drink very much as usual, as if nothing had happened which might have weakened my appetite! Look!—now the cascade leaps high into the moonlight; it was like one of those vigorous thrilling thoughts of revenge which career through the heart at times."

"Revenge!" said Jacob, thoughtfully; "yes, if by revenging oneself one could alter that which has been done; if one could, by taking the life of a man, reverse his deeds."

Josinski turned round and gazed at him: "Thou hadst not such thoughts as those when thou lay in delirium, and murmured the name of the man who has robbed thee of thy bride; no, not when thou spakest with a fervour which caused the blood to flow from thy breast."

"That was, perhaps, in the horrible feeling that I could not revenge myself; yet neither could I give up revenge. That was the despairing desire for revenge, when oneself unconsciously knew how weak one was. Yes, in those first moments, then I could have fallen upon him like a wild beast! But now, since then, when I have imagined to myself that he was in my power, and I have gone through all the possible means by which I might do him injury whilst I myself remained happy, I have felt myself compelled to give them up, one after another, and to content myself merely with the consolation of believing that vengeance alone belongs to God!"

"It becomes you very well to be religious," said Josinski, derisively,—and left the room.

Jacob remained sitting in silence. After a short time he rose, went to the table, and took up Josinski's sword, as if to examine it. He bent over it; he brought it nearer and nearer to himself, and lastly pressed it to his lips, as quickly and mysteriously as if he feared lest any one should see him."

Shortly after Josinski re-entered the room; he seized Jacob's hand, and said, with tears in his eyes, "Forgive me, dear Bendixen, for being so short-tempered and unkind. I am just now so unhappy, I feel bitter against myself and against the whole world."

"Oh, no, Josinski; I will be candid with thee. I confess that thou wast right. This religious feeling is, I often fear, at bottom a sort of hypocrisy which I practice towards the Divinity. I know not sometimes, whether there really exists such a power; I believe it, nevertheless, to be probable, and I fear to displease it, lest in wrath it should deprive me of the only thing, the last thing which I worship in this world. Oh, Josinski, our souls are enigmas to themselves!"

"My dear friend! Dost thou really believe that God will perform a miracle for thee—that *she* is still faithful to thee?"

"I do not know, Josinski; but it seems to me so natural, I cannot give up the thought that it may perchance be so. If you had known her—if you had only seen that lovely creature! I could love God and the whole world, if she has only retained her love for me; I could clasp every Christian to my heart, and call him brother, because she is a Christian. I amuse myself by imagining things about her; of how it might be if I went home and saw her again. Sometimes I have fancied her standing at the altar with him; the priest has opened the holy book and repeated the prayers; he asks the question, 'Wilt thou take this man for thy husband?' She moves her lips—then I suddenly step forward, and, with a shriek, she throws herself into my arms. But this idea was quite irrational, I confess. At other times I have seen their house. She was sitting beside him at the tea-table; he was reading a newspaper, and yawning; she was pale and thoughtful. Then came the servant in, and announced that a foreign gentleman, an officer, was without, and wished to speak with the lieutenant. He went into his own room; I advanced towards him, and challenged him—now that I, too, am an officer. Then rushed she in, exclaiming, 'Spare him! spare the father of my child! If thou wilt have satisfaction, thou shalt have it. Here, in my husband's presence, I tell thee, my beloved, that I only loved thee, and shall love thee for ever!' Then went I away, and sacrificed my life for some beautiful and sacred Christian cause. Oh, Josinski, you know not, under circumstances of noble generous excitement, of what I am capable! It is no fable that Christ might die even for his cruellest enemies—in my own soul I feel that such self-sacrifice is possible. Perhaps God will enable me to begin my life anew in some other place, for I see plain enough that here all has gone wrong."

"We will be cheerful this evening," cried Josinski; "I will prepare a festal bowl. We will partake of it together, till my horse comes to the door. I will sing once more the song of Poland, and thou shalt sing about happy love. Perhaps our hearts will break, and then we shall have no need to part!"

"I must not die yet," murmured Jacob.

They sat for some time silent. Josinski again spoke. "It is so hard," said he, "for me to part with thee, Bendixen. When thou art gone, I shall first feel truly the loss of my fatherland. I can remember that when, as a child, I was sent from my father's estate to the military school in Warsaw, I did not begin to cry till the carriage which had brought me drove back again. And now, also, I shall have to endure the tortures of conscience, because thou hast sacrificed so large a part of thy fortune—perhaps the whole of it—for the sake of poor Poland. It is the son's duty to pay his father's debts, that he at least may lie with honour in his grave; but thou knowest that I have nothing left."

"Dear Josinski, it is painful to me to hear thee talk thus," returned Jacob. "Why wilt thou look upon me as a stranger? Besides, I am not poor; I have yet wealth in my own land; my father was rich. It is, therefore, not the anxiety about the means of life which is our heaviest grief."

"The day begins to dawn," said Josinski, as he turned towards the window; "now we may count the minutes that we have to remain together. I would so gladly hold them fast, and yet I wish that it was over. Indulge me in one thing, my friend. Let us two ride together from this place. On the way, we will suddenly turn our horses, each to his own side; we will not look back for several hours,—thus it will be over."

CHAPTER XLIV

The steam-vessel cast anchor, and boats came alongside to land the passengers.

One was met on the steps of the Custom-house by wife and children; to another a friend spoke a joyous welcome; a third was received by his servant, who, with active solicitude, busied himself in looking after his luggage. One only passed through the crowd without any eye noticing him, and with feverish excitement pursued his solitary way along the streets.

Now and then a faint ray of joy flashed through his soul, at the sight of well-known places; but directly afterwards his mind seemed to check itself, as if afraid of giving itself up to glad emotions.

He stole past the house of the Fangels: now he had once more seen it! The blinds were down, and he said to himself, "I didn't think of that; they are at their country-house this evening."

He turned his steps in the direction of Martin's abode, and he smiled as he pictured to himself the joyful astonishment of his friend.

Martin had left the hospital, and now for some time had lived with Jacob's old hostess.

"Good heavens! is it you, Mr. Doctor?" cried the old lady; "I really did not know you till you spoke. Be so good as to come in and sit down. Nay, but how you are changed! You really look as if you were ten years older—yes, that you do! Ah! you young fellows," said she, holding up her forefinger upbraidingly, "you lead pretty lives when you go into foreign parts, especially in Paris, where people are so very gay—yes, that you do!"

"Tell me, dear madam, where is Martin?"

"He is gone out a-walking—yes, that he is. I fancy he went with Mr. König. He came and fetched him; and you know very well what young men are. But he is such a capital young fellow, Mr. Doctor! that you may believe. It quite goes to my heart that he is now going abroad."

"Is Martin going abroad?"

"Yes, that he is; he is going to Sweden, to study the cholera. Yes, you young fellows—it is so easy for you to go up and down the world; there is nobody to trouble yourselves about——. Are you going so soon, Mr. Doctor? Won't you call again this evening? Mr. Martin is sure to be at home then; he is such a regular young man."

"No; I shall be in the country this evening. But will you tell him that I lodge at the *Hôtel du Nord?*"

"Ah! in the country—on a visit to some kind friends," said the old lady; "yes, that will do you good. I will be sure and tell Mr. Martin. Good-bye, Mr. Doctor."

"It is, perhaps, as well that I did not meet with him," thought Jacob, as he left the gate; "and now——" He laid his hand upon his heart, as if to still its violent, anxious throbbing.

CHAPTER XLV.

It was an evening in September. The full moon, red as blood, rose above the Sound from a dark mass of cloud; by degrees it became paler and paler, until it shone forth in its clear, golden brightness, while before its onward course was driven a mass of white cloud in the form of an arch. The mild light illumined the sea, and the hilly breadth of shore and meadow, in which the corn crops lay, either in swath or piled up in shocks. A deep quiet rested upon the whole scene; not a breath of air moved the leaves of the trees. From the shore alone was heard a low sound of water, as if of softly-stealing footsteps.

Jacob approached the fence which surrounded the garden of the country-house of the Fangels; here he paused. The faint sound of violins and flutes was heard from the house, which was lighted up as if for a festal occasion.

"There is music!—they are rejoicing," said he, as he stood in trembling expectation; "Oh, now I remember—this is her birthday."

He entered the grounds, and walked towards a little summer-house. "Here," continued he, "she used often to come; here I will wait for her this evening, and every evening until chance or fate leads her hither. At this moment, perhaps, she is dancing; once she danced with me. What if I now were to enter the room quite calmly, and say to them, 'Good evening!'"

A sound was heard on the path; some one approached: it was Thora!

She advanced slowly and thoughtfully towards the place where he stood. Thus was he once more near to her! He could have fallen on his knees and worshipped her. Lost in contemplation, he did not stir; he wished, as it were, to prolong the joy of recognition to the latest moment.

She passed an opening in the trees; the light of the full moon fell on her countenance and figure. She seemed to have grown in stature; she had lost somewhat of the grace and buoyancy of youth, but her figure was beautifully rounded, and full of womanly dignity. The crimson of excitement was on her cheek, however, and it seemed to Jacob that that strange, glassy, introverted gaze was in her eye, which he had occasionally seen before, and which he knew not why, always repelled him. Her manner was hurried; she seemed to be full of expectation, as if some secret purpose had brought her thither.

The next moment a second footstep was heard, and turning quickly she met a young man to whom she gave her hand, and both entered the summer-house, where they seated themselves side by side.

"Where is my husband?" asked she in a hoarse whisper.

"He was quite drunk when I left him," said the young man.

"My God!" exclaimed Thora; but you will do this for me, dear Grabow," said she, the next moment; "you will find me the money? I cannot ask it from my father. I have no hope but in you!"

"I will do it, my adored Thora—I will do this, and much more for you!" said the young man, passionately, and pressed the hand which he still held to his lips.

Thora was either too much absorbed by her own thoughts to notice this passionate demonstration, or else she willingly permitted it; the silent spectator believed the latter.

"Yes," said she, "I rely on you; you will provide this money; you will keep my secret; you are my only friend!"

"Ask anything from me!" began the young man again, with passionate emphasis.

"Hist!" said Thora, interrupting him, and snatching away her hand; "I thought I heard a sigh—oh! such a fearful sigh!"

"It was the wind in the leaves," said the young man; "do not trouble yourself about it."

"No, there was some one!" persisted Thora. "Hark! I hear some one moving behind the summer-house! There *is* somebody—go and look!"

When he came back, he said, "There was certainly somebody leaning against a tree; but he went as soon as he saw me. He looked like an old man. You can go out and look yourself; there is nobody now."

"We understand one another," said Thora, "let **us** now return to the house."

"Rather, let us walk together for awhile in this heavenly moonlight," said the young man.

She drew her shawl around her, put her hand within the young man's arm, and Jacob, as he once more looked from the outer fence into the garden, saw two figures slowly moving side by side among the trees.

CHAPTER XLVI.

"Bendixen is come!" shouted Martin to Gröndal, as they met early on the morrow in the Östergade.

"That is the reason why you are going at full gallop. When did he arrive?"

"He called yesterday afternoon, and inquired for me. Will you go with me to him? He lodges at the hotel."

"Yes, if I can depend upon his being shaved; for we shall certainly kiss one another."

"No, I think of meeting him just as if he had never been away. How astonished he would look if we were to go in quite coolly, with a 'Good morning!' instead of falling on his neck."

"Excellent! That is á la Wessel* I will go with you."

"And afterwards we will give him a little entertainment at the hospital, to set all right after our coolness!"

"Oh, yes! you have excellent ideas to-day."

"I must now go, and practise the face I must make when I see him. It is a good thing that you are with me, else we should very likely begin to talk about that affair with Thora Fangel. You remember, don't you, that he was betrothed to her?"

"Yes, who has not been a fool in his young days?"

* Wessel the Danish poet, who, from the window of Dreier's, a celebrated literary club, seeing a friend, who had taken a solemn leave on setting out on a long voyage, coming up the street, having been driven back by contrary winds, suggested to the club to pass this joke upon him."

"You talk like a book. Now, let us go and look after his quarters; stay, here it is on the card—'Bendixen, No. 54.' Good; now make a proper face. Are you ready?"

"Now hear, Martin. I really at bottom like Bendixen very much; let us in, and shake him cordially by the hand—and even give him a hearty kiss, if it cannot be otherwise."

"Now I believe, God forgive me! that your heart fails you," cried Martin.

"Before you shall think so disparagingly of me," returned Gröndal, "I will go in and make a face as if I was going to eat him. My heart fail, indeed!"

Without waiting for the permission to enter, Martin opened the door the moment after he had knocked, and Gröndal followed.

Jacob lay, dressed as he had been the evening before, upon his bed, and slept; a wax-light stood upon the table; it was burned down to the socket, and with a dying flame flickered up and down with a long wick.

"Where the devil can he have been last night?" said Martin.

"He lay thus in camp, don't you see?" returned Gröndal. "He fancies that he is still in Poland; now I know that we might surprise him without opposition! Do you take him by the arms, I will take him by the feet."

"No, it is cowardly to surprise a sleeping foe; let him rather sleep it out. Hark! do you run down to the hospital, and arrange a forenoon entertainment; I will wait for him till he wakes."

"If one could only carry him out," said Gröndal, "and then wake him up during the feast with the ringing of glasses and bottles, then he might be ready to think, by all the gods! that he had never once been away."

"Gröndal, you are poetical; you would enact one of the Thousand-and-One Nights"

"Would I?" said Gröndal,—"then good-by."

When he was gone, Martin drew the curtains of the bed, and extinguished the light. He seated himself by the bed, and contemplated the pale, sunken features of his friend; suddenly Jacob began to sigh, and Martin then called out "Bendixen! Bendixen!" first in a low voice, then louder and louder, until at last he took him in his arms and shook him.

"Who is there?" cried Jacob, and rose up.

"Good friend! a Pole, by the father's side!"

"Martin!—is that you?" exclaimed Jacob, and sprang from the bed.

"Who else should it be? Who else beside me would sit a long hour by the clock, watching by his friend whom he has found once more?"

"Was it a dream?" said Jacob, and rubbed his eyes.

"What! that I woke you? If so, it was a cursedly life-like dream."

"Yes, that also was a cursedly life-like dream," said Jacob.

Martin was silent, and gazed at him.

"Martin!" said Jacob—and seized both his hands; "and we see one another again! Now I have nothing left in the world but you!"

"Not so!—where are you, yourself? Have you lost yourself in Poland?"

"No, but now there is no one else whom I care about."

"May I depend upon that? Not even——"

"Do not mention her! Let me not hear her name!"

"Bravo! That is the way you should talk! Only you need not scream so loud; but the sentiment is good. Still you may follow the prescription."

"Oh, yes! I am now cured!" said Jacob, and began to walk about the room.

Martin accompanied him; and said, as he looked at him askance—

Yes, let us take a little exercise. The peripatetic philosophy is not to be despised. No, since you are in such good health, what need you trouble yourself about how you behave among the children of men, either for their profit or your own?"

"I have thought for a moment of going out into the street with a knife in each hand, and striking every one, as long as I could move!" said Jacob.

"Death! it's a good thing I came before you went out."

"But then I considered that they would overpower me, and carry me to Amage, and try, and condemn me, and then the whole city would turn out to see the Jew beheaded!"

"That was quite rational. You have returned from the campaign in Poland, to study Danish law and justice."

"Or else," continued Jacob, "to set fire to the whole city at all quarters; but then they would send me to the House of Correction, or else to Bedlam."

You reason most sensibly. What harm has the poor city done to you?"

"You know that that was a mere fancy; I let the city stand."

"Yes, that was all very well, and you ought to receive thanks for so doing; but it strikes me, nevertheless, that there is a little fever in this fancy. Listen to me; did not you tell my landlady that you were going into the country? Now I suspect that you went out last night, and have taken cold."

"No; it must have been only a dream!"

"What?"

"That I saw her!"

"Did you not also dream that you talked with her?"

"No; there was a man that prevented that."

"Ah!—What! you dreamed, then, that her husband came in the way?"

"Yes, her husband!"—and Jacob laughed.

"You laugh very heartily," said Martin; "was his conversation, then, so very amusing?"

"I did not say a word to him."

"Where is Benjamin?" asked Martin, abruptly; and then added, half aloud to himself, those sort of people know by instinct all that happens to those that they attach themselves to."

"Benjamin!—he is dead?" said Jacob.

"Dead?—Benjamin! What did he die of?"

"Of cholera."

"Hem! Nay, I will say a prayer for the dead over him, for he deserved it! But tell me now, without any reservation, Bendixen, have you had conversation with any of the Fangels?"

"No."

Good; and in future let me advise you to take care how you dream about seeing any of them. One might fancy that you had been dreaming that Engborg might become a familiar friend of yours?"

"Ha! ha! It would be a very crazy idea, if people fancied such a thing."

"Of what faith do you acknowledge yourself? Is not your heart oppressed by some disbelief?"

"No; I cannot disbelieve my own senses. I am quite rational."

"That is a very good thing. Well, then, come with me to the hospital; thou canst not in any case suffer by becoming still more rational?"

"Martin!" returned Jacob, "it is now seven years since thou first induced me to mix with people—what has it led to? No!—suffer me to remain alone—I hate people."

"What injury have the earth's thousand million of people done to thee?" said Martin. "They may, it is true, have shown themselves very ungrateful for the many benefits thou hast conferred on them, since thou no longer wilt let the light of thy countenance shine upon them."

"Listen to me, Martin," returned Jacob; "my love for the Christians is gone. If I could root them out all at once I would do it; but they are too mighty for me. Let me, therefore, at least go out of their way; let me not more frequently than is needful have to experience that the commonest fellow, if he is a Christian, is better than I am. I will endeavour to put a curb over myself; I will live retired and quiet, nor have intercourse with any one but thyself."

"My good fellow, I thank thee infinitely for the honour thou wouldst do to my humble person," said Martin; but to-morrow morning I set off for Sweden, where I shall remain some time."

"Cannot I go with thee?" asked Jacob.

"Not well, I fear," replied Martin. "If I am at the Swedish hospital, I cannot perform my duty as nurse."

"Oh, I can do very well; I can stand on my own legs."

"Yes, thou has learned to stand very cleverly," said Martin; "thou art a grown man; and yet thou canst get such foolish notions in thy head as to take a knife in each hand and kill everybody! Thou art come to years of discretion truly."

"That was a frenzy! Thou makest me ashamed of myself, Martin."

"Yes, as long as thou art in good company. Now, come with me?"

"No, let me rather remain at home."

"Just come and try how things are outside; perhaps thou mayst recover thy taste after a little Danish punch. Come along!"

"And if I should meet Wilhelm Fangel?"

"Gröndal will have arranged the entertainment, and of course he will have sent to invite Fangel. Of course!" said Martin, laughing. "And even if thou didst meet him, my good fellow, it is not the thing for the man who has fought with Diebitsch Sabalkansky and Paskewitsch Erivansky to be afraid of Wilhelm Fangel! Come along, I say!"

CHAPTER XLVII.

"Welcome to the noble hero!"

Sang the students as they stood in double file within the door, each in his loose undress coat and with a full glass in his hand.

Martin led Jacob into the room with a low bow; and when the song was ended, Gröndal stepped forward, and said:

"I have a word to say. As president of this feast, I propose a hurrah for the hero Bendixen—who has taught the Russians what sort of metal we fellows of the Royal Danish Hospital are made of. Now, therefore, let us give a thundering hurrah for this man, who has been highly serviceable to the hospital! And further, I have to remark that you must not shout too loud, because a sick woman is lying just below us. Drain your glasses, therefore, to the last drop; that is as good as the best hurrah; and as for Bendixen himself, he shall be crowned with a garland by way of compensation!"

The door opened, and a student, dressed as a young woman, entered with a garland made with the leafy twigs of the linden tree, and advanced towards Bendixen.

"It is Victoria!" said Gröndal, "and the garland is a laurel-wreath. With a gracious movement the goddess places the garland on his head. Denmark is a grateful country!"

The goddess was so clumsy in her endeavours to make the garland fit to the brow for which it was intended, that she tore away many of the green leaves in so doing, and when at length it was fixed it resembled rather a crown of thorns, which gave to Jacob's pale and attenuated countenance a death-like expression.

"Thou seemest too grand with thy laurel-wreath," said Martin, and took it off.

"To table, gentlemen!" cried Gröndal; "what is the hero Bendixen without meat?"

Jacob was seated at the upper end of the table; behind him was arranged a collection of the largest surgical instruments, so as to represent a warlike trophy.

"Bendixen!" cried one, after a few moments' stillness had prevailed during the meal, "now tell us some of your adventures. The Polish ladies are handsome, are they not; with dark hair and rosy lips?"

"Gentlemen," said Martin, rising, "our esteemed president has allowed me to speak first. A long time, gentlemen, will elapse before you again hear this voice, because I am going to leave you. Weep not, my friends, we shall meet again; if not here, why then, elsewhere. Like the Indian warrior, it will console me in my hour of departure if I can take the assurance with me that my wigwam will not be deserted when I am gone. I propose to you, therefore, that you allow Bendixen to stand in my stead: the pipe which I have smoked, he will also smoke of; the glass which I have emptied, will he also drain,—and if at any time he shall have drunk too freely therefrom, you will give him a bed, and coffee next morning; you will watch over his morals and his good behaviour as if they were in my own person; let none of the masters' daughters steal away his heart. Promise me this?"

"We promise!" exclaimed all, and raised their glasses aloft.

"Then I am at peace! Then will not my memory die from among you!" exclaimed Martin. "Now, let us drink!"

All filled their glasses, and drank.

"By all that's sacred, here comes my merry Holstein cousin!" exclaimed one; "I hear his spurs in the passage—come in!"

"Good day, Lieutenant Grabow! Welcome! Come and drink with us!" was cried on all sides.

"Thank you,—I will not drink just now; I got tipsy last night."

"Is that a reason? Then you might never drink in the day. Will you have wine, or cold punch?"

"Let me first have some herring-salad, if you have any," said Grabow.

"That is a standing dish here at the hospital. Sit you down there, by the side of Bendixen. He is a prodigal son, who has come home again; we've killed the fatted calf for him. Bendixen! this is Grabow! More I will not say in his commendation. You must become good friends."

Bendixen looked closely at Grabow,—almost more closely than politeness warranted.

He had one of those careless, untroubled, merry countenances which wins the beholder even against his own convictions. One meets such men occasionally, and involuntarily one feels a species of envy, because fortune seems to have written upon their brows, "I will that all love this bad young fellow!"

"Make a little room for him, Bendixen," said some one; "you two warriors may very well agree in one bed."

"I have made room for the lieutenant," said Jacob, drawing still further to one side.

"Nay, that will never do! He must not sit beneath the trophy!" exclaimed Gröndal. "Bendixen shall not be shoved aside for any one; that I, as manager and president of the feast, will not allow."

"I was not shoved aside; I gave up the seat voluntarily," said Jacob.

"I am much obliged to you for your politeness," said Grabow; and seated himself.

"You are not in a good humour to-day, lieutenant," said one of the company.

"Oh, I was cleared out last night."

"Did you pay your debts?" asked the cousin.

"Yes, as far as I could; but I have given my word for a deal more. But I am pretty well convinced that one of my partners was guilty of false play—the other was as drunk as a pig."

"Who were you playing with?"

"Nay, I am not going to tell that. But on what occasion is this forenoon feast?"

"It is in honour of Bendixen, who is come home after a long journey."

"Bendixen," exclaimed König, "you will not take your examination now, will you? You'll live rather on your wealth, and become the Mæcenas of your old comrades."

"Yes, that would do very well," said Jacob.

"How many Mæcenases would you have?" asked Gröndal. "You would go and cure the old gentleman to get the post of army-surgeon."

"Ah, my love has not been returned; Banner has got the office."

"That was—I had nearly said something very bad. But he was a younger candidate, and had not nearly so good a character as you."

"Yes! but then he is of an older and better family."

"And who will have the situation at Veile?"

*   *   *   *   *

Whilst part of the company were carrying on a lively conversation relative to the affairs of the medical class, Lieutenant Grabow turned politely towards Jacob, and began to converse with him. He possessed, in a high degree, the talent of maintaining a conversation alone. Jacob emptied one glass of wine after another, and laughed loud at several of the lieutenant's stories.

Martin bent towards them, and asked:

"Pardon me, but have you two ever met before? You seem as if you were a pair of most excellent friends."

Jacob laid down the knife with which he had been idly playing as he talked.

Grabow replied, "Mr. Bendixen belongs to the cavalry service as well as myself. People of similar tastes soon become acquainted."

"Yes; we have similar tastes," said Jacob, and smiled.

"Bendixen and Grabow are very like one another," said the student who sat by Jacob. "Don't you all think so?"

When the general attention was turned to this subject, all agreed that there was a striking resemblance between the two countenances, although the features were different.

"Yes, truly; we might, perhaps, be mistaken for one another," said Jacob, and began to sing.

"Well, I will not exactly say so," replied one of the company, "for without flattery, Grabow is the handsomer of the two. But that was right, Bendixen, give us a song? Let us have a Polish song,—you must have them at first hand?"

Jacob sang several of the wild and melancholy airs of Poland; he seemed to throw his whole soul into them, and sang with a strange enthusiasm and pathos which carried away the hearts of all who heard him.

When he had ended, the tone of the whole party seemed changed; each one wished to bear away with him the deep impression unimpaired, and soon after the party broke up.

When Martin, Grabow, and Jacob stood together outside the door, Martin said,—

"I am going down to the Custom-house to speak to the

captain, and afterwards I shall come round and say farewell. Shall you be at home in a couple of hours, Bendixen?"

"Yes, I am going straight home."

"If you will walk up the King's New Market," said Grabow, when Martin was gone, "we can have the benefit of each other's society for a little while longer?"

Jacob made no objection; and they walked on together.

"It is extraordinary," began Grabow, "that we have only known each other for a few hours, and yet it seems to me as if we were old friends. Listen now. You must give me some good advice as to how I shall get out of a dilemma."

"Do you think I am the right person for you to ask?" remarked Jacob, with a smile.

"Yes; why not? However, we can try. You see, I lost, as you have already heard, all my money last night; I shall not have another penny till the end of the month. But that would not so much matter, if only myself was concerned; but I have promised a friend to advance a sum of money for a good-for-nothing fellow who has got into trouble. I have given my word of honour to do it, and I must,—even if I sell my soul!"

"But why cannot your friend do it, as it is for his friend?"

"My good fellow," returned Grabow, "it is a fair lady that I wish to oblige."

"Oh, indeed! That is quite another thing," said Jacob; "and if I may suggest, since you have done me the honour of acquainting me with your private affairs—the lady is married, and you would oblige the husband through the wife?"

"The devil!—but you're a conjuror. However, I will be candid with you,—you are right. I was acquainted with her some years ago, over in Holstein, when I lay in garrison there; and now that I am stationed here, I have been lucky enough to knit up the old acquaintance. She is married to a brute of a husband—a drunken gambler; she had much better have had me at first."

"You were an old lover, then?" asked Jacob.

"One out of half a score. She was my first angel; but that is neither here nor there. I have given her my word of honour to pay a debt for the husband, the amount of which she dare not ask from her own family. The man deserves shooting that subjects such a woman to such a humiliation."

"Then you have, perhaps, already a little *liaison* with her—eh?"

"No! by Heaven, no! But give me, my good fellow, your best advice; how am I to raise five hundred rix-dollars to-day?"

"Is the husband's debt so much?"

"No, it is not exactly so much; but I have had a little miniature portrait of myself painted. I am to fetch it to-night, and the cursed painter will not give me credit; I cannot get it else until the end of the month."

"Then, in Heaven's name, let your portrait be till the end of the month; you can content yourself for so long by admiring yourself in the glass."

"Ha, ha, ha! That's very well said; but no, I wish to make a present of the portrait to the lady. Yesterday was her birthday, and I would have given it then but it was not ready; besides, now she has asked a favour from me. Tell me, now, where can I borrow this five hundred rix-dollars?"

"There are people enough in Copenhagen who lend money," returned Jacob, curtly.

"God knows there are!" replied Grabow; "but those fellows do not lend without security of one kind or another. I have none to give—I will be candid with you, Mr. Bendixen. I will treat you as a friend; I have opened my heart to you already—lend me the money yourself? My cousin tells me that you are rich—you can do it without any inconvenience, and you will oblige both me and my fair lady. Lend me, I say, five hundred rix-dollars?"

"I lend them? Ha, ha, ha! It is a laughable idea, truly!"

"Why is it laughable?" asked Grabow, gravely. "I ask nothing unreasonable. On my soul! I will pay whatever percentage you may demand."

"Nothing unreasonable!" repeated Jacob, with a laugh, the bitterness of which Grabow did not perceive. "Oh! yes—it would be excellent; it would deserve a high per-centage!"

"You shall yourself fix the rate—I will object to nothing. The money I *must* have: I will put my name to whatever conditions you please, without questioning them!"

"Done, lieutenant!" said Jacob, striking him on the shoulder; "you shall have the money!—and on very reasonable terms."

"Hurrah!" shouted the gay lieutenant; "can I go home with you now, and fetch the money?"

"No, you cannot have it for a few days."

"Just like any other Jew," murmured Grabow to himself. "But, my dear Bendixen," added he aloud, "I want them to-day; that poor devil, the husband, may be in jail else. I have given my word of honour to pay the money to-day. I would not disoblige her for the world; like so many other women, she is a fool to her husband. I must oblige her in her own way, and that is, by saving her husband from disgrace. I must have the money, or he must go to prison."

"Let him go to the devil!" exclaimed Bendixen, with a degree of warmth which made Grabow stand still and look at him. "But on my honour," continued he, again speaking calmly, "I have not the money to-day. I must myself make arrangements before I can lend it to you."

"When can I have it?"

"In two days you may render this service to your fair lady," returned Jacob. "Come to me then, and you shall have the money. Adieu! lieutenant."

"The day after to-morrow?" said the lieutenant, as Jacob turned to leave him.

"Yes, the day after to-morrow."

CHAPTER XLVIII.

"Well, have you got all ready?" asked Grabow on the appointed morning.

"Yes," returned Jacob.

"Can I have the money, then? But you look as if something were amiss. Have you altered your mind?"

"No; but the question is, will you agree to my conditions?"

"Name your own per-centage: as I have told you, I will not object to any amount."

"It is not any money per-centage; it is quite another thing which I require."

"Shylock and his pound of flesh!" thought Grabow to himself. "What is it?" said he, aloud; "if, my dear Bendixen, it is any service which I can render you, I will do it with the greatest pleasure?"

"It is merely this," returned Jacob, "that I will send a little note with the portrait."

"What can that mean? Perhaps a *billet d'amour?*"

"You have not mentioned the lady's name."

"True; but perhaps you will tell her that you lent me the money?"

"Why should I do that? What an absurd idea!"

"No, you look too sensible for that! What, then, can be the meaning of it?"

"It is a little whim of mine, that is all," said Jacob.

"And a cursed queer whim it is—and besides, she is now not well."

"Has she taken cold, then?"

"What made you think of that?"

"Oh, that is always the excuse with people; they have taken cold."

"Ha, ha, ha!—you are right there! But as I said, she is not well; it is a most difficult thing to get anything to her; she lives very retired, and sees no one. Report says that she is very unhappy; but I have had the good fortune to please her."

"If you can send the portrait to her, you can send also my note," returned Jacob.

"Hum!—But I have not exactly a fancy for the thing! What the devil could put such an idea into your head?"

"Those are the conditions on which you have the money," said Jacob.

Again Grabow thought of Shylock and the pound of flesh. "It is like cutting my own throat," said he. "But I tell you what," added he the next moment, "you must do me a service, then, in return?"

"What is that?"

"You must lend a Kammer-junker of my acquaintance two hundred rix-dollars."

"On these terms are you agreed?" asked Jacob.

"There is my hand!"

"Good; I will now write the letter."

He went to another table and wrote:—

"The dead may even return to warn the living of danger."
                                    "Jacob Bendixen."

"Nay," said Grabow, who had watched him narrowly; "it is short, it cannot be very dangerous."

"Nay, hold! if you have any tender words to write which shall accompany your miniature, write them now; my note must be inclosed in yours. After that we will fetch the miniature, and, in my presence, a messenger shall be sent with both. You can easily manage so that I do not know to whom they are sent. Do this, and here are the five hundred rix-dollars which shall be laid in your hands."

"You are a capital fellow!" said Grabow. "Well, let us now set about it—a capital fellow, for all your pound of flesh," repeated he to himself.

CHAPTER XLIX.

Jacob had not the heart to mix with his fellow-men; he passed his time alono; sometimes he read; but for hours together he sat as if sunk in profound thought. His mind dwelt much on Josinski; and, at times, a strong impulse within his soul urged him to return to the desolation of Poland, between the state of which unhappy country and his own individual condition, he imagined he saw so strong an affinity. Nevertheless, a still stronger impulse kept him fixed, as it were, to the spot, waiting for what next might occur. At times he was restless, and passed hours in walking up and down his room: there was a void in his soul, and he said to himself that it was the absence of Martin or Josinski which caused it—but his thoughts dwelt on another object.

On one of these occasions of restless excitement, about two days after the transaction with Grabow, he went to the hospital.

Grabow's cousin and some of the other younger students were sitting together, in deep conversation, and smoking their pipes the while.

When Bendixen entered, though all eyes were turned on him, they took no further notice, but continued to speak in a lower voice.

Shortly afterwards, one of the young men went out and

returned with a couple of old coats on his arm, and advancing towards Jacob, he thus addressed him:

"Bendixen, how much will you lend me on these old clothes?"

"What is the meaning of this?" asked he, crimsoning to his forehead.

"Nay, what's the use of making so much ado! We know all about the transactions with Grabow and the Kammerjunker; it was soon done. You have not been into Poland for nothing!"

"You shall have all the business of the hospital!" said Grabow's cousin; "they won't forget you, just for old acquaintance sake!"

The crimson flush of Jacob's countenance had now changed to a deathly pallor. He folded his arms over his breast, and demanded,—

"What has Grabow told you?"

"Oh, nothing at all remarkable," replied the cousin, stretching himself on a chair, and putting both his hands in his pockets; "it was merely a scene of every-day life. A young lieutenant is in difficulty for money, and lays open his case to Mr. Moses. Mr. Moses says that he can assist him; but that moneys are high at this time. It does not matter; the lieutenant says, 'I must have the money at any cost.' 'Yes, but I have not got it at this time,' says Mr. Moses; 'but I can obtain it for you in a couple of days.' The lieutenant goes and tells everybody what a fine fellow Mr. Moses is. But before many days are over, Mr. Moses has thrown a bucket of water over the lieutenant's enthusiasm; and the lieutenant then tells his friends, and they all believe him, that that money has been the dearest money to him that he ever had!"

Jacob moved not a muscle; and still standing, with his pallid countenance and folded arms, he asked, in a low, firm voice,—

"Did Grabow tell on what conditions he had that money?"

"Good Heavens! No; he was more discreet than that. He said that he was bound in honour to silence."

"Enough!" said Jacob; "I am satisfied!"

"Bendixen," said another, "it was doing a good stroke of business—two at once; but you always had the character of having a good head for business!"

Now came Gröndal forward, who had entered during this scene.

"Listen to me, Bendixen," said he. "The pipe which Martin smoked from, you shall not smoke,—neither from his glass shall you drink; as for the rest, we will not cast you out for the sake of Martin, who was the most upright of men; so you may come and eat at the hospital table whenever you will."

Jacob could not make any reply; he looked round upon the jeering circle of his late friends with a sentiment of deep sorrow, not unmingled with anger, and left the room in silence.

"There has been a gentleman asking many times after you," said his landlady, as Jacob entered his lodgings; "he seemed to have something very much on his heart."

"Did he not leave his name?"

"No; but he looked like an officer. He will not be long before he is here again, for I told him that I expected you soon back."

"Good!" said Jacob; and entered his room.

"Oh, heavens! are you ill, Mr. Bendixen? You look so deadly pale," said the woman, who now had looked at him for the first time; "let me make you a good warm cup of coffee?"

"No, thank you," said Jacob; and went into his own chamber.

Before long, Grabow came.

"She is dead!" exclaimed he, standing before Jacob, as if in an attitude of accusing horror.

"Who?" asked Jacob, catching hold of the table.

"The lady to whom you sent that letter."

"Nay! what had I to do with her death?" cried he; and again supported himself.

"What had you to do with it? What was there in the letter which you sent to her?" demanded Grabow, looking deathly pale, and yet with fury in his eye. "There must have been something mysterious in the letter; she lay for ever crying about the letter, and who it had come from."

"Lay! Was she then so ill?"

"She had brain fever—she was delirious—no one but her mother was with her."

"It is not extraordinary for people to rave in delirium," said Jacob, scarcely knowing what he said.

"It drives me mad to see you so calm. I could almost believe that you had written the letter on poisoned paper."

Ha! ha! ha! what an absurd idea!" and Jacob laughed.

"Yes," said Grabow; "and now she is dead!—and I have paid her husband's debt. Heaven knows what is become of the portrait; but she was not delirious till the next night, and her mother was a discreet woman. But this I have to say to you: do you never, if you come across Lieutenant Engborg—for it was his wife, and this I say in confidence, now she is dead—do you never say a syllable about that portrait!"

"No, that shall I not," said Jacob.

"Again listen to me, Bendixen. I now come to you once more as a friend, man. Lend me twenty rix-dollars to get myself a suit of mourning, otherwise I cannot be at the funeral."

"Grabow!" said Jacob, resuming somewhat of his former composure, "if you would sell yourself body and soul to me, I would not do it."

"That is truly enough spoken, for I have no security to give you beyond my own person. But I can insure my life, if you like."

Jacob raised his head, and gazed at him.

"There is no need of that," said he.

"Well, lend me the money in any case."

Jacob continued to look at him, without replying.

"Do me this service," continued Grabow. "I cannot think how you can be so hard. Such a rich fellow as you are has immense power over us poor Christians."

"Once more," said Jacob, rising with a grave dignity of demeanour which cowed the otherwise imperturbable Grabow, "I will not lend you the money! The woman is dead whom you would have injured, under the plea of obliging her husband; what matters it, then, whether you have a suit of mourning for her burial or not?"

"That is it, is it?" said Grabow, with a tone of hatred and derision. "You *are* Shylock, and will have your pound of flesh!"

"Leave me!" said Jacob.

When he was gone, Jacob bolted the door; and sat through the whole of that day and the next night alone in his chamber.

* * * * *
* * * * *

CHAPTER L.

BEFORE a small house, in Pile-street, stood, one winter forenoon, the black Jewish hearse. A corpse was carried out, followed by a throng of poor Jews, who, after the coffin had been placed in the hearse, struggled each one for a seat in the carriages which stood behind for the accommodation of the funeral attendants.

People thrust into some of the carriages from both sides at once, so that there was a fearful crowd inside; they shouted, contended for precedence, and made a great disturbance. In others, they only entered at one side; and sometimes it happened that a person rushed in so violently at one door that he flew out again at the other. In short, it was one of the old-fashioned Jew burials.

After the funeral train came the higher class of Jews on foot, as well as such of the poor as could not obtain by force a seat for themselves in any of the vehicles.

A rabble rout accompanied the hearse, who shouted, and flung stones at it; the police rushed among the crowd, and administered blows to those who threw stones as well as to those who did not.

Seven elderly Jews sat in one of the carriages; and these, after having mutually crushed and cursed one another, gradually subsided into peace. Next they looked round, to see who they really were who had thus come together.

"On my life, Mausch Ringstedt!" cried one, and stretched forth both his arms, as far as there was a possibility of doing so, towards another man who sat in an opposite corner, "how came you here?"

"Ephraim Gedaljo, as I live!" cried he who was thus accosted, and endeavoured to get a hand at liberty that he might offer it to his recognised friend.

"When did you come?" asked Ephraim.

"Last night. How are your wife and children?"

"They are quite well. Why did you not come on Friday evening? You might have had brown soup with me on Sunday! By my life you poor rogue, that you must travel in such winter weather!"

"Oh, no; I hope to do a good stroke of business, therefore I hurried here. A man must sell his last shirt, if he would get rich, you know."

"Did you only come last night—and yet are here?"

"Nay, a poor man must look at all chances. There will be good alms given." *

"And why not? He was rich, and there are no poor heirs who need begrudge the poor man's little bit of service."

"What was he, properly? I know nothing about him. He was called Rabbi Jacob, was he not?"

"Who he was, and where he came from, I know not. I only know that there will be a good almsgiving, and therefore I am here."

"I knew him," said one of the others—who, being somewhat genteeler than the others, talked Danish, whilst they spoke in their Hebrew dialect."

All the other six turned towards the present speaker, as quickly as their squeezed condition permitted.

---

* At a Jewish funeral, alms are given to the poor in proportion to the wealth of the deceased.

"Who is that?" asked Mausch Ringstedt, in an undertone, of his neighbour.

"It is Schaie Yisroel. He has a deal more money than you and me put together, and yet he goes for the alms!"

"He was a pious man!" began Schaie Yisroel, and lifted his eyes devoutly towards the carriage-roof.

"Pious?" interrupted one of the others. "One never saw him at the school."

"No, he had his own notions. Once a year he went to synagogue, on the Feast of Reconciliation, and he stayed there, spite of everybody, the whole day. He had his seat just beside mine; I know all about him," said he, in an authoritative manner.

As no one ventured to contradict him, he continued—"That was a pious man! He gave more free-will donations to the free school than all the rest of the community put together. He was a member of every benevolent institution; and whenever he saw a Jew lad getting his learning among the Christians, he took upon himself all the expense of immediately putting him under a Jewish master; or if a young man set himself down to their cursed studies, which spoil the best Jew that ever was born, he was at hand like a good friend, and set him at once behind a desk. Blessed be his memory!"

"What trade did he carry on?" inquired Mausch Ringstedt.

Schaie Yisroel's countenance gloomed over at this question, and he replied—"God forgive him, and let not the earth lie heavily upon him, because he took the bread from other children of Israel! Therefore I am going to-day, that I may get back a little of that of which he robbed me during two long years. He discounted bills, and how did he discount them? All the great folks were mad after him, and would not have anything to do with us others, as long as he lived, although he took a higher per-centage than I did. Not long since the fat Kammer-junker came to me."

"'It is a long time since I had the pleasure of serving the Mr. Kammer-junker,' said I.

"He laughed and replied, 'Why you see Bendixen is now ill, and probably may not recover.'

"'What then, is not my money as Bendixen's?' asked I, 'Mr. Kammer-junker.'

"'Yes,' said he, 'but then Bendixen was so like a gentleman, and treated me like a gentleman, and even though he had the face to take his hundred per cent., yet I would rather have paid him that than you your fifty per cent. And if one happens to be pinched on an occasion, and has not anything to leave with him as security or pledge, he will except one's word of honour, as if he himself understood what word of honour meant. That's what you do not, Mr. Yisroel!' That was what the Kammer-junker said.

"'No, God forbid, Mr. Kammer-junker,' says I; 'any solid pledge for me, but not your word of honour. I have already as many words of honour from lieutenants lying by me, as would equip a whole regiment!' On that the Kammer-junker laughed, and left me in pledge a new pair of epaulettes which he had just fetched from the goldsmith, whom he paid with his word of honour."

"*Gentleman?*" asked Mausch Ringstedt of his neighbour, "what does that mean?"

"How can I tell," replied the interrogated; "one, I suppose, who takes a hundred per cent."

"All lesser concerns," continued Schaie Yisroel, "he turned over to me, probably because we stood side by side every Yohmkipur (Feast of Reconciliation). The profit is very good; one gets in reality more by lending a few shillings on a coat or shirt, than by a hundred rix-dollars on a nobleman's pledge. But then there is such cursed crying and sobbing, and one so soon gets set down for a hard-hearted wretch! He would have nothing to do with this sort of thing; he would not, in fact, lend to them. If a poor woman came to his door, begging for a shilling on a gown, though it might be worth five rix-dollars, he would not let her in. Yet for all that, he was helpful to the poor in a hundred ways. It is unknown what he did to help the needy; yet he would not *lend* to them. No, that business he turned over to me! And I've heard that he sent a power of money into Poland; and every Pole had a friend in him. Yet the Christians called him a usurer, a blood-sucker, and a Jew-smaus!—Jew-smaus! they are so fond of that name. There lives next door to me a Christian, who takes two hundred per cent, and him also they call a Jew-smaus!"

"To hell with the smauses!" shouted the rabble outside, and a stone was dashed through the coach-window.

"I'll bide at home for the future!" cried Mausch Ringstedt, and drew back into his corner. The police ran after the rude boys, along the lanes outside the city gate.

After a little time of anxious silence, curiosity again awoke among the passengers, and Mausch Ringstedt asked, as if his mouth watered at the very idea, "And is there really such a good profit?"

"That you may believe. He had more than he could do; I might have been in partnership with him."

"You, Schaie Yisroel!" exclaimed they, in amazement.

Schaie Yisroel kept silence for a little that he might enjoy the curiosity of his hearers, and then continued, "Last Yohmkipur, as we were standing together as usual, who should come up but Dr. Martin, and stood just opposite to us——"

"Dr. Martin," interrupted Mausche Ringstedt, "is that a son of Liebsche Martin, who married a daughter of Mendel Kaun?"

"No," replied Ephraim Gedaljo, "he is a son of Martin Butcher."

"Oh! of little Martin Butcher? I know him. And his son is a doctor? Is he clever? Has he much to do?"

"And how? He is only lately come back from Sweden, where they have made much of him."

"That is really a pleasant thing to hear! Well, and what of him, Mr. Yisroel?"

"You might let me say my say, and let your questions be," returned Schaie Yisroel, in a tone of vexation at being interrupted. "No, he set himself, this Dr. Martin, as I said, over against us. He fixed his eyes on Bendixen, and that made me look at him. Poor fellow! he was quite pale; he could not bear the fasting. So, says the doctor, 'How are you, Bendixen? Full of business?' 'It's nearly all over with me,' says he. 'What,' says the doctor, 'have you more to do than you can manage? You should take Mr. Schaie Yisroel in as a partner.' I winked at the doctor, as much as to say I should be willing enough. 'Yes,' says Bendixen; on that I took him by the arm and said, 'We will talk about that to-morrow morning; I will call on you.' On that he turned round to me, and stared at me; and then all at once, down drops he; and the doctor conveyed him home. From that day he never again carried on business, but got weaker and weaker, till he died. Thus near was I to a capital thing."

"What did he die of?" asked Mausche Ringstedt.

"They say of an old wound," replied Schaie Yisroel; "he had been in the war in his youth."

"In his youth? Why I thought that he was not an old man?" said another.

"No, not exactly so; but he looked older than he really was."

"In the war?" asked Ephraim Gedaljo; "how could he there eat koscher and keep the Sabbath?"

"He was not very pious in his youth. He was even betrothed to a Christian. But the Spirit of the Lord came over him; he left her, and became an orthodox Jew. You know Reisches Aaron, Ephraim Gedaljo? Now, he watched beside him, together with Dr. Martin, during the last days of his life. All the last night he spoke not a word. Just as he was dying, he raised himself up, gazed wildly round him, and called upon the Law of Moses, upon the blessed Thora."

"Did he not say his Schema Yisroel?" asked the obstinate doubter.

"No; but he cried, as I tell you, upon the Law of Moses, the blessed Thora. He was a pious man. Blessed be his soul!"

They had now reached the burial-ground, and the coach released its company.

Whilst the body, according to the rites of the Jewish Law, was washed both in warm and cold water, in the dead-house, sat Uncle Marcus and his two sons, together with the funeral company, and sang, with low voices, the apointed Psalms of David, whilst the rest of the attendants waited backwards and forwards in the passages and in the burial-round.

When the body was wrapped in the tallis, and laid in the shallow, unplaned coffin, Uncle Marcus and his two sons were summoned; they rose weeping, and advancing to the coffin, besought of the dead who lay therein forgiveness of the wrong which they might possibly have done to him during his lifetime.

The lid was placed upon the coffin, and the bearers were ordered to come forward.

The bearers raised it upon their shoulders and advanced towards the burial-ground, whilst the chief-mourner went about through the company rattling the poor's box, whilst he exclaimed,—

"Benevolence frees from death!"

When they had entered the burial-ground, between the rows of hoar-frost-covered trees, the bier was placed upon the ground, and all assembled round it in a circle, repeating, in a low monotonous voice, the customary prayer—"The deeds of the Creator are righteous;" after which, and still amid the murmuring of prayers, it was again placed on the shoulders of the bearers, and carried to the grave, on which was repeated the prayer,—"Yauseif beseiscr elyaun." ("Him who is throned in the shadow of eternity.")

Once more the assembly stood in a circle around the little heap of soil and the hollowed grave. A deep silence prevailed. The lid of the coffin was removed, and a little bag containing earth was laid under the head of the corpse; the lid was then screwed down, and the coffin lowered into the grave.

Outside the rabble was heard shouting, "Bloodsucker! Jew-smaus!" and stones were thrown and yells raised in spite of the staves of the police. One stone was thrown into the grave, and fell upon the coffin. It sent forth a dull sound, as if the dead had uttered a groan.

A locked padlock was cast into the grave as a sign that with this burial all further mortality was at an end, on which Uncle Marcus came forward and flung in the first three shovel-fulls of earth; after him his two sons, and then the others who were present. As soon as any one had thrown in the earth, he went his way out of the burial-ground and washed his hands in the court.

When the crowd was gone, one alone remained standing by the grave: this was Martin.

He stood gazing for some time after the departing throng, and when he was alone he knelt down and prayed an inward prayer. After that, he took a little of the soil from the grave, wrapped it in paper, and laid it upon his breast.

As he was about to go, he turned round yet once more; he looked long over the city towards the woodland country where he had seen the deceased in the joyful animation of youth, and said,—

"He then believed 'in eternal poetry and eternal life!'"

THE END.